Netherlands Yearbook of International Law

Volume 42

For further volumes:
http://www.springer.com/series/8913

I. F. Dekker · E. Hey
General Editors

Netherlands Yearbook of International Law 2011

Agora: The Case of Iraq: International Law and Politics

T·M·C·Asser Press   Cambridge University Press   Springer

General Editors
I. F. Dekker
School of Law
Utrecht University
Janskerkhof 3
3512 BK Utrecht
The Netherlands

E. Hey
Erasmus School of Law
Erasmus University Rotterdam
Burgemeester Oudlaan 50
3062 PA Rotterdam
The Netherlands

Managing Editor
M. Ambrus
Erasmus School of Law
Erasmus University Rotterdam
Burgemeester Oudlaan 50
3062 PA Rotterdam
The Netherlands

ISSN 0167-6768 ISSN 1574-0951 (electronic)
ISBN 978-90-6704-961-0 ISBN 978-90-6704-849-1 (eBook)
DOI 10.1007/978-90-6704-849-1

Softcover reprint of the hardcover 1st edition 2012

This Volume is also available as a journal product, either as part of the subscription to Volume 58 of the Netherlands International Law Review, or as a stand-alone journal, both through Cambridge University Press. In addition to the electronic version published on http://www.springerlink, the Yearbook is also available online through the Cambridge Journals Online service.

Published by T.M.C. ASSER PRESS, The Hague, The Netherlands http://www.asserpress.nl
Produced and distributed for T.M.C. ASSER PRESS by Springer-Verlag Berlin Heidelberg

Printed on acid-free paper

Springer is part of Springer Science+Business Media (www.springer.com)

Board of Editors

Aims and Scope

The Netherlands Yearbook of International Law (NYIL) was first published in 1970. It has two main aims. It offers a forum for the publication of scholarly articles of a more general nature in the area of public international law including the law of the European Union. In addition, it aims to respond to the demand for information on state practice in the field of international law. Each Yearbook therefore includes an overview of state practice of the Netherlands.

The NYIL is published under the auspices of the T.M.C. Asser Instituut.

T.M.C. Asser Instituut

Located in the 'international zone' of The Hague—the City of Justice, Peace and Security, The T.M.C. Asser Instituut is a leading, inter-university research institute operating in the broad field of international law.

Founded in 1965, the Institute's international community of scholars is engaged in research, postgraduate training and dissemination of knowledge in furtherance of the purposes and principles of international law. This inter-university institute cooperates closely with and supports the Dutch universities' activities in the relevant disciplines. The academic fields covered by the Institute are Private International Law, Public International Law, Law of the European Union, International Commercial Arbitration, International Humanitarian Law, International Criminal Law and International Sports Law.

The Institute enjoys an excellent reputation at national and international level for its development, organisation and hosting of conferences and academic meetings, demand driven postgraduate programmes and training. Its ancillary websites and data collections all contribute to a coherent and integral strategy in the area of knowledge transfer.

The Institute has its own publishing house, T.M.C. Asser Press. T.M.C. Asser Press not only serves the publishing needs of the T.M.C. Asser Instituut, but also those of academics and practitioners worldwide in the fields of International and European Law.

T.M.C. Asser Instituut
Institute for Private and Public International Law
International Commercial Arbitration and European Law

Institute Address:
R. J. Schimmelpennincklaan 20-22
2517 JN, The Hague
The Netherlands

Mailing Address:
P.O. Box 30461
2500 GL The Hague
The Netherlands
Tel.: +3170 342 0300
Fax: +3170 342 0359
Internet: www.asser.nl

Publisher's Note

In the interests of timely publication and wide dissemination of the Documentation Section of the *Netherlands Yearbook of International Law*, T.M.C. Asser Press is pleased to announce that from now on, this section will only be made available online (free of charge) at www.asser.nl/NYIL/documentation. This brings the added benefit of documentation that is fully searchable, thereby more easily serving the needs of scholars, students and practitioners.

Contents

Abbreviations

AA	Ars Aequi
Aanh. Hand. I/II	Aanhangsel tot het Verslag der Mededelingen van de Eerste/Tweede Kamer der Staten Generaal
AB Kort	Administratiefrechtelijke Beslissingen Kort
AB	Administratiefrechtelijke Beslissingen
AJCL	American Journal of Comparative law
AJIL	American Journal of International Law
ASIL Proc.	American Society of International Law Proceedings
Australian YIL	Australian Yearbook of International Law
BDIEL	Basic Documents of International Economic Law
BGBl	Bundes Gesetzblatt
BNB	Beslissingen in Belastingzaken Nederlandse Belastingrechtspraak
Buffalo CLR	Buffalo Criminal Law Review
BVerfGE	Entscheidungen des Bundesverfassungsgericht
BYIL	British Yearbook of International Law
California LR	California Law Review
Calif. Western ILJ	California Western International Law Journal
CMLRev.	Common Market Law Review
Columbia JEL	Columbia Journal of European Law
Columbia JTL	Columbia Journal Transnational Law
Columbia LR	Columbia Law Review
Cornell ILJ	Cornell International Law Journal
DD	Delikt en Delinkwent
Denver JIL and Pol.	Denver Journal of International Law and Policy
ECR	European Court Reports
EJIL	European Journal of International Law
ETS	European Treaty Series
European LJ	European Law Journal
European LR	European Law Review

GA Res.	UN General Assembly Resolutions
Georgia LR	Georgia Law Review
G Washington ILR	George Washington International Law Review
GYIL	German Yearbook of International Law
Hand. I/II	Verslag der Handelingen van de Eerste/Tweede Kamer der Staten Generaal
Harvard HRJ	Harvard Human Rights Journal
Harvard ILJ	Harvard International Law Journal
ICJ Rep.	International Court of Justice Reports
ICLQ	International and Comparative Law Quarterly
ILM	International Legal Materials
ILR	International Law Review
IRRC	International Review of the Red Cross
JB	Jurisprudentie Bestuursrecht
JV	Jurisprudentie Vreemdelingenrecht
Kamerstukken I/II	Bijlagen bij het Verslag der Handelingen van de Eerste/Tweede Kamer der Staten Generaal
Leiden JIL	Leiden Journal of International Law
LJN	Landelijke Jurisprudentie Nummers website with full text Dutch case law <www.rechtspraak.nl>
M en R	Milieu en Recht
MRT	Militair Rechtelijk Tijdschrift
NAV	Nieuwsbrief Asiel- en Vluchtelingenrecht
NILR	Netherlands International Law Review
NIPR	Nederlands International Privaatrecht
NJ	Nederlandse Jurisprudentie
NJB	Nederlands Juristenblad
Nordic JIL	Nordic Journal of International Law
NYIL	Netherlands Yearbook of International Law
OJ	Official Journal of the European Communities
RdC	Recueil des cours
RGDIP	Revue Générale de Droit International Public
RIAA	Reports of International Arbitral Awards
RSV	Rechtspraak Sociale Verzekeringen
RV	Rechtspraak Vreemdelingenrecht
RvdW	Rechtspraak van de Week
SEW	Sociaal-Economische Wetgeving—Tijdschrift voor Europees en Economisch Recht
Stb.	Staatsblad van het Koninkrijk der Nederlanden
Stc.	Nederlandse Staatscourant
St. John's LR	St. John's Law Review
USZ	Uitspraken Sociale Zekerheid
Valparaiso Univ. LR	Valparaiso University Law Review
Virginia JIL	Virginia Journal of International Law
Yale JIL	Yale Journal of International Law

Yale LJ	Yale Law Journal
Yearbook ILC	Yearbook of the International Law Commission
ZaöRV	Zeitsschrift für ausländisches öffentliches Recht und Völkerrecht

General Information for Authors

1. **Embargo**
Articles submitted to NYIL should not be simultaneously under consideration elsewhere. Acceptance of the Editors offer to publish implies, that authors agree to an embargo on publication elsewhere, either in English or another language, for a period of two years following the year of publication of the Yearbook containing the article in question.

2. **Copyright**
Copyright is exclusively reserved to the author(s), but T.M.C.ASSER PRESS has the full exploitation of the contributions, both in hardcopy and electronic formats.

3. **Fees**
Authors will not receive a fee, but will be presented with a copy of the Yearbook containing their article and a free PDF file of their article.

4. **Editorial policy**
All papers are refereed by the Board of Editors. The Board of Editors reserves the right to suggest modifications and/or additions to the paper submitted, and further reserves the right to reject, or to revoke acceptance or to withhold publication of any paper.

5. **Language**
Authors are requested to submit their paper in English. Papers accepted for publication may, at the discretion of the Editors, be linguistically revised.

6. **Submission of papers**
Manuscripts should be sent in Word format to the Managing Editor at nyil@asser.nl. A hard copy will only be requested if necessary. The length of the manuscript should not exceed 15,000 words, including footnotes. Together with the manuscript an abstract of 150-250 words, and a list of 10 keywords should be submitted. The first footnote of your contribution (marked with an asterisk) should contain name, position, (institutional) affiliation and the e-mail address of each author. The text should be clearly divided in sections and subsections. Authors should carefully

check for errors before submitting. Authors are responsible for accuracy of quotations, for supplying complete and correct references, and for obtaining permission, where needed, to cite another author's material.

For house-style information please contact the Managing Editor at <nyil@asser.nl>.

Part I
General Articles

Chapter 1
T.M.C. Asser and Public and Private International Law: The Life and Legacy of 'a Practical Legal Statesman'

Geert De Baere and Alex Mills

Abstract This contribution commemorates the award of the tenth ever Nobel Peace Prize to Tobias Michael Carel Asser on 10 December 1911, and examines his life and his lasting contribution to scholarship and practice in private and public international law. After a biographical sketch, it considers the scholarship of TMC Asser, including his part in the foundation of the *Revue de droit international et de législation comparée*, and his international institution-building, particularly his role in the foundation of the *Institut de droit international*, the International Law Association, the 'Hague Conferences on International Private Law' (which ultimately became the international institution of the Hague Conference on Private International Law), the Permanent Court of Arbitration, and the Hague Academy of International Law. It also explores his legal and diplomatic practice, for example his important role as a Dutch delegate at the 1899 and 1907 Hague Peace Conferences. The article concludes with a reflection on Asser's contribution to public and private international law, and concludes that while he was no doubt a very talented scholar, it was the combination of this with his skills and initiative as a negotiator, diplomat and international institution builder which secured his reputation and his legacy.

The quotation in the title is from an award ceremony speech by Jørgen Gunnarsson Løvland, Chairman of the Nobel Committee, 1911, available at http://nobelprize.org/nobel_prizes/peace/laureates/1911/press.html. The authors wish to thank Ms Hanne Cuyckens and Mr Janek-Tomasz Nowak for research assistance, and Dr Kimberley Trapp and Mr Hans van Loon, Secretary General of the Hague Conference on Private International Law, for helpful comments.

G. De Baere (✉)
Department of International and European Law, Leuven Centre for Global Governance Studies, University of Leuven, Leuven, Belgium
e-mail: Geert.DeBaere@law.kuleuven.be

A. Mills
Faculty of Laws, University College London, London, UK
e-mail: a.mills@ucl.ac.uk

I. F. Dekker and E. Hey (eds.), *Netherlands Yearbook of International Law 2011*,
Netherlands Yearbook of International Law 42, DOI: 10.1007/978-90-6704-849-1_1,

Keywords TMC asser · Nobel peace prize · Public international law · Private international law

Contents

1.1 Introduction: The 1911 Nobel Peace Prize Winner, a Century On

1.1.1 Biographical Sketch

On 10 December 1911, the Norwegian Nobel Academy[1] awarded the tenth ever Nobel Peace Prize to Tobias Michael Carel Asser.[2] This contribution commemorates that event a century on, and examines the life of the 1911 Nobel Prize

[1] Which from 1907 to 1912 consisted of Jørgen Løvland, John Lund, Hans Jakob Horst, Georg Francis Hagerup and Carl Berner, available at http://nobelprize.org/nobel_prizes/peace/articles/committee/nnclist/index.html.

[2] Shared with Alfred Fried (11 November 1864–5 May 1921), an Austrian-born journalist and peace activist. See further Haberman 1972.

winner and his lasting contribution to scholarship and practice in private and public international law.[3]

Asser was born in Amsterdam on 28 April 1838 to Carel Daniel Asser, a prominent lawyer and sometime member of the *Hoge Raad der Nederlanden*, and Rosette Henry Godefroi, both of well-known Jewish families.[4] His maternal uncle, Michaël Hendrik Godefroi, for example, was minister of justice from 1860 to 1862. Asser's family had been involved in the Jewish community of Amsterdam for generations. His great-great-grandfather, Moses Salomon Asser, a trader in cacao and a lawyer, was an important representative of the Haskala or Jewish enlightenment in The Netherlands and the driving force behind the *Felix Libertate* society for the equal treatment of Dutch Jews. Asser himself was a member of the Curatorium of the Dutch–Jewish Seminarium from 1882 to 1887, but broke with Judaism around 1890 and became a member of the protestant church.

Asser took up the study of law at the *Athenaeum Illustre* in 1856.[5] On 8 February 1858, he won a gold medal for his reply to a prize question set by the University of Leiden with his thesis on the economic conception of value.[6] Less than 10 days before his twenty-second birthday, he obtained his doctorate *utriusque iuris* (literally 'of both laws', that is to say in both Roman law and canon law) in Leiden on 19 April 1860 under the supervision of Professor S. Vissering, with a thesis on the history of the principles of Dutch constitutional law relating to foreign policy.[7] It provided a critical analysis of the *ad hoc* involvement of the Dutch parliament in foreign policy and pleaded for the subjection of all treaties to parliamentary approval. After obtaining his doctorate, Asser practiced law in Amsterdam. He was appointed a professor of law at the Athenaeum in 1862, where he taught civil and commercial law, as well as criminal law and criminal procedure. He married Johanna Ernestina Asser on 22 June 1864, and together they had three sons and one daughter. In 1877, he became a part-time professor of commercial law and private international law at the same institution when it was restyled the Municipal University of Amsterdam ('Gemeentelijke Universiteit van Amsterdam'), all the while continuing his legal practice; something quite uncommon for a professor of that era.[8] He continued in this post until 1893, when he was appointed a Member of the Council of State, the highest administrative

---

[3] Among the numerous biographical essays, see, for example, van der Mandere 1946; Haberman 1972; Westenberg 1992; Voskuil 1995.

[4] Voskuil 1995, pp. 6–7.

[5] Considered to be the predecessor of the University of Amsterdam, the *Athenaeum Illustre* was founded in 1632. At the time of Asser's student years, law was taught by only two professors, viz. Jeronimo de Bosch Kemper and Martinus des Armorie van der Hoeven. See Westenberg 1992, p. 55.

[6] Asser 1858. The front cover identifies Asser as 'T.M.C. Asser, student in de rechten aan het Athenaeum Illustre te Amsterdam' (T.M.C. Asser, law student at the Athenaeum Illustre in Amsterdam).

[7] Asser 1860.

[8] See further Sect. 1.4 below.

body in the government. As a professor, he had a particular reputation for being a practical teacher, with an emphasis on mooting sessions. While his practical approach to teaching was innovative and must have gained him popularity with his students,[9] it also attracted criticism from some of his colleagues at the university, who took the view that his concentration on the practical application of the law implied that his teaching was more superficial.[10]

Asser developed an interest in international law, particularly private international law, quite early on in his academic career. Together with Gustave Rolin-Jaequemyns[11] and John Westlake,[12] he founded a journal of international law, *Revue de droit international et de législation comparée* ('RDI') in 1869.[13] He was one of those invited by Rolin-Jaequemyns to take part in the conference at Ghent on 8 September 1873 which founded the *Institut de Droit International* (Institute of International Law).[14] A strong believer in the avoidance and peaceful settlement of disputes through international conferences where principles for conflict solution could be agreed, he managed to persuade the Dutch government to call several conferences on the codification of private international law at The Hague in 1893, 1894, 1900 and 1904 over which Asser presided.[15] Asser later also presided over both Hague Conferences on the Unification of the Laws on Bills of Exchange and Cheques, held in 1910 and 1912, respectively.[16] He further acted as his country's delegate to the Hague Peace Conferences of 1899 and 1907.[17] He was part of The Netherlands delegation to the Congo conference in 1884–1885 and the Suez Canal Conference of 1885.[18] Asser was a member of an international committee for the abolition of tolls on the Rhine River (established in 1860), reflecting his support for free trade and for Dutch interests in having access to German markets. Navigation on the Rhine would become one of Asser's favourite subjects for scholarship.[19] The Dutch government appointed him a member of the Central Commission for the Navigation of the Rhine, in which he served from 1888 until 1895. Noted as a negotiator, Asser was involved during this period from 1875 to 1913 in virtually every treaty concluded by the Dutch government. Noted also as an arbiter of international disputes, he was a member of the Permanent Court of

---

9 Though his first lecture was apparently attended by only two students: van der Mandere 1946, p. 172.

10 Voskuil 1995, p. 9.

11 See further Nys 1910; Koskenniemi 2004.

12 See further AJIL Editorial Comment 1913.

13 See Sect. 1.2.2 below.

14 See Sect. 1.3.1 below.

15 See Sect. 1.3.3 below.

16 See Sect. 1.4.5 below.

17 See Sects. 1.4.2 and 1.4.4 below.

18 See Sect. 1.4.1 below.

19 See Sect. 1.2.1 below.

Arbitration ('PCA'),[20] and sat as an arbiter in its first case: the Pious Fund dispute between the United States and Mexico (1902).[21] Asser had a reputation for pragmatism, a skill that allowed him to broker compromises and break stalemates in international negotiations. An interesting example is the 'reverse' ratification process designed by him for the 1912 Opium Convention, which involved accession first by other invited states and only afterwards by the state parties who negotiated the text.[22] The grace and seeming effortlessness with which Asser moved in international circles will have been aided by the fact that, by all accounts, he was a gifted linguist, speaking 'German with ease and grace, French with the accent, fluency and precision of a native, and English with little or no trace of a foreign accent',[23] as well as his native Dutch.

Asser also participated in the political life of The Netherlands. In 1875, minister Van der Does de Willebois appointed him legal adviser to The Netherlands Ministry of Foreign Affairs, a position he kept until 1893, when he became a member of the Council of State. He served as the first president of the Standing Government Committee on Private International Law, established in 1897 by Queen regent Emma, until his death in 1913, and was also President of the State Commission for International Law from 1898. He even stood for election to the Dutch parliament in 1891, but failed to get elected.[24] He was appointed minister of state (without portfolio) by the Dutch government in 1904, a position he also held until his death.

He received numerous honours, including Cross of a Commander of the Order of The Netherlands Lion; of the Order of Orange-Nassau; and of the Baden Order of the Lion of Zähringen; Order of the Crown of Italy; and the Luxemburg Order of the Oak Crown. He also became an officer of the Belgian Order of Leopold, and Knight of the Legion of Honour. He received honorary doctorates from the Universities of Cambridge, Edinburgh, Bologna, and Berlin, and a posthumous honorary doctorate from the University of Leiden, at the occasion of the opening of the Peace Palace in The Hague in 1913. A library of international law, which he gathered with the help of contributions from 20 countries, has been named 'The Asser Collection' and is housed in the Peace Palace. Asser was also involved in the efforts to establish what would become the Academy of International Law in the same Peace Palace, although died before being able to witness its establishment.[25]

---

[20] See Sect. 1.4.2 below.

[21] See Sect. 1.4.3 below.

[22] van der Mandere 1946, pp. 195–197.

[23] AJIL Editorial Comment 1914a, p. 344.

[24] Asser's run for office was satirised by Johan Braakensiek with a cartoon in the journal *De Groene Amsterdammer* of 6 September 1891. It depicts Asser in courtly dress with ermine cape, with the superscript 'Prof. Asser's Candidatuur voor de Tweede Kamer' and the subscript: 'Tobi or not Tobi—that is the question'.

[25] See Sect. 1.3.5 below.

Tobias Asser passed away in The Hague on 29 July 1913, precisely 14 years to the day after the adoption of the 1899 Hague Convention and just under a month before the inauguration of the Peace Palace on 28 August 1913.

1.1.2 The Nobel Peace Prize

When Alfred Nobel drew up his will in Paris on 27 November 1895,[26] he provided for part of his estate to constitute a fund, the interest on which was to be annually distributed in the form of prizes 'to those who, during the preceding year, shall have conferred the greatest benefit on mankind'.[27] The said interest was to be divided into five equal parts, one of which was to go to 'the person who shall have done the most or the best work for fraternity between nations, for the abolition or reduction of standing armies and for the holding and promotion of peace congresses'.[28] Asser appears to fit the ticket admirably.

The award ceremony was held on 10 December 1911 in the auditorium of the Nobel Institute. Jørgen Gunnarsson Løvland, Chairman of the Nobel Committee, welcomed the audience. He then called upon Professor Fredrik Stang,[29] who addressed the assembly on 'Nordic Cooperation in Unifying Civil Law'. This address was followed by Mr. Løvland's announcement that the Nobel Peace Prize for 1911 was to be shared by Mr. Asser and Mr. Fried, neither of whom was able to be present at the ceremony and neither of whom delivered a Nobel lecture. Mr. Løvland then gave a biographical account of each laureate and, since 1911 was the tenth anniversary of the first prize presentation, concluded with some brief comments on the basis for awarding the prizes. After a brief biographical sketch, Løvland emphasised the fact that Asser was above all 'a practical legal statesman', comparing his position in the sphere of international private law to that enjoyed by Louis Renault in international public law.[30] While Løvland placed most emphasis on Asser's public activity, he noted that Asser's scholarly writing was 'of great importance in its own right'. He described Asser as 'a pioneer in the field of international legal relations' with a reputation 'as one of the leaders in modern

[26] The full text of Alfred Nobel's will in the original Swedish is available at http://nobelprize.org/alfred_nobel/will/testamente.html and in English translation at http://nobelprize.org/alfred_nobel/will/will-full.html.

[27] In the original Swedish: 'åt dem, som under det förlupne året hafva gjort menskligheten den största nytta'.

[28] In the original Swedish: 'åt den som har verkat mest eller best för folkens förbrödrande och afskaffande eller minskning af stående armeer samt bildande och spridande af fredskongresser'.

[29] Himself a member of the Committee since 1921 and its chairman from 1922 to 1941.

[30] Louis Renault (1843–1918) was a professor of international law at the University of Paris and, like Asser, also involved in the practice of international law, becoming the 'one authority in international law upon whom the Republic relied' and even 'the very oracle of international law', Scott 1918, pp. 607 and 610. He was awarded the 1907 Nobel Peace Prize.

jurisprudence', and concluded that it was 'only natural' that his countrymen should see him as a successor to or reviver of The Netherlands' pioneer work in international law in the seventeenth century by the likes of Hugo Grotius;[31] an assessment which appears still to hold a century on.[32] Løvland then turned to what, judging from Nobel's will, would appear to have been the core of the reason why Asser was awarded the Peace Prize: the fact that it was at his instigation that the Dutch government summoned the four Hague conferences in 1893, 1894, 1900 and 1904 on private international law; all of which he presided over.[33] These conferences prepared the ground for conventions which would establish uniformity in international private law 'and thus lead to greater public security and justice in international relations'. As a result, Løvland noted before the lecture rather abruptly ends, seven Conventions had been concluded on different aspects of civil procedure and of family law. It is perhaps rather striking that Løvland nowhere mentions Asser's important (though granted less central) role in the two major Peace Conferences held in The Hague in 1899 and 1907.[34]

1.2 Scholarship

1.2.1 A Selection of Asser's Scholarly Writings

Asser approached legal scholarship and writing in the same manner in which he approached law as a discipline in general: as first and foremost a practical tool, rather than an object of abstract analysis. He was more interested in how law could be used in practice than in systemic questions pertaining to areas of law or to law in general.[35] Asser's approach to legal scholarship was therefore one inspired by his own combination of practice and academia. The following contains a selection of his writings that illustrate that approach. Asser's own selection of his scholarly work between 1858 and 1888 was published in 1889 under the title *Studiën op het Gebied van Recht en Staat*.[36] It contained a rather wide selection of writings, ranging from an excerpt of his prizewinning 1858 thesis on the economic conception of value to extracts from his doctoral dissertation and various articles on

[31] However, Koskenniemi points out that Asser (like the other men behind the Revue de droit international et de législation comparée) did not come from the tradition of Grotius, Koskenniemi 2002, p. 17. Note that Asser himself wrote an essay at the occasion of the tercentenary of Grotius' birth, Asser 1883.

[32] See, for example, Vlas 2010, p. 169.

[33] See Sect. 1.3.3 below.

[34] See Sects. 1.4.2 and 1.4.4 below.

[35] Voskuil 1995, p. 8.

[36] Asser 1889.

private international law, but equally on such subjects as corporate law, criminal law, the life of Grotius or the revision of the Dutch constitution.

His celebrated *Schets van het Nederlandsche Handelsrecht* offers some insights into Asser's approach to scholarship. Rather than an exhaustive theoretical account of Dutch commercial law, it limits itself to a clear and concise exposition of the key concepts, avoiding 'lofty legal reasoning or historical reflections or comparative legal considerations'.[37] He continued defending this approach to teaching and scholarship in his farewell lecture, arguing that 'no thorough, i.e. scientific approach to trade law is possible without having clearly understood trade itself'.[38] However, another theme in Asser's work is present in the *Schets*: Asser emphasises the importance of international commerce and of unification of commercial laws, as trade is hindered by divergence of laws. Asser's international interest and his practical orientation may also be gleaned from the fact that one of the three parts of the *Schets van het Nederlandsche Handelsrecht* is devoted to shipping law, which is both an internationally oriented part of the law and at the same time formed an important part of Asser's practice as a lawyer.[39] It is therefore unsurprising that Asser would go on to write a similarly concise and practically oriented *Schets* of private international law. The two *Schetsen* combine these features with a further important virtue: clarity of exposition. Especially as regards private international law or conflict of laws, which has the (not entirely unmerited) reputation 'of being a specialized, somewhat strange and very complicated legal discipline',[40] that is quite a feat. In his foreword to the French translation by his hand, Alphonse Rivier notes that Asser's *Schets* is characterised by a focus on the principles of the law without losing sight of the necessities of legal practice, and without committing the error of confusing expositions *de lege lata* with reflections *de lege ferenda*.[41] Although the Dutch have played a significant role in the development of private international law,[42] the *Schets van het internationaal privaatregt* was the first Dutch textbook on the subject and was, in addition to French, translated in German, Romanian, Serbian and Spanish.[43] The book does more or less precisely what one might expect from Asser: it provides a rather exhaustive sketch of private international law as it stood at the time, without going very deep into any particular topic.

---

37 In the original: 'breedvoerige juridische redeneeringen of geschiedkundige bespiegelingen of vergelijkende rechtsbeschouwingen', Asser 1885a, p. v.

38 Quoted in van der Mandere 1946, pp. 172–173 (translation by authors).

39 See further Sect. 1.3.4 below.

40 Remien 2001, p. 79.

41 Asser 1884, p. II.

42 Which Asser explains by the fact that the autonomy of the cities in the Republic of the United Netherlands (1581 to 1795) as regards civil and commercial law was thus that it caused no end of conflicts between the different sets of laws: Asser 1880a, p. 6; Asser 1885a, pp. 5–6. See further *e.g.* Mills 2009, p. 45 *et seq.*

43 Voskuil 1995, p. 10.

Asser's scholarship was, however, by no means predominantly descriptive. In one of the first articles published in the newly established RDI, entitled 'De l'effet ou de l'exécution des jugements rendus a l'étranger en matière civile et commercial', Asser addresses the issue of the recognition and enforcement of judgments in civil and commercial matters.[44] He does so in a manner characteristic of the double role he would later develop as a lawyer and a political figure, by combining analysis with a clear plea for his project of unification of private international law. The analysis in the article leads up to a conclusion in twelve points, in which Asser argues that the execution of judgments without revision cannot be stipulated in a law which applies equally to judgments originating from every different country, but must rather be provided for in international agreements. An important aspect of Asser's proposal is that these agreements must be accompanied by a further international understanding on the jurisdiction of courts, the principal procedural formalities, and the laws with respect to private international law. The result must be that the court seised with the request for execution of a judgment with the authority of *res judicata* should not examine whether the judgment was rendered by a court having jurisdiction, nor whether it infringes provisions of public order, public morality or the public law of the State in which the execution is requested. Asser adds that it is to be understood that these rules only apply *inter partes* and not to judgments delivered by States not party to the treaties he proposes, which will remain subject to a complete revision before being granted a *pareatis*.[45] In other words, when an agreement whereby two States grant each other's judgments the benefit of reciprocal execution without revision goes together with the adoption of uniform rules on jurisdiction, the foreign judgment must be treated equally with judgments rendered by a national court. Any other solution would, according to Asser, not be in accordance with the confidence that must underlie international agreements on the execution of judgments without revision.[46]

Asser seems well aware of the fact that this is a rather revolutionary proposal. He recounts how, at the 1863 conference of the International Association for the Progress of Social Sciences,[47] everyone was in agreement that execution of a foreign judgment could only be granted after an examination of the competence of the foreign court. Undaunted, Asser tried to argue the contrary position, referring to a law of the North German Confederation of 5 June 1869, which obliged the courts of the confederation to execute judgments of other courts in the confederation without examining their competence.[48] Moreover, by defending the position that a court asked to enforce a foreign judgment need not examine whether the award infringes provisions of public order, public morality or the public law of the

[44] Asser 1869.

[45] Ibid., pp. 490–492. '*Pareatis*' is a term used by Asser as a synonym for 'exequatur', which is now in desuetude. For an extensive analysis of Asser's article, see Laufer 1992, pp. 39–65.

[46] Asser 1869, p. 477.

[47] See Sect. 1.2.2 below.

[48] Asser 1869, pp. 478–479.

State in which the execution is requested, Asser expected to encounter 'vivid protestations'. 'That will not', he declared, 'prevent me from developing entirely freely my ideas on this subject'.[49] Asser's fundamental proposition is therefore that unification of private international law must be brought about through international agreements, which would form the core of what Asser calls a 'Judicial Union' (*Union Judiciaire*). There is a striking parallel between Asser's ideas and some of the fundamental principles underlying the Brussels Convention on Jurisdiction and the Enforcement of Judgments in Civil and Commercial Matters,[50] concluded almost 100 years later on 27 September 1968, and its successor Council Regulation (EC) No 44/2001 of 22 December 2000 on jurisdiction and the recognition and enforcement of judgments in civil and commercial matters.[51] Asser's strong belief in the necessity for unification of private international law through international agreements would perhaps become the *Leitmotiv* of his career, driving for example his instigation of the Hague Conferences on Private International Law,[52] and eventually leading to his receipt of the Nobel Peace Prize.

Asser would return to this idea on many occasions. For example, the twelfth year of the RDI opens with an article by his hand entitled 'Droit international privé et droit uniforme'.[53] Voskuil has observed that it signifies a shift away from the scholar, and more in the direction of the fulltime diplomat and civil servant he would become.[54] The article, which both outlines the activities of the International Law Association,[55] the RDI and the *Institut de Droit International*, and sets out a strategy for the codification of private international law,[56] is certainly a step along the way from his early writing, including his still rather scholarly and theoretically inclined doctoral dissertation, towards finding his own voice as a practical legal scholar and statesman. Recalling Rolin-Jaequemyns' description of the progress of solidarity between peoples as *'l'esprit d'internationalité'*,[57] Asser proposes a pragmatic examination of whether that 'esprit' has led to any great achievements in private international law, but not before explaining why public international law

[49] Ibid., pp. 481–482 (translation by authors).

[50] [1972] OJ L299/32. On the parallel with the Brussels Convention, see Laufer 1992, pp. 131–158.

[51] [2001] OJ L12/1. The Regulation and Convention permit only very limited review of the jurisdiction of the judgment court under Article 35. Although they do allow for review of a judgment for compatibility with the public policy of the enforcing state under Article 34(1), this has been interpreted narrowly in practice. See *e.g.* Case C-7/98 *Krombach* v *Bamberski* [2000] ECR I-1935, para 21; Case C-420/07 *Apostolides* [2009] ECR I-3571, para 55. See De Baere 2010, pp. 1145–1149 and 1151–1155.

[52] See Sect. 1.3.3 below.

[53] Asser 1880b.

[54] Voskuil 1995, pp. 13–14.

[55] See Sect. 1.3.2 below.

[56] As Asser himself indicates in his introduction to the reproduction of the article in Asser 1889, p. 314.

[57] See Sect. 1.2.2 below.

will not be the subject of his enquiry. No progress in that respect is possible, says Asser, as long as 'ambitions, jealousy, and secular antipathies masked as State interest continue to dominate the notions of justice and right in important international questions'.[58] However, he continues, 'let us not despair of the future—far away though it may be'. Academic lawyers, Asser adds, may even in public international law eventually convince Statesmen of the necessity of subjecting interest to justice by preparing general rules that may be accepted by governments in their external relations.[59] Asser then turns to the topic of private international law and its unification. After a historical overview, he considers and accepts the benefits that uniform laws would provide. At the same time, his practical mind militates against adding to the many resolutions and declarations adopted by various international fora calling for such uniform laws, which have not had any significant results. He therefore takes the view that the primary means of resolving international conflicts must be the adoption of uniform rules of private international law, and that uniform legislation is only to be used as an exception, to regulate certain matters in which the need for uniformity is particularly acute. Asser's conclusion is that an international conference should be called, or several of them with regard to specific topics, to reach an agreement on the principles of private international law, with national laws following as needed to ratify and implement those treaties. Only in that manner, says Asser, may we hope to gain sympathy with statesmen, whose fear of 'exaggerations' has led to the failure of previous attempts at unification. It would then be permitted to hope for 'practical results'.[60] It is characteristic of Asser's career that he took action to turn this proposal into a reality, by initiating the Hague Conferences on Private International Law, as discussed below.[61]

In 1901, Asser had the satisfaction of reporting on one of the successes of his approach by publishing an account of the 1896 Hague Convention on Civil Procedure, which had emerged out of the first two conferences.[62] Written, as Asser notes in his foreword, 'more with my scissors than with my pen', it is essentially a guide to the convention and the *travaux préparatoires*, with the addition of Asser's personal reflections. Asser emphasises the historical importance of the entry into force, on 25 May 1899, of The Hague Convention of 14 November 1896, establishing common rules regarding several matters pertaining to civil procedure. He also takes the opportunity to confirm his hands-on approach to law, by explaining that, for many lawyers, the difficulties for the codification of private international law seemed insurmountable. However, Asser argues, postponing the codification of private international law until all authors were agreed on uniform rules would be like the farmer who, wanting to cross the Seine, waited patiently on the riverbank until the water would finally stop flowing. That would clearly not do for

---

[58] Asser 1880b, pp. 5–6 (translation by authors).

[59] Ibid., p. 6.

[60] Ibid., p. 22.

[61] See Sect. 1.3.3 below.

[62] Asser 1901. See further Sect. 1.3.3 below.

Asser. The results of research on private international law were, he argues, already enough to 'cross without fear'.[63]

A final and perhaps rather peculiar example of Asser's combination of statesmanship and scholarship can be found in the piece Asser published in May 1885 on the General Act of the Berlin Conference on West Africa of 26 February 1885.[64] It sets out Asser's experiences as part of The Netherlands delegation—one of the many international conferences at which he represented The Netherlands following his appointment as Legal Advisor in 1875.[65] At the Berlin Conference, he was principally responsible in particular for matters pertaining to shipping, and his article provides an analytical account of the Act. For present-day readers, the article has at least two rather striking features. First, it describes the proceedings and the result of the conference from the rather detached standpoint of the diplomat assigned to perform a particular task and assessing the outcome. Second, Asser appears to be quite positive about the Berlin Conference and about the recognition of the *Association internationale du Congo* as possessing sovereignty over the Congolese territory, describing the future state as having been founded 'not with the usual narrow-minded intent to which European statecraft has accustomed us, but to ensure civilization and wealth in general', which are, Asser adds, 'the best guardians of the freedoms which the Conference wished to guarantee to trade and shipping for all'.[66] Asser also credits German Chancellor Otto von Bismarck, who had taken the initiative for the conference, with having brought the conference to a successful result. He describes how Bismarck, who had no interest in the legal debate on the status of the *Association*, lobbied for the recognition of its sovereignty, which was first recognised by the United States of America on 10 April 1884, followed by Germany on 3 November 1884, and the United Kingdom on 16 December 1884.[67] The *Association* would, of course, become the vehicle for the foundation of King Leopold II of the Belgians' Congo Free State, and the system of wealth-extraction and servitude that characterised his rule.[68] The Berlin Conference would later be sarcastically referred to by Joseph Conrad in his *Heart of Darkness* as 'The International Society for the Suppression of Savage Customs'.[69] It would, however, be unfair to reproach Asser's lack of prescience as regards the tragic turn events in the Congo would take. He was at the conference to negotiate free navigation of the river Congo and that is what he did and reported on in this article.[70]

---

[63] Ibid., pp. 4–5.

[64] Asser 1885b.

[65] See further Sect. 1.4.1 below.

[66] Asser 1885b, p. 373 (translation by authors).

[67] Ibid., pp. 372–373 and 392.

[68] Koskenniemi 2002, pp. 156–157.

[69] Conrad 1902, p. 71.

[70] Moreover, Rolin-Jaequemyns, Asser's friend and co-founder of the RDI, had written favourably in the *Revue* about what he perceived to be the scientific and philanthropic endeavours of King Leopold II, Rolin-Jaequemyns 1877. See further the account of the Berlin Conference in Koskenniemi 2002, pp. 121–127.

1.2.2 The Foundation of the Revue de Droit International et de Législation Comparée

It might be argued that Asser's most important contribution to scholarship in public or private international law was not his own writings, but his role as a co-founder, with John Westlake and Gustave Rolin-Jaequemyns, of the first international law review,[71] the *Revue de droit international et de législation comparée.* The three founders had met at the first session of the *Association internationale pour le progrès des sciences sociales* (International Association for the Progress of Social Sciences) in September 1862.[72] The Association had been established, in the words of its secretary-general Couvreur, as a 'vast instrument of enquiry' to examine the opinions in different countries as regards questions of general interest in the social sciences, especially regarding civil and criminal law.[73] Koskenniemi notes that certain French members of the Association wished to use it for 'revolutionary purposes', which led to the break-up of the society after four conferences.[74] However, Asser, Rolin-Jaequemyns and Westlake kept in contact, and it was during a walk in Haarlem along the *Dreef* to the woods of the *Haarlemmerhout* when Rolin was in The Netherlands for business in July 1867 that he and Asser came up with the plan of an international legal journal.[75] After enlisting the support of Westlake and of Pasquale Mancini, professor of public, foreign and international law in Turin, on the basis of a prospectus drawn up by Asser, the journal was founded with Asser, Rolin-Jaequemyns and Westlake as principal editors.

In an essay in the inaugural 1869 volume, Rolin-Jaequemyns explains the importance of the study of international and comparative law, thereby setting out the programme for the RDI. After referring to Grotius, Montesquieu and Bentham,[76] to make the point that not just statesmen can have an impact on what is to be done for the good of humanity, Rolin argues that nowadays everyone is a statesman in some way and not 'absolutely incompetent' to engage in debates over 'a science that forms, after all, the supreme *desideratum* of every straight and honest soul.' That science must, however, neither remain vague or abstract, nor limit itself to one single existing legislation. The object of study must therefore be the comparative legislation of various civilised countries.[77] The time at which

---

[71] AJIL Editorial Comment 1914a, p. 344.

[72] See Association Internationale pour le Progrès des Sciences Sociales 1863, pp. 3–5. Westlake and Asser are listed as secretaries of their respective national associations, and Rolin-Jaequemyns is also mentioned as attending in various places throughout the report.

[73] Asser 1880a, p. 7.

[74] Koskenniemi 2002, p. 13. Note, however, that Asser proposed the unification of the law relating to negotiable instruments during the second session. See Hudson and Feller 1931, p. 339.

[75] Asser 1902, p. 111; van der Mandere 1946, p. 176.

[76] Note that Asser published the text of and a brief commentary on an unedited letter from Jeremy Bentham to King William I of The Netherlands, Asser 1893.

[77] Rolin-Jaequemyns 1869, p. 3.

Rolin was writing was, in his assessment, also characterised by a cosmopolitan movement, whereby ideas come into existence through interactions between civilised nations, which take each other as examples and thereby learn from each other. Indeed, says Rolin, sometimes the same issues arise simultaneously and almost in the same terms in countries that have nothing apparent in common. Some of these issues have already been resolved, such as the abolition of slavery. Other issues, however, require the attention of the legislators, such as the utility of the death penalty and the equality between the sexes as regards civil and political rights. Still other issues require more study and raise particular difficulties. It is especially this category of issues that is susceptible to learning from experiences acquired by other peoples. Examples range from the organisation of the penitentiary system to the organisation of representative government and of the judiciary. The RDI, argues Rolin, ought to be the forum for the free discussion of all such issues, regardless of whether they have become part of the political debate.[78] The study of comparative legislation makes every nation conscious of the fact that it is morally obliged to act in accordance with the principles of universal justice, and it reinforces what Rolin calls '*l'esprit d'internationalité*'.[79] Rolin argued for the necessity of reconciling 'the legal and historical spirit, which takes into account *what has been* and *what is* with the philosophical spirit, which is concerned with *what ought to be*', and this both in the comparative study of legislations and even more in the study of international law.[80] As regards the latter, Rolin takes its ultimate source to be the conscience of humanity as manifested through public opinion, that is to say the opinion of enlightened men. The fact that that opinion is constantly subject to evolution makes international law eminently progressive.[81]

It should be noted that, as was typically the case for Asser, this reference to public opinion at the inception of the RDI could not remain a purely theoretical matter. Together with the Russian delegate Friedrich Von Martens, Asser urged the German delegation at the 1899 Hague Conference to consider the pressure of world public opinion and accept the establishment of an arbitral tribunal.[82] In his inaugural essay to the RDI, Rolin further notes that public opinion is, albeit unanimous on certain issues, far from set as regards many others. The double aim of the study of international law is therefore to register the agreement between men on a given question and to derive the principles from that agreement, and to clarify other issues that are subject to doubt. Rolin lists a number of issues in international law that may be of interest for the RDI to study, including: what is a nation or a State and what rights attach to that status? What is the status of property under international law? And even, rather topically even for the twenty first century: is there a right to intervene abroad for the benefit of non-nationals and in the general

78 Ibid., pp. 11–12.

79 Ibid., p. 17.

80 Ibid., p. 225.

81 Ibid., pp. 225–228.

82 See Caron 2000, p. 16. See further Sects. 1.4.2 and 1.4.4 below.

interest of humanity? Apart from these issues of public international law, most issues of private international law remain to be settled.[83] All these issues, concludes Rolin, are part of the field that the new RDI aims to study through the calm pursuit of truth and justice, which is 'stronger than revolutions, diplomatic intrigues or war'.[84]

The RDI reflected the interests and intentions of its founders, by featuring articles on such varied subjects as the reform of penal law and social law (*e.g.* child labour), as well as articles on various aspects of private international law, such as jurisdiction and the recognition of judgments, among which of course several were by Asser. The RDI's reformist agenda was also pursued by reporting on various proposals for peaceful settlement of disputes through arbitration and on various meetings of international societies. It became a successful forum for publications within its purview from across the world. However, it gradually moved more in the direction of public international law. Unfortunately, the number of different contributors remained low, and further decreased after the establishment of the *Revue générale de droit international public* in 1894 in Paris. By the time the final issue of the Revue appeared in 1939, it had become identified as a mostly Belgian journal.[85] Nonetheless, as the first international law journal, the RDI left behind a lasting contribution to the scholarly analysis of public and private international law and to their development as academic disciplines. Moreover, the RDI led to the establishment of networks of scholars and diplomats from around the world, which precipitated the founding of the *Institut de Droit International* in 1873 (see below), which in turn would have a lasting impact on international law.[86]

1.3 International Institution Building

The most significant and enduring contribution which Asser has made to international law is not, perhaps, his scholarship, but his role in establishing leading international institutions dedicated to furthering international law and dispute resolution. In the speech given at his Nobel award ceremony, it was indeed observed that 'his public activity has overshadowed his scholarly writing'.[87]

[83] Ibid., pp. 238–245.

[84] Ibid., p. 245.

[85] For the account see Koskenniemi 2002, pp. 12–19. Note that Gustave Rolin-Jaequemyns was succeeded as editor by his son Edouard and his brother Albéric Rolin, whose son, Henri Rolin, in turn co-founded the still-running *Revue belge de droit international/Belgisch Tijdschrift voor Internationaal Recht* in 1965.

[86] Indeed, it has even been argued that together the founding of the RDI and of the IDI marked the beginning of international law as we know it today, Koskenniemi 2004, p. 5.

[87] See http://nobelprize.org/nobel_prizes/peace/laureates/1911/press.html. As previously noted, his scholarly work was, however, also considered worthy of praise. See Sect. 1.1.2 above.

The continued success of a number of the institutions he played a part in establishing in making a positive contribution to the development and furtherance of international law is testament to both the skill with which they were established, and the importance of the role which each institution plays.

1.3.1 Institut de Droit International

One of the immediate impetuses for international institution building in Asser's time was the Franco-Prussian War of 1870–1871. In some ways the war was a predictable consequence of long-running balance of power concerns in Western Europe, with a unifying Germany matched against Napoleon III of France. Advances in military technology, however, made the conflict particularly bloody, culminating in the brutality of the Siege of Paris and the indiscriminate shelling of the besieged city by Prussian artillery to damage French morale. The events of this conflict would have stood in stark contrast to the success of the Alabama Claims Arbitration between Great Britain and the United States, which handed down its final award on 14 September 1872. The arbitral award peacefully resolved a highly contentious and politically charged dispute which had arisen out of British violations of neutrality in the American Civil War, through a failure to exercise due diligence in allowing the construction of Confederate vessels in British territory. In the aftermath of these events, desiring to facilitate more peaceful means of managing international relations or at least regulating the conduct of warfare, Asser and 10 other like-minded academics, lawyers and diplomats[88] convened in Ghent on 8 September 1873, and founded the 'Institut de Droit International' ('IDI'), in order 'to encourage progress in international law'.

Although a relatively informal academic body, the IDI has played a very important role in the progressive development of international law, as a forum for discussion and a focus for efforts towards codification. It is notable that its influence has, from its beginning, encompassed matters of both public and private international law. The first resolution passed on 5 September 1874 by the IDI at its inaugural meeting in Geneva (held in the very same room used by the Alabama Claims Arbitration) called for international agreement on the unification of rules of private international law—a project at the heart of Asser's scholarship, as discussed above, and to which he would make an extremely significant further contribution through the Hague Conferences on Private International Law, discussed below. At the same meeting, the Institut also established a committee to

[88] See generally Koskenniemi 2002, p. 39 *et seq*. Other notable founders of the IDI included Rolin-Jaequemyns (co-founder with Asser of the *Revue de droit international et de législation comparée*—see Sect. 1.2.2 above; Westlake was unable to attend), Mancini, Calvo, Field (see *infra*, note 92), Bluntschli, Lorimer, and Moynier (co-founder of the 'International Committee for Relief to the Wounded' in 1863, which changed its name to the 'International Committee of the Red Cross' in 1876. See further *e.g.* Durand 1994.

study and develop proposals for furthering the 'Brussels Declaration' of 27 July 1874 concerning the laws and customs of war, the result of an international conference which had met on the initiative of Tsar Alexander II of Russia. The IDI's work on the matter led to the adoption of a 'Manual of the Laws of War on Land' at its meeting in Oxford on 9 September 1880.[89] This in turn formed the foundation of the Hague Conventions on land warfare adopted at the Peace Conferences in The Hague in 1899 and 1907, in which Asser also played a leading role, as discussed below.[90] As a mark of its early successes, the IDI was itself awarded the Nobel Peace Prize in 1904.

1.3.2 International Law Association

The founding of the IDI was quickly followed by the establishment of another major international organisation on 10 October 1873 in Brussels, the 'Association for the Reform and Codification of the Law of Nations', later renamed the 'International Law Association' ('ILA').[91] Although overlapping with the IDI in its concerns, and more of an American initiative (directly inspired by the success of the Alabama Claims arbitration), the ILA was consciously intended to complement rather than compete with the IDI, which would remain the principal 'scientific' international legal codification body. The ILA was indeed founded with the support of the IDI (who had agreed at their first meeting a month earlier to send a delegation to Brussels), and the first president of the ILA, the American supporter of international legal codification David Dudley Field,[92] was also one of the founders of the IDI. It was envisaged that the ILA would have a much broader membership, not limited to leading academics, but 'to consist of Jurists, Economists, Legislators, Politicians and others taking an interest in the question of the reform and Codification of Public and Private International Law, the Settlement of Disputes by Arbitration, and the assimilation of the laws, practice and procedure of the Nations in reference to such laws'[93]—in summary, anyone 'interested in the improvement of international relations'.[94] It is notable that, like the IDI, the ILA was and remains concerned with the progressive development of both public and private international law.

---

[89] Available at http://www.idi-iil.org/idiF/resolutionsF/1880_oxf_02_fr.pdf. Note also, *e.g.*, the IDI's 1877 Resolution on the laws of war, adopted in response to the commencement of hostilities between Russia and Turkey, available at http://www.idi-iil.org/idiF/resolutionsF/1877_zur_04_fr.pdf.

[90] See Sects. 1.4.2 and 1.4.4 below.

[91] See generally *e.g.* Abrams 1957.

[92] Perhaps best known for Field 1876—a proposed international code dealing with both public and private international law.

[93] See generally *e.g.* Bewes 1925.

[94] Ibid.

The first national sub-branch of the ILA was The Netherlands Society of International Law, established in 1910. The Centenary of the Society was celebrated in the hosting of the ILA biennial meeting in The Hague in 2010, for the fourth time in its history, and in a number of articles in a special edition of The Netherlands International Law Review (volume 57(2), 2010), examining the development of international law in The Netherlands, with one article specifically dealing with the history of The Netherlands Society of International Law.[95] Although Asser had no role (or at least no public role) in the founding of the ILA in general, it is no surprise that he was one of the 33 founding members of the board of The Netherlands Society. Further proof of his strong support for the Society may be found in the report that he donated to it part of the proceeds of his Nobel Prize award.[96] While Asser's direct influence on The Netherlands Society of International Law was of course curtailed by his death in 1913, his legacy was nevertheless extended and may easily be identified through his influence on others. The President of the Society for its first 15 years was Daniel Josephus Jitta, who had succeeded Asser at the University of Amsterdam when the latter had retired from academic office in 1893, and had also succeeded him as a member of The Netherlands Council of State in 1903. Jitta inherited and furthered Asser's legacy as a scholar and practitioner of both public and private international law. His successor in turn as President of the Society in 1926 was another student of Asser, Bernard Cornelia Johannes Loder, who had significantly contributed to the drafting of the Statute of the Permanent Court of International Justice, and then served as the Court's first President from 1922 to 1924. The international impact of Dutch international lawyers during this period must surely be attributed to some degree to the role played by Asser in establishing The Netherlands as a leading centre of international law.

1.3.3 The 'Hague Conferences on International Private Law'

As noted above, in September 1874 the IDI passed a resolution calling for international agreement on the unification of rules of private international law, felt by Asser among others to be an important and realistically achievable objective in the progressive development of international law. In February 1874, the government of The Netherlands had indeed already issued an international call for action on the matter, noting:

> how desirable it would be for the conclusion of arrangements relative to the reciprocal execution of judicial decisions pronounced in civil and commercial cases to be rendered possible, or at least facilitated, by the adoption, on the part of the governments interested, of uniform rules in regard to judicial competence.[97]

---

[95] Eyffinger 2010.

[96] Ibid., p. 149.

[97] United States Department of State 1874–1875, p. 790.

In particular, The Netherlands proposed that:

> [i]n order to attain this end, which consists in rendering possible … the conclusion of conventions regulating the reciprocal execution of decisions pronounced in civil and commercial cases … the best way would be to confide this important and difficult matter to an international commission, whose duty it should be to draw up a body of rules which the governments interested should pledge themselves to introduce into their legislation or to follow in their treaties.[98]

While the call was specifically directed to the governments of Germany, England, Austria, Belgium, France and Italy, it was also more widely distributed—a copy was, for instance, forwarded by the Ambassador of The Netherlands to the United States[99] to the US Secretary of State, Hamilton Fish (who had, incidentally, also negotiated the terms of the Alabama Arbitration with Great Britain). The accompanying memorandum drew particular attention to the importance of the issue in light of what we might today describe as 'globalisation', making the strikingly modern argument that:

> [t]he extension of international relations of all kinds, the improvement and the multiplication of the means of transportation and communication, have, by facilitating the removal of individuals and of fortunes, and by giving a truly cosmopolitan character to commercial and industrial relations, rendered most desirable the adoption of a reform based upon the solidarity of the interests of all civilised nations.
> The rapidity with which it is now possible to travel from one end of the world to the other is by no means in harmony with the tardy movements of judicial decisions, which, in principle, do not go beyond the frontier of the country in which they were rendered.[100]

If this memorandum was not at least in part the product of Asser's pen, it bears very clear evidence of his influence, not just in the fact that it cites his academic writing to support its analysis—his 1869 article in the first edition of the *Revue de droit international et de législation comparée*[101] noted above—but also in its broader appreciation of the importance of the issue. This particular initiative did not, however, proceed further. On the part of the United States, Hamilton Fish replied that 'the difficulties are so great in the way of carrying into effect the project, arising from the nature of the organic Constitution of the United States and the relations of the States to the Federal Government, that it is not thought best to attempt it'[102]—an objection which again has a strikingly modern tone, resonating in the present federalism difficulties facing the United States in implementing treaties, including treaties of private international law harmonisation.[103]

---

[98] Ibid.

[99] Ibid., p. 789 *et seq.*

[100] Ibid., p. 791.

[101] See Sect. 1.1 above. The US record (p. 791) is slightly inaccurate, citing to 'F.M.C. Asser [sic] on the effect or the execution of decisions rendered in a foreign country in civil and commercial cases. (*Revue de droit international et de legislation comparée*, 1869.)'.

[102] United States Department of State 1874–1875, p. 795. See further *e.g.* Alexander 1928, p. 222 *et seq.*

[103] See *e.g.* Mills 2010, p. 451; Brand 2009, p. 368; Ku 2008.

The perceived importance of the issue was, however, such that it received continued and frequent attention. The issue of the harmonisation of international rules for the recognition of foreign judgments was discussed periodically by the IDI,[104] and at almost every ILA meeting from 1877 until the end of the century, but with little progress. An inter-state conference to replace the failed Dutch effort of 1874 was proposed to be held in Rome in 1884, with the support of Mancini[105] (the then Italian Minister of Foreign Affairs), but apparently cancelled due to a cholera outbreak.[106] Greater progress was made in South America, with the adoption of a regional private international law harmonisation treaty at a Congress in Montevideo in 1889.[107] Although in part this achievement may have been assisted by pre-existing similarities in the legal systems of the states involved, its significance as a model for later projects, not just American but also European and international, should not be underestimated. Partially inspired by this development,[108] at Asser's initiative and with Asser presiding, a conference to consider the issue of international harmonisation of private international law was convened in 1893 in The Hague, and attended by almost all European states (with the perhaps notable exception of Great Britain). This was, in fact, to be the first of four conferences held over the next decade or so,[109] with further meetings in 1894, 1900 and 1904, at each of which Asser was re-elected as President. All were widely attended by European states, with the interesting appearance of Japan at the 1904 meeting, but with no British or American participation. Although intended to engage generally with harmonisation of private international law, the conferences in practice focused on quite particular issues as realistic starting points. The major product of the first two conferences, for example, was the 1896 Convention on Civil Procedure (which came into effect in 1899), focusing on coordination of rules dealing with such matters as the communication of judicial and non-judicial acts and the execution of letters rogatory, and outlawing discrimination against foreign nationals regarding the provision of security in civil proceedings or the possibility of imprisonment for debt. The 1900 conference produced treaties dealing more with choice of law issues, focused on the validity of marriage, divorce, and guardianship of infants, all of which came into force in 1904. At the 1904 conference, further treaties were prepared on such matters as succession,

---

[104] See *e.g.* the 1878 Resolution on 'Execution of Judgments', with Asser as the reporter, available at http://www.idi-iil.org/idiF/resolutionsF/1878_paris_01_fr.pdf.

[105] See *e.g.* Lipstein 1993, p. 554 *et seq.*; the initiative is also mentioned in the *Mémoire* annexed to the 'Note pour Messieurs les Délégués à la Conférence de Droit International Privé' of August 1893', in Actes de la Conférence de La Haye 1893, p. 6.

[106] See International Law Association 1885, p. 48. Later reports suggest that this may have provided convenient diplomatic cover for failure in the efforts to establish the conference.

[107] See *e.g.* Bewes 1920.

[108] The work of the Montevideo conference is discussed in the *Mémoire* annexed to the 'Note pour Messieurs les Délégués à la Conférence de Droit International Privé' of August 1893', in *Actes de la Conférence de La Haye* 1893, p. 6.

[109] See generally *e.g.* van Loon 2005; Lipstein 1993.

marital relations, lunacy, and bankruptcy, as well as an amendment to the 1896 Convention on Civil Procedure.

These conferences thus marked an important and successful shift in strategy in the harmonisation of private international law. Where the ILA and IDI had struggled to make progress in the general project of harmonisation of jurisdiction and the recognition and enforcement of civil judgments, the success of Asser's initiative could be attributed to a change in both forum (an inter-governmental rather than academic conference) and approach (a focus on achievable fragments rather than an all-embracing but unattainable ideal). Although this change may have been the product of necessity rather than intention,[110] it was nevertheless to Asser's credit in presiding over these conferences that he was able to judge the limits of possible consensus. The success of the conferences thus clearly owed a great deal to Asser's skill as a diplomat as well as his technical expertise—he was described by one participant as 'so much the soul of the whole enterprise as always to discover a solution at the proper time'.[111]

The Hague conferences were to meet again in 1925 and 1928, but without great success. It was not until 1951 that the project was re-established, this time with the adoption of a Statute which came into force in 1955—largely again under a Dutch initiative.[112] The modern Hague Conference on Private International Law, a formal international organisation dedicated 'to work for the progressive unification of the rules of private international law',[113] is thus a direct and worthy legacy of Asser's initiative more than a century ago.

1.3.4 Comité Maritime International

One of the other projects which received significant attention in the early years of the ILA and IDI was the international codification or harmonisation of maritime law. The subject was considered to be a particularly appropriate area for such attention because of its necessarily international subject matter, and because, as a result, national law had already developed very much with an international consciousness of the need for coordinated rules. After limited progress was made through diplomatic conferences in the 1880s or within the ILA, it was agreed that a separate organisation should be formed to continue the project. Around 1897, the 'Comité Maritime International' (CMI) was thus established, with Asser's

[110] At the 1893 Conference, Asser initially proposed the development of general principles, but quickly accepted the proposal of the French and Swiss delegates for an approach that was more concrete, practical and tangible: see Actes de la Conférence de La Haye 1893, pp. 29–31; van Loon 1989, p. 1134.

[111] Universal Congress of Lawyers and Jurists 1904, p. 137.

[112] Note also Gutzwiller 1945.

[113] Statute of the Hague Conference on Private International Law, Article 1, available at http://www.hcch.net/index_en.php?act=conventions.text&cid=29.

involvement once again, for the purpose of encouraging and supporting codification of international maritime laws. As an aspect of this, it was envisaged that one of the functions of the CMI was to serve as an umbrella association for national maritime law associations, who are counted among its membership. As a body more focused on industry and commercial interests, it continued to draw upon the expertise of academic and practising members of the ILA, to aid its codification efforts.[114] With the emergence of this institution we can again see the evidence of Asser's astuteness, in his recognition of the role that focused and specialised institutions can play in the progressive development of international law.

1.3.5 Hague Academy of International Law

Although the Hague Academy of International Law did not hold its first session until 1923, Asser may also certainly be credited with contributing significantly to its establishment.[115] Prior to the First World War, he was president of the Dutch committee which negotiated the founding of the Academy.[116] It was agreed that the Academy should operate, like the Permanent Court of Arbitration (established in 1902 as a product of diplomatic efforts in the 1899 Hague Peace Conference, as discussed below[117]), from the Peace Palace, built in The Hague from 1907 to 1913, to whose library Asser also contributed.[118] The idea for such an academy had long been supported by the IDI and ILA, but it was Asser who finally planned and shaped its practical formation, contributing further a part of his Nobel Prize award to the project,[119] and apparently even contributing part of his estate to its foundation.[120] Funding for the Academy came principally from the Carnegie Endowment for International Peace, established in 1910. The first President of the Endowment, the renowned international lawyer Elihu Root (a former US Secretary of State and also at the time a Senator and President of the American Society of International Law), was himself awarded the Nobel Peace Prize in 1912.

114 See International Law Association 1899, p. 91.

115 Asser also wrote an essay on the establishment of the Academy: Asser 1912, pp. 282–292.

116 See *e.g.* AJIL Editorial Comment 1914b, p. 353.

117 See Sect. 1.4.2 below.

118 See http://nobelprize.org/nobel_prizes/peace/laureates/1911/asser.html.

119 See http://www.vredespaleis.nl/default.asp?pid=101&tl=1.

120 See *e.g.* AJIL Editorial Comment 1914b, p. 356 (thanking 'the heirs of Mr. Asser'), and also noting Asser's contribution to the drafting of the Statutes of the Academy (a copy of which is at p. 357 *et seq.*). A memorial to Asser's passing is, rather sadly, found in the same volume of the journal, p. 343.

1.4 Legal and Diplomatic Practice

It is a defining characteristic of Asser's life that he pursued a diversity of interests and activities. During his time at the University of Amsterdam, for example, he was an active practitioner and a prominent figure in the Amsterdam business and banking community. While his private practice was an enduring part of his career, over time it was increasingly dominated by a sense of public service, particularly following his appointment as Legal Advisor to The Netherlands Ministry of Foreign Affairs in 1875. As noted above, he became a part-time professor in 1877 to allow him to continue these activities alongside his academic work.

1.4.1 Legal Advisor

As Legal Advisor, Asser counselled and represented The Netherlands in a variety of contexts. As noted above, he was, for example, a member of the Dutch delegation to the Congo conference of 1884–1885 in Berlin.[121] This conference attempted to establish legal regulation of European claims to African colonial territory, although its major effects were an acceleration of the colonial 'Scramble for Africa' and the establishment in 1885 of the (ultimately notorious) quasi-privatised 'Congo Free State' (under the control of the Belgian 'International Association of the Congo'). Asser played a more significant role in the contemporaneous negotiations to neutralise the Suez Canal (following British occupation in 1882), securing a seat for The Netherlands on the Suez Canal Commission, which drew up the Convention of Constantinople in 1888.[122] Continuing an early interest in problems of international communications and transport regulation, Asser also served as a representative to the International Conference for the Protection of Submarine Cables in 1882,[123] the International Conference on International Legislation Governing the Transport of Goods by Rail (which adopted the International Convention concerning the Carriage of Goods by Rail in 1890), and (as noted above) the Central Commission for Navigation on the Rhine.

1.4.2 1899 Hague Peace Conference

The establishment of the IDI and ILA were, as previously noted, directly inspired by the success of the Alabama Claims Arbitration, and consequently these

---

[121] See generally *e.g.* Koskenniemi 2002, p. 121 *et seq*. See further Sect. 1.2.1 above.

[122] See http://nobelprize.org/nobel_prizes/peace/laureates/1911/asser.html. Note also the 1879 Resolution of the IDI on the neutrality of the Suez Canal, available at http://www.idi-iil.org/idiF/resolutionsF/1879_brux_01_fr.pdf. See further Asser 1888.

[123] Once again, drawing on the work of the IDI, in its 1879 Resolution on the subject, available at http://www.idi-iil.org/idiF/resolutionsF/1879_brux_02_fr.pdf.

organisations gave particular attention during their early years to the development of the possibility for the arbitration of international disputes. This issue, alongside questions of disarmament and the conduct of warfare, was considered at two major 'Peace Conferences' held in The Hague in 1899 and 1907 (a third conference scheduled for 1915[124] was, for obvious reasons, never held), in which Asser played an important role.[125] Although neither conference successfully established any form of compulsory arbitration, one of the major successes of the 1899 conference, a product of Asser's direct involvement and skill as a negotiator, was the adoption of a Convention for the Pacific Settlement of International Disputes,[126] which founded the Permanent Court of Arbitration ('PCA'). The PCA is of course not a 'court', but an international organisation dedicated to assisting states (and increasingly also international organisations and private parties) in the peaceful resolution of their disputes.[127] To this end, it provides a facility including a panel of potential arbitrators to assist in resolving disputes through binding arbitration, where the parties to the dispute consent, which remains active and important today.[128]

1.4.3 Arbitrator

In 1902, Asser served as an arbitrator in two very important inter-state disputes—a sign of the great esteem in which he was held as (in the words of a US diplomat) 'an unimpeachable authority upon international law'.[129] The first was as sole arbitrator (with the agreement and at the joint request of the United States and Russia)[130] in the *US-Russian Sealing Arbitration,*[131] a claim made by the United States on behalf of US sealing ship owners for compensation for the seizure of four US ships by Russia outside Russian territorial waters. Russia admitted that one

---

124 See *e.g.* Scott 1908a.

125 See generally *e.g.* Aldrich and Chinkin 2000.

126 See *e.g.* Eyffinger 1999, including the Convention, p. 416 *et seq.*; United States Department of State 1899, p. 521.

127 Asser was rather critical of the PCA: 'Instead of a Permanent Court, the Convention of 1899 only created the phantom of a Court, an impalpable ghost, or, to speak more plainly, it created a clerk's office with a list', cited in Kebede Tiba 2006, p. 203; Spiermann 2005, p. 4.

128 See further http://www.pca-cpa.org/.

129 See *e.g.* United States Department of State 1900, p. 859.

130 See *e.g.* United States Department of State 1900, p. 799. The US Ambassador to The Netherlands reported back that Asser, when asked what compensation he would require to act as arbitrator, 'assured us he regarded it as a great honor to be selected, and that the honor was more to him than any consideration of money, and that he preferred to leave the amount of his compensation to be determined by the parties', p. 800.

131 See generally United States Department of State 1902. *Appendix I—Whaling and sealing claims against Russia.*

ship was mistakenly seised, and another had its cargo seised without proof of illegality, and the only issue for these cases was calculation of compensation. The justification for the seizure of the other two ships, that Russia was in 'hot pursuit' from illegal sealing within its territorial waters, was rejected by Asser as unfounded in international law, and compensation was awarded to the US. Although the US had unsuccessfully argued for extensive territorial seas in the region in its pleadings for the 1893 *Bering Sea Arbitration* with Great Britain (in which the US had itself seised British ships on the high seas, and been found liable for compensation), it was held not to be 'estopped' by these claims, and the generally accepted 3 mile territorial limit was applied. The amount of compensation was calculated with the assistance of commercial experts, nominated by the parties at Asser's request, and included damages for lost profits for the time the ships were out of service. The arbitral award appears to have been happily accepted by both states as a successful resolution of a difficult diplomatic problem.

The second dispute in which Asser served as an arbitrator in 1902 was the PCA's very first case, the *US-Mexico Pious Fund Arbitration.*[132] Asser was appointed by Mexico and served as one of five arbitrators, each appointed from the permanent panel of arbitrators (nominated by states) which had been established for the PCA. This dispute arose out of a trust fund established in the seventeenth and eighteenth centuries, to support religious activities in the Californias, which came ultimately under the control of the Mexican government.[133] With the cession of 'Upper California' from Mexico to the United States in 1848, the fund ceased payments to churches based in Upper California. After those churches complained to the United States, the dispute was submitted to a 'mixed claims commission' in 1869, finally resulting in an 1875 award of 21 annuities, covering the years from 1848 to 1869, which were paid to the church by Mexico. Subsequent annuities were, however, not paid, and a later dispute then arose as to whether the payment obligation continued. In 1902 the US and Mexico agreed to refer the claim to an arbitral tribunal established under the auspices of the PCA, authorised 'to render such judgment or award as may be meet and proper under all the circumstances of the case'. The tribunal ultimately found (unanimously) that the amount of annuity determined in the 1875 award was payable by Mexico in perpetuity, and thus ordered payment of past dues (since 1869) as well as a continuing annual contribution.[134] Two aspects of the decision are particularly notable. The first is the exclusion by the tribunal of Mexico's reliance on its domestic law as a defence against an international obligation—an early affirmation of a now well-accepted

[132] The Pious Fund Case. *United States of America v. the United Mexican States.* Protocol signed at Washington, 22 May 1902. Decision at The Hague, 4 October 1902. UN Reports of International Arbitral Awards, Vol. IX, p.1. See generally United States Department of State 1902. *Appendix II—United States vs. Mexico. In the matter of the case of the Pious Fund of the Californias*; Penfield 1902.

[133] See generally Weber 1963.

[134] Payments lapsed during the Mexican Revolution; a final settlement was only made in 1967. See Weber 1969.

principle of international law.[135] The second is the fact that the award drew heavily on the private law (and private international law) principle of *res judicata*, determined to be a general principle of international law, to find that the decisions of fact and law under the 1875 award should continue to determine Mexican obligations under the fund. While it may be impossible to attribute any of this reasoning to individual arbitrators, it is not unreasonable to suppose that Asser's particular interest in the harmonisation of private international law principles played a role in the approach of the arbitral award.

1.4.4 1907 Hague Peace Conference

The second Hague Peace Conference, held in 1907,[136] focused predominantly on regulating the conduct of warfare, particularly at sea. The conference also, however, gave significant attention to the further development of inter-state arbitration, and produced a revised Convention on the Pacific Settlement of International Disputes.[137] A further Convention dealing with the Limitation of Employment of Force for Recovery of Contract Debts was also established, which essentially made international arbitration compulsory for the recovery of debts owed by foreign states to private parties, with force only permissible if an offer to arbitrate were refused or an arbitral award not complied with.[138] While this may not seem a major development when viewed with modern eyes, the use of force to reclaim private debts was considered at the time a significant potential source of international conflict. It had, for example, been one of the issues at the heart of the 1902 Venezuela Crisis, in which Great Britain, Germany and Italy imposed a naval blockade on Venezuela for several months.[139] Consideration was also given at the 1907 Conference, but without success, to a 'Treaty of Arbitration', through which states would give general consent and thereby more widely commit themselves to compulsory arbitration.[140]

---

[135] Reflected in *e.g.* Articles 3 and 32 of the International Law Commission's Articles on Responsibility of States for Internationally Wrongful Acts (2001).

[136] See generally *e.g.* Scott 1908a; Eyffinger 2007; AJIL Colloquium 2007; Daudet 2008.

[137] See generally *e.g.* Hershey 1908.

[138] See generally *e.g.* Scott 1908b.

[139] Venezuela accepted the validity of the claims of the blockading powers; a copy of the protocol is available at 2 American Journal of International Law 1908, p. 902. A further dispute arose as to whether the blockading powers should have priority over other Venezuelan creditors, and under US pressure this was submitted to the PCA in 1903; a copy of this further protocol is available at 2 American Journal of International Law 1908, p. 905. The dispute was resolved by an arbitral award on 22 February 1904, somewhat surprisingly in favour of the blockading powers.

[140] The mechanism is supported by Article 53 of the 1907 Convention on the Pacific Settlement of International Disputes. See further *e.g.* Hull 1908.

Substantial progress was also made at the conference on the establishment of a 'Court of Arbitral Justice',[141] with a permanent membership representative of the international community, to complement the more flexible but ephemeral PCA. Agreement on the formation of the Court was reached in principle, and 35 articles forming the basis of a convention for this purpose were endorsed at the conference. However, progress was frustrated by a lack of agreement on the means of appointing judges, and how states were to be represented on the court without its membership becoming unwieldy or their sovereign equality unacceptably compromised. Nevertheless, it is evident that at this conference and in many of the articles it discussed and agreed the seeds were sown for the foundation of the Permanent Court of International Justice in 1922,[142] and its successor the International Court of Justice.

1.4.5 Conferences on Unification of the Law of International Bills of Exchange

The account above should by no means be taken to indicate a complete shift in Asser's interests, away from private international law considerations to matters of greater concern to the public international stage. Asser continued to be interested in and emphasise the importance of matters of private international law, reaffirmed by his presiding role in two conferences, hosted in The Hague in 1910 and 1912, on the unification of the law relating to international bills of exchange.[143] The result of the second conference was the adoption of a convention on the subject, which was widely signed, not only by European and South American states, but also by China and Japan,[144] perhaps signifying a growing internationalisation of the project of legal harmonisation. Although ultimately not widely ratified, the uniform rules which were agreed at the conference formed the basis of future legal codification efforts, including the Convention Providing a Uniform Law For Bills of Exchange and Promissory Notes negotiated under the auspices of the League of Nations at Geneva in 1930.[145] The 1912 Convention was printed, with a posthumous introduction by Asser,[146] perhaps his final publication, in the inaugural 1913 edition of the *Grotius Internationaal Jaarboek*, renamed in subsequent editions as the *Grotius Annuaire International*, which from 1913 to 1946 essentially served as

[141] See *e.g.* Scott 1908a, 1916.

[142] See *e.g.* the many references to the 1907 draft convention and discussions in the documents and proceedings of the 1920 Advisory Committee of Jurists, available at http://www.icj-cij.org/pcij/other-documents.php?p1=9&p2=8; Spiermann 2003.

[143] See *e.g.* Ellinger 2000, pp. 35–36.

[144] Lorenzen 1916, p. 138.

[145] See *e.g.* Guerrico 1944, p. 3.

[146] Noted in Engert 1914.

one of the distinguished predecessors to The Netherlands Yearbook of International Law.

1.5 A Legacy in Public and Private International Law

It should be readily apparent from the outline above that Asser was at the heart of much of the development of international law in the critically formative period of the late nineteenth and early twentieth centuries. His 'fingerprints' may be found on almost any area of international law, public or private, and summarising this legacy necessarily involves omission and simplification. But with these provisos, we may perhaps identify four key legacies of Asser's professional life.

First, Asser played a critical role in the development and gradual institutionalisation of legal internationalism. At a time of growing European nationalism, with the emergence of unified German and Italian states, he shared with a number of his key contemporaries a belief in the importance of a global perspective and the potential importance of law in regulating relations between nations. With them, he established informal global networks of like-minded scholars and diplomats (including the Institut de Droit International), largely academic groups who would work for the expansion of the scope and influence of these ideas. Seeking to give these initiatives a greater impact and effect, he would also be involved in the establishment of associations of international lawyers (including the International Law Association), and the growth of 'international law' itself as a new field of academic and practical work devoted to the legalisation of international relations. Finally, progressing the development of this field further, he would be heavily involved in building enduring international institutions (including the Hague Conference on Private International Law, and The Hague Academy of International Law) which today continue to embody those ideas of internationalism. One aspect of Asser's professional life is therefore the transformation of the idea of internationalism, through socialisation and legalisation, into concrete institutions with real social products, designed to outlast and overshadow their founders. Asser would, one might suspect, be delighted that it is today so difficult to believe that one man was at the heart of the foundation of so many of the key institutions of legal internationalism.

Second, Asser was not simply an organiser or facilitator of these organisations or conferences; he was a very active contributor to their work. In so doing, he played a further central role in the early emergence of formalised dispute resolution on the international plane. In the 1899 Hague Peace Conference, he played an important part in the establishment of the Permanent Court of Arbitration, and his work as an arbitrator in two major international disputes in 1902 contributed to the credibility of the institutionalisation of international dispute resolution. Asser was involved in further work on a proposal to augment the PCA with the establishment of an additional, more judicial, international institution during the 1907 Hague Peace Conference, which very much laid the foundations for the emergence of the Permanent Court of International Justice in the aftermath of the First World War. Asser was, however, by no means a naïve internationalist. He made it quite clear that, if international arbitration as a means of peaceful settlement of disputes was to flourish, the 'fantastical-sentimental' attitude that divests the institution of its legal character and thus of its true meaning was to be strongly opposed. Part of that was Asser's plea for a careful examination of the applicable law, arguing against an automatic preference of international over national law in that respect. 'Nobody', stated Asser, 'will suspect me of not caring for international law. However, it would be difficult to deny that this part of law does not yet deserve the palm when it comes to legal certainty'.[147] Nonetheless, the development of institutions of international dispute settlement was a key complement to the development of substantive international law during this period. Without them, international law might struggle to differentiate itself from politics, as no distinctly legal forum or procedure would be available to engage with disagreements over the interpretation or application of substantive rules of international law. In them, we see the beginnings of a conception of an international 'rule of law', where disputes over the rules governing international relations may be peacefully resolved through legal processes.

Third, Asser played a major role in establishing the reputation of The Netherlands as an important neutral power in the development of international law, and of The Hague as a capital of international law and legal institutions, a status which it continues to have and promote today.[148] The relationship between The Hague and international law has long been somewhat symbiotic—international law has perhaps contributed as much to The Hague as The Hague has contributed to international law. As one scholar has put it, 'it was the law that, around 1900, gave a new lease of life to the dreamy, backward township'.[149] The success of The Hague in attracting international conferences and institutions during Asser's time has continued to serve it well, giving it a natural prominence when a location is being considered for any new institution. It has equally given The Netherlands an impetus to participate fully in international lawmaking activities, to justify its geographic centrality. This is, of course, a role which The Netherlands has long played, reflected in its 'Grotian tradition', as a small and somewhat vulnerably positioned state with a great strategic interest in the promotion of international peace and free trade, including through the progressive development of both public and private international law. The significance of The Hague as a centre of international law and institutions cannot of course be attributed to any one individual. It may nevertheless be suggested that the decision to hold the 1899 Peace Conference in The Hague, which went some way to establishing or confirming its status, was likely to have been influenced at least to some extent by the successful

[147] Asser 1903, pp. 245–258, especially p. 258.

[148] Celebrated in van Krieken and McKay 2005.

[149] Eyffinger 2010, p. 144.

hosting in The Hague, at Asser's instigation, of the Conferences on Private International Law held in 1893 and 1894.

Fourth and finally, Asser may be viewed as having a particularly important legacy in the field of private international law, through The Hague Conference on Private International Law and more broadly the internationalist perspective it embodies. One of Asser's principal areas of work was on the international harmonisation of rules of private international law, which he clearly viewed as an important matter of international concern. But in this he was swimming against a tide. In the late nineteenth century, the traditional understanding of private international law as part of the law of nations was being eroded by a range of factors, including the rise of 'positivist' international legal theory.[150] Although legal practitioners like Asser have always remained more conscious of the functional and practical entanglement of public and private international law, Asser's lifetime saw a growing doctrinal division between the two subjects, as public international law was increasingly viewed as a formal system for documenting agreements between equal and sovereign states. In contrast, by the middle of the twentieth century, much of private international law had been reconceptualised (perhaps even misconceptualised) as a matter of purely national concern—as part of the law of civil procedure, or private law seeking to determine the just outcome in individual cases. This has perhaps left its strongest legacy in the various states of the United States, where private international law rules are frequently viewed as serving substantive domestic policy interests. In Europe, however, this understanding has been overturned in recent decades by the development of European private international law rules, focused on systemic objectives principally associated with the efficient functioning of the internal market. In the modern era, private international law is in the process of re-emerging, in something like its original conceptualisation, as a form of public law dealing with the distribution of national regulatory authority between states. On the international stage, this means it is closely linked with public international law rules of jurisdiction and their shaping of national sovereignty. The Hague Conference on Private International Law, refounded as a permanent international institution in the 1950s, carries the torch for this internationalist perspective on private international law, through the support it provides for private international law harmonisation efforts. It is not merely the direct inheritor of the forum for negotiation provided by the conferences hosted by Asser in The Hague in 1893, 1894, 1900 and 1904, but an inheritor of the spirit of internationalism, and the internationalist perspective on private international law, which inspired those conferences. It is no coincidence that other international bodies which Asser contributed to creating, including the Institut de Droit International, the International Law Association and The Hague Academy of International Law, are all at least formally engaged in both public and private international law. These all continue to carry the hallmarks of the beliefs of Asser and his collaborators—the importance of the development of both public

[150] See further *e.g.* Mills 2009, Chap. 2.

and private international law as a matter of international justice and the peaceful relations between states.

Tobias Michael Carel Asser's legacy in public and private international law is both broad and deep. He had an impact on the substantive development of international law, the professionalisation of the study and practice of international law, and on its institutionalisation. His obituarist in the *American Journal of International Law* in 1914 summed up Asser's contribution well in the following tribute:

> [i]t is not given to many men to take part in such important creations, and the evidences of his constructive imagination and his well directed zeal will long survive him and make his name one to conjure with in the international world.[151]

Asser's professional life coincided with a period of great change in the development of international law, and we should of course be wary of attributing too much significance to the contribution made by any individual in such large and global social transformations. Nevertheless, his individual contribution as a 'practical legal statesman' was indisputably worthy of the distinction it received through the award of the Nobel Peace Prize in 1911.

References

Abrams I (1957) The emergence of the international law societies. Rev Politics 19:361–380

Actes de la Conférence de La Haye (1893) Chargée de réglementer diverses matières de droit international privé, Septembre 1893, p 12–27

Aldrich GH, Chinkin CM (eds) (2000) Symposium: the Hague peace conferences. Am J Int Law 94:1–101

Alexander AA (1928) Foreign judgments—enforcements of—under the comity of nations. Georgetown Law J 17:221–233

American Journal of International Law: Colloquium (2007) The second Hague peace conference: a centennial commemoration. Neth Int Law Rev 54:195–413

American Journal of International Law: Editorial Comment (1913) Professor John Westlake (1828–1913). Am J Int Law 7:582–584

American Journal of International Law: Editorial Comment (1914a) In Memoriam T.M.C. Asser. Am J Int Law 8:343–344

American Journal of International Law: Editorial Comment (1914b) The Academy of International Law at The Hague established in co-operation with the Carnegie Endowment for International Peace. Am J Int Law 8:351–360

Asser TMC (1858) Verhandeling over het staathuishoudkundig begrip der waarde. Johannes Müller, Amsterdam

Asser TMC (1860) Het bestuur der buitenlandsche betrekkingen volgens het Nederlandsche staatsregt. Johannes Müller, Amsterdam

Asser TMC (1869) De l'effet ou de l'exécution des jugements rendus a l'étranger en matière civile et commercial. Revue de droit international et de législation comparée 1:473–493

Asser TMC (1880a) Schets van het internationaal privaatregt. De Erven F Bohn, Haarlem

Asser TMC (1880b) Droit international privé et droit uniforme. Revue de droit international et de législation comparée 12:5–22

---

151 AJIL Editorial Comment 1914a, p. 344.

Asser TMC (1883) Hugo De Groot—1583—10 April—1883, De Gids. Reprinted in: Asser TMC, Studiën op het gebied van recht en staat (1858–1888). De Erven F. Bohn, Haarlem, 1889, pp 337–348

Asser TMC (1884) Eléments de droit international privé ou du conflit des lois. Ouvrage traduit, complété et annoté par Alphonse Rivier. Arthur Rousseau, Paris

Asser TMC (1885a) Schets van het Nederlandse handelsrecht. Vierde, vermeerderde druk. De Erven F. Bohn, Haarlem

Asser TMC (1885b) De Congo-Akte, De Gids, May 1885. Reprinted in: Asser TMC, Studiën op het gebied van recht en staat (1858–1888). De Erven F. Bohn, Haarlem,1889, pp 357–392

Asser TMC (1888) La Convention de Constantinople pour le libre usage du Canal de Suez. Revue de droit international et de législation comparée 20:529–558

Asser TMC (ed) (1889) Studiën op het gebied van recht en staat. De Erven F Bohn, Haarlem

Asser TMC (1893) Een onuitgegeven brief van Jeremias Bentham aan koning Willem I. In: Verslagen en mededeelingen der Koninklijke akademie van wetenschappen. Afdeeling letterkunde. 3de reeks. Müller, Amsterdam, pp 179–182

Asser TMC (1901) La Convention de La Haye Du 14 Novembre 1896 relative a la procedure civile. Les héritiers F, Bohn, Haarlem and Belinfante Frères

Asser TMC (1902) Fondation de la revue. Revue de droit international et de législation comparée 34:109–116

Asser TMC (1903) Nationaal recht en international scheidsgerecht. In Verslagen en mededeelingen der Koninklijke Akademie van wetenschappen. Afdeeling letterkunde. 4de reeks. Müller, Amsterdam

Asser TMC (1912) De Akademie voor internationaal recht. In:Verslagen en mededeelingen der Koninklijke akademie van wetenschappen. Afdeeling letterkunde. 4de reeks. Müller, Amsterdam

Association Internationale pour le Progrès des Sciences Sociales (1863) Annales de l'Association internationale pour le progrès des sciences sociales—Première Session—Congrès de Bruxelles, Bruxelles (etc.). Lacroix, Paris: Guillaumin

Bewes WA (1920) The Treaties of Montevideo (1889). Trans Grotius Soc 6:59–79

Bewes WA (1925) Transactions of the International Law Association, 1873–1924. Sweet & Maxwell, London

Brand RA (2009) The European magnet and the U.S. centrifuge: ten selected private international law developments of 2008. ILSA J Int Comp Law 15:367–394

Caron DD (2000) War and international adjudication: reflections on the 1899 peace conference. Am J Int Law 94:4–30

Conrad J (1902) Heart of darkness. Penguin, London

Daudet Y (ed) (2008) Topicality of the 1907 Hague conference, the second peace conference. Martinus Nijhoff, The Hague

De Baere G (2010) Case C-420/07, Meletis Apostolides v. David Charles Orams, Linda Elizabeth Orams, Judgment of the Grand Chamber of 28 April 2009, [2009] ECR I-3571. Common Mark Law Rev 47:1123–1159

Durand A (1994) The Role of Gustave Moynier in the founding of the Institute of International Law (1873)—the war in the Balkans (1857–1878). The manual of the laws of war (1880). Int Rev Red Cross 34:542–563

Ellinger P (2000) Negotiable instruments. In: Zweigert K (ed) International Encyclopedia of Comparative Law, Instalment vol 9. Martinus Nijhoff, Den Haag

Engert AVH (1914) Untitled book review. Am J Int Law 8:414–415

Eyffinger A (1999) The 1899 Hague peace conference: the parliament of man, the federation of the world. Kluwer, Dordrecht

Eyffinger A (2007) The 1907 Hague peace conference: the conscience of the civilized world. Judi Cap, The Hague

Eyffinger A (2010) 'A caravan passes by...'—The centenary of The Netherlands society of international law. Neth Int Law Rev 57:143–166

Field D (1876) Outlines of an international code, 2nd edn. Baker Voorhis, New York

Guerrico HMB (1944) Unification and present status of negotiability legislation in America. Minn Law Rev 29:1–21

Gutzwiller M (1945) Das internationalprivatrecht der Haager Konferenzen: Vergangenheit und zukunft. Annuaire Suisse de Droit International 2:48

Haberman FW (ed) (1972) Nobel lectures. Peace 1901–1925. Elsevier, Amsterdam

Hershey AS (1908) Convention for the peaceful adjustment of international differences. Am J Int Law 2:29–49

Hudson MO, Feller AH (1931) The international unification of laws concerning bills of exchange. Harv Law Rev 44:333–377

Hull WI (1908) Obligatory arbitration and the Hague conferences. Am J Int Law 2:731–742

International Law Association (1885) Report of the Twelfth Conference

International Law Association (1899) Report of the Eighteenth Conference

Kebede Tiba F (2006) What caused the multiplicity of international courts and tribunals? Gonzaga J Int Law 10:202–225

Koskenniemi M (2002) The gentle civilizer of nations. The rise and fall of international law 1870–1960. Cambridge University Press, Cambridge

Koskenniemi M (2004) Gustave Rolin-Jaequemyns and the establishment of the Institut De Droit International (1873). Revue belge de droit international 37:5–11

Ku JG (2008) The crucial role of the states and private international law treaties: a model for accommodating globalization. Mo Law Rev 73:1063–1070

Laufer H (1992) La libre circulation des jugements dans une union judiciaire. Une idée géniale de T.M.C. Asser, visionnaire de la Convention de Bruxelles. Peter Lang, Bern

Lipstein K (1993) One hundred years of Hague conferences on private international law. Int Comp Law Q 42:553–653

Lorenzen EG (1916) The Hague convention of 1912, relating to bills of exchange and promissory notes. Ill Law Rev, 11:137–158 (part 1), 247–267 (part 2)

Mills A (2009) The confluence of public and private international law: justice, pluralism and subsidiarity in the international constitutional ordering of private law. Cambridge University Press, Cambridge

Mills A (2010) Federalism in the European Union and the United States: subsidiarity, private law and the conflict of laws. Univ Pa J Int Law 34:369–455

Nys E (1910) Notice sur Gustave Rolin-Jaequemyns. In: Annuaire de l'Académie royale des sciences, des lettres et des beaux-arts de Belgique. Hayez, Brussels, pp 53–87

Penfield WL (1902) The 'Pious Fund' arbitration. North Am Rev 175:835–843

Remien O (2001) European private international law. The European community and its emerging area of freedom, security and justice. Common Mark Law Rev, 38:53–86

Rolin-Jaequemyns G (1869) De l'étude de la législation comparée et de droit international. Revue de droit international et de législation comparée 1:1–17

Rolin-Jaequemyns G (1877) L'oeuvre de l'exploration et de civilization de l'Afrique centrale. Revue de droit international et de législation compare 9:288–291

Scott JB (1908a) Recommendation for a third peace conference at the Hague. Am J Int Law 2:815–822

Scott GW (1908b) Hague convention restricting the use of force to recover on contract claims. Am J Int Law 2:78–94

Scott JB (1916) The status of the international court of justice. Oxford University Press, Oxford

Scott JB (1918) In Memoriam Louis Renault. Am J Int Law 12:606–610

Spiermann O (2003) 'Who attempts too much does nothing well': the 1920 advisory committee of jurists and the statute of the permanent court of international justice. British Year B Int Law 73:187–260

Spiermann O (2005) International legal argument in the permanent court of international justice. The rise of the international judiciary. Cambridge University Press, Cambridge

United States Department of State (1874–1875) Foreign relations of the United States. http://digital.library.wisc.edu/1711.dl/FRUS.FRUS187475. Accessed 2 Sept 2011

United States Department of State (1899) Foreign relations for the United States. http://digital.library.wisc.edu/1711.dl/FRUS.FRUS1899. Accessed 2 Sept 2011

United States Department of State (1900) Foreign relations for the United States. http://digital.library.wisc.edu/1711.dl/FRUS.FRUS1900. Accessed 2 Sept 2011

United States Department of State (1902) Foreign relations for the United States. http://digital.library.wisc.edu/1711.dl/FRUS.FRUS1902. Accessed 2 Sept 2011

Universal Congress of Lawyers and Jurists (1904) Official report of the universal congress of lawyers and jurists, held at St. Louis, Missouri, U. S. A., September 28, 29, and 30, 1904, under the auspices of the universal exposition and the American bar association

van der Mandere HChGJ (1946) Tobias Michael Carel Asser. In: Sevensma TP et al. (eds) Nederlandsche helden der wetenschap. N.V. Uitgevers-maatschappij Kosmos, Amsterdam, pp 167–200

van Krieken PJ, McKay D (eds) (2005) The Hague: legal capital of the world. TMC Asser Press, The Hague

van Loon JHA (1989) Quelques réflexions sur l'unification progressive de droit international progressive du droit international privé dans le cadre de la Conférence de La Haye. In: Erauw J et al (eds) Liber Memorialis François Laurent. E. Story-Scientia, Brussels, pp 1810–1887

van Loon JHA (2005) The Hague conference on private international law: an introduction. In: van Krieken PJ, McKay D (eds) The Hague: legal capital of the world. TMC Asser Press, The Hague

Vlas P (2010) On the development of private international law in The Netherlands: from Asser's days to the codification of Dutch private international law (1910–2010). Neth Int Law Rev 57:167–182

Voskuil CAA (1995) Tobias Michael Carel Asser—1838–1913. In: The moulding of international law: Ten Dutch Proponents. TMC Asser Institute, The Hague, pp 5–25

Weber FJ (1963) The pious fund of the California. Hispanic Am Hist Rev 43:78–94

Weber FJ (1969) The United States versus Mexico: the final settlement of the Pious Fund. Historical Society of Southern California, Los Angeles

Westenberg JW (1992) Tobias Michael Carel Asser (1838–1913). Een pragmatisch jurist. In: Blom JCH, Leupen PHD, De Rooy P, Veen TJ, Kooymans L (eds) Een brandpunt van geleerdheid in de hoofdstad. De universiteit van Amsterdam rond 1900 in vijftien portretten, Uitgeverij Verloren. Amsterdam University Press, Hilversum, pp 53–76

Chapter 2
Legal Aspects of the Transfer of Authority in UN Peace Operations

Terry D. Gill

Abstract United Nations Peace Operations and UN mandated Peace Enforcement Operations, which are usually conducted by regional organizations or *ad hoc* coalitions of States, are wholly dependent upon the voluntary contribution of troops by Member States. This involves transferring parts of command authority to the United Nations or to the regional organization which has undertaken the mission under UN mandate, while other aspects of authority over the troops remain under the control of the State which is contributing its troops. This partial transfer of authority results in complex multilayered command structures which has given rise to certain legal and practical questions relating to the attribution of conduct in relation to allegations of possible violations of international law and the most appropriate remedies in such cases. This article provides an overview of the types of command structures most often used in both UN and UN mandated operations and explores the questions resulting from these in relation to attribution of conduct. It also discusses possible shortcomings in the provision of remedies and offers some suggestions as to how these might be addressed.

Keywords UN peace operations · UN mandated peace enforcement operations · Attribution of conduct · Control · Command structures · Accountability

Professor of Military Law, University of Amsterdam and Netherlands Defence Academy; Associate Professor Public International Law, Utrecht University

T. D. Gill (✉)
University of Amsterdam and Netherlands Defence Academy, Amsterdam,
Utrecht University, Utrecht, The Netherlands
e-mail: T.D.Gill@uu.nl

I. F. Dekker and E. Hey (eds.), *Netherlands Yearbook of International Law 2011*,
Netherlands Yearbook of International Law 42, DOI: 10.1007/978-90-6704-849-1_2,

Contents

2.1 Introduction

United Nations peace operations have evolved over the past half century into a multifaceted instrument for carrying out a number of main tasks of the UN, including, in particular, the maintenance of international peace and security, the promotion of conflict resolution, and increasingly, the protection of human rights. They are often referred to as a 'flagship activity' of the Organization and have become a well established and recognized instrument within the UN System, despite the fact that no specific reference to such operations exists in the UN Charter. Their evolution from traditional forms of peacekeeping, following inter-state conflicts involving the monitoring of ceasefire agreements into much more challenging missions which often combine elements of traditional peacekeeping with aspects of peace enforcement, alongside peace-building activities, such as post-conflict reconstruction, promotion of the rule of law, and other efforts aimed at building a lasting stable environment, has led to a dramatic increase in the number of missions and peacekeeping personnel and to a corresponding increase in the complexity of missions and of the arrangements and agreements which regulate them.[1]

[1] For a description of the various types of UN (authorized) peace operations see *inter alia* Findlay 2002, pp. 3–7; White 1993, p. 199 *et seq.* The official UN typology can be found in the Secretary-General's Reports 'An Agenda for Peace' 1992 and 'Supplement to an Agenda for Peace' 1995. The official UN

All UN Peace Operations are dependent upon the voluntary contribution of personnel by Member States to the Organization to carry out the tasks set out in the mandate issued by the UN Security Council. In order to ensure that the mandate is carried out in an impartial manner and in recognition of the specific and primary role of the UN in maintaining international peace and promoting conflict resolution, the States contributing troops to a specific mission will in many cases transfer part of their authority over the troops and other formed units to the UN for the duration of their participation in the operation. This normally involves placing the troops contributed to the mission under some degree of UN command, while retaining the authority to withdraw from the mission and control over a number of other matters, including the exclusive exercise of criminal jurisdiction over the troops and the maintenance of discipline within the contributed units. These arrangements result in a multilayered authority structure, with the UN and the troop contributing countries jointly exercising different degrees of authority over the troops participating in the mission. While normally the operational conduct of the mission would be transferred to UN authority as will be explained at more length below, other levels of authority at the strategic and internal level normally remain within the control of the contributing State. The general exception to this would be in the event the operation involved the high risk or near certainty of sustained high intensity combat against organized armed opposition, in which case the UN would normally delegate command and execution of the mission to a regional organization or coalition of States willing to undertake it and enforce a Security Council mandate.[2] In such cases, OPCOM, or at least some elements of it, is often transferred to a lead nation or regional or other organization which has been mandated by the UN Security Council to enforce the mandate.

The partial transfer of authority and control over troops participating in UN-led peace operations and in UN Security Council mandated enforcement and peace enforcement operations gives rise to certain operational and legal questions. These include how such transfers are carried out, what kind and degree of authority and control is involved in such a transfer, and what the legal consequences of such transfers are, including those relating to accountability and possible legal responsibility (see Sect. 2.4.1 below for definitions of how these terms are used in this article) for misconduct and possible violations of international law. The legal personality of the UN and its attendant immunity before national courts imply that there will be some aspects relating to such operations which fall outside the normal legal oversight of national authorities, including municipal courts. At the same

(Footnote 1 continued)
Doctrine for Peace Operations is contained in 'United Nations Peacekeeping Operations: Principles and Guidelines' 2008, hereinafter cited as Capstone Doctrine.

[2] For a description and explanation of the complex UN command and authority structure see 'Managing United Nations Peacekeeping Operations', in Capstone Doctrine, p. 67 *et seq.* For an analysis of this structure see Cammaert and Klappe 2010, p. 159 *et seq.* For an analysis of the reasons why the UN command structure is generally not employed in (peace) enforcement operations involving the risk of sustained high intensity combat see Gill 2010, pp. 92–93.

time, there are at present, few (judicial) remedies available at the international level to ensure that all aspects of a mission are carried out in conformity with international law. It is of the utmost importance both in terms of compliance with the law and in terms of the legitimacy of the mission and the UN and other relevant actors that there are adequate mechanisms in place to ensure both accountability and to address the consequences of possible breaches of legal obligations in the conduct of the mission. The United Nations is a creation of international law and is committed to conducting its operations in conformity with all applicable rules and norms governing the conduct of operations. Failure to do so, or even the appearance of impunity can have a major impact upon the legitimacy of such operations and ultimately upon the organization itself.

This article will give a description and analysis of the types of operations carried out by the UN or under UN mandate and will attempt to provide some answers to the abovementioned issues, including whether there are currently gaps in ensuring legal accountability which need to be addressed to ensure that all such operations meet the highest standards of compliance with relevant norms and rules of international law.

This article is structured as follows. Firstly an overview is given in Sect. 2.2 of the various categories of UN and UN mandated operations. These different categories have implications for the type of command arrangements which are employed and the type and degree of authority which is usually transferred by the States providing troops to carry out the operation. In Sect. 2.3, a description is provided of the different levels of command in military operations and the command structure which is employed in both operations conducted directly by the UN itself under its direct authority and operations authorized under a mandate of the UN Security Council, which are conducted and carried out either by regional organizations or by one or more Member States acting under the overall authority of the mandate issued by the Council. The present section reflects to a large extent the typology of operations discussed in the previous paragraph and is important in understanding what is meant by 'transfer of authority' and the implications this has for attribution of different types of conduct to the organization or State which exercises authority over the operation. Section 2.4 discusses issues of responsibility and accountability related to the transfer of authority and command structure used in the various types of operations conducted by the UN or under UN mandate set out in the previous two sections. It is subdivided into subsections dealing with definitional issues for the purposes of this article, issues relating to attribution of conduct in the light of the abovementioned command structures employed in different types of operations and the level of authority normally exercised by the respective actors, the primacy of the UN in the maintenance of peace and security and the implications this has and does not have for purposes of attribution of conduct, and finally discusses the question of how transfer of command and authority and the resulting implications for attribution of conduct relate to the provision of effective remedies for possible breaches of conduct and of international obligations. In this context, a number of recommendations are proposed relating to how to better assess questions of attribution of conduct based upon the actual command structures and degree of authority exercised in different types of operations and a number of gaps in existing remedies are given attention. Finally, some overall conclusions are drawn in the final section.

2.2 Classification of Peace Operations in UN Doctrine and Practice

2.2.1 Enforcement and Peace Enforcement Operations

The UN Charter, as stated above, makes no reference to Peace Operations, much less any classification of the various categories of such operations, such as (peace) enforcement, peacekeeping, or peace-building operations. Nevertheless, these categories have emerged in UN doctrine and practice relating to peace operations and reflect to a significant extent the underlying purpose and character of the operation and of the Charter itself.[3] The Charter, for example, makes a distinction between powers of the Security Council in relation to the peaceful settlement of disputes and conflict resolution on the one hand, and the powers and authority it wields in relation to the maintenance of international peace and security on the other. Peace Operations, based upon the former, have been often referred to as 'Chapter VI' operations, while those related to the maintenance of peace and security have often been designated as 'Chapter VII' operations to reflect this difference in purpose and character. Operations with the overall purpose of promoting a peaceful resolution of (post-)conflict situations, not involving the use of force beyond self-defence, which in contemporary UN doctrine includes defence against forcible attempts to frustrate the execution of the mandate, usually on the part of 'spoilers' differ conceptually and in practical terms from those which have as their purpose and are mandated to suppress a breach of the peace or act of aggression, or to restore and maintain international peace and security as a response to an ongoing threat to it. While many post-Cold War Peace Operations, including approximately half of the currently 15 operations being conducted by the UN Department of Peacekeeping combine aspects of both, involving a certain degree of overlap in purpose and are confronted with challenges which require a multifaceted response, there is still a fundamental difference between peace operations which are governed by the bedrock principles of peacekeeping: consent of the parties, impartiality, and limited use of force on the one hand, and operations which are intended and mandated to impose the will of the international community 'by all necessary means' on the other.[4] Although many contemporary operations, such as those currently underway in Eastern Congo, Darfur, South Sudan, Ivory Coast and Haiti

[3] See *supra*, note 1.

[4] The fundamental principles of United Nations Peacekeeping Operations are longstanding and are set out in 'Basic Principles of United Nations Peacekeeping', Capstone Doctrine, pp. 31–35.

cannot always be neatly fit into a particular category, there can be no doubt that the distinction between the objectives and purposes of these two broad categories are fundamental, both conceptually and in more practical terms.[5]

Operations which have as their overriding purpose the enforcement of the will of the international community within the context of the maintenance of international peace and security are not governed by the abovementioned principles of consent, impartiality, and limited use of force and will differ radically in terms of their mandates, force composition, and application of force and coercion from those which are subject to these principles. This distinction is reflected in UN doctrine and is widely referred to as 'enforcement action or operations' on the one hand and 'peace (keeping) operations' on the other. Enforcement action is by its nature, neither reliant upon consent, nor impartial and will be directed against a particular State or entity. This in turn may involve the use of proactive measures, including the application of force and coercion going far beyond what is required for self-defence and response to incidental attempts to interfere with the conduct of the mandate.[6] Enforcement action can even involve the use of offensive force directed against a State or other entity with the object of imposing a military solution and involving sustained high intensity combat amounting to involvement in an armed conflict as a party to it. This was the case, for example, in the Korea conflict (1950-3) and in the UN mandated 'Operation Desert Storm' (1990-1), which had as their purposes the suppression of serious breaches to international peace and the reversal of the actions of North Korea and Iraq respectively.

Not all enforcement action is necessarily so far-reaching in terms of its objectives or involvement in an armed conflict or the use of force and coercion and this justifies a further subdivision within the overall category of enforcement measures of a military character between enforcement operations and what have come to be referred to as peace enforcement operations. The former are in fact UN mandated war-fighting operations designed to impose a military solution in response to a particularly serious breach of international peace, while the latter, while sharing the abovementioned characteristics of not being reliant upon consent of all parties, impartiality and limitation of force to self-defence, do not involve the attempt to impose a purely military solution and do not invariably imply the involvement of the UN (mandated) Force as a party to an armed conflict. While consent is not a requirement for either enforcement or peace enforcement operations, in the former it will be irrelevant, while in the context of peace enforcement, it can be a useful supplement to the extent feasible to the existence of a Chapter

---

[5] 'The Normative Framework for United Nations Peacekeeping Operations', Capstone Doctrine, para 1.4; 'Security Council Mandates', pp. 16–19. See also Gill 2010, pp. 81–88 (enforcement and peace enforcement characterization and legal basis) and pp. 135–142 (*idem.* in re. consensual peacekeeping, peace making and peace building operations).

[6] For an analysis of the nature of enforcement action see e.g. Simma et al. 2002, pp. 754–759; Franck 2002, p. 20 *et seq.*; Bowett 1964, pp. 266–267. For a clear distinction between enforcement and peace enforcement operations see Findlay 2002, pp. 6–7; Gill 2010, pp. 86–88.

VII legal basis for the operation and the successful execution of the mandate. Although both enforcement and peace enforcement share the characteristics of not requiring consent of the parties and the ability to engage in the proactive use of coercion, they differ in their objectives, the applicability of the humanitarian law of armed conflict, and their possible relation to the host government. Peace enforcement may or may not involve the sustained conduct of hostilities against an organized armed opponent and the applicability of humanitarian law will be limited to situations where this results in involvement as a party to a (non-international) armed conflict, while enforcement operations of the Korea or Desert Storm variety will automatically result in the full applicability of the humanitarian law relating to an international armed conflict to all parties.

Examples of peace enforcement operations include, in addition to the latter stages of the ONUC operation of the 1960s conducted by the UN itself, more recent examples such as the stabilization forces in post-conflict Bosnia (SFOR and IFOR), Kosovo (KFOR), Iraq (MNFI) and the post invasion phase in Afghanistan (ISAF); all of which in recent years have been conducted under UN mandate by regional organizations, or arrangements, or by coalitions of States acting under the overall authority of the Security Council.

2.2.2 *Peace Operations*

Peace Operations, by contrast, are normally conducted under the direct authority of the UN itself, or in some cases by or in close cooperation with regional organizations operating under UN mandate, but within the framework of and in conjunction with diplomatic (peacemaking) and peace-building efforts aimed at conflict resolution and promoting a durable peace and the rule of law. Many contemporary mandates are quite detailed and multifaceted and may even include certain elements of peace enforcement alongside traditional and more robust peacekeeping and peace-building activities. Nevertheless, they differ conceptually and in practical terms from enforcement action in that they still are essentially reliant upon consent, impartiality, and force limited to response to direct attack or incidental armed attempts by ‘spoilers’ to interfere with the carrying out of the mandate and are not intended or set up to impose the mandate by force of arms. Examples of such peace operations include the ongoing operations in the Congo (MONUC and since July 2010 renamed MONUSCO), the Ivory Coast (UNOCI), Haiti (MINUSTAH), South Lebanon (UNIFIL), and the African Union/UN Hybrid Operation in Darfur (UNAMID), to name some of the most well-known current operations. While traditionally, the demarcation in the legal literature between the two (enforcement/peacekeeping) has been the question whether the operation is conducted on the basis of a Chapter VI or VII mandate, in actual contemporary practice this is not the determining factor. Of the 15 operations currently being conducted under the authority of the UN Department of Peacekeeping, approximately half are being conducted under a Chapter VII mandate.[7] This does not, however, automatically make them enforcement or even primarily peace enforcement operations in the way they are conceived and are carried out, notwithstanding a certain degree of overlap between robust peacekeeping and peace enforcement. They still rely upon the bedrock principles of peacekeeping and are essentially consensual in nature. They are not mandated, comprised, or equipped to carry out sustained combat operations against an organized armed adversary with a view to imposing a military solution. They are expected to cooperate with and essentially dependent upon the consent of the main parties involved although they are capable of using force if necessary to *react* to armed attempts to frustrate the mandate, rather than *proactively* seeking out and neutralizing, including through the use of *offensive* force, any armed opposition which threatens the execution of the mandate. This distinction is probably more important in practice than whether the mandate is based on Chapter VII, which is utilized in relation to these types of contemporary peace operations by the Security Council to signal resolve and the seriousness of the situation, rather than as a mandate to impose a solution through the use of proactive force. Where more sustained force against an organized adversary is necessary to achieve the mandate, the UN Peacekeeping Forces are generally dependent upon outside assistance acting under Security Council mandate, as was the case in the latter stages of the Yugoslavia conflict when the NATO Rapid Reaction Force was deployed to apply pressure upon the (Bosnian) Serb leadership to accept a negotiated solution, in Eastern Timor, where Australia provided the military 'muscle' to ensure withdrawal of Indonesia, in Kosovo, where NATO provided a large well-equipped force to ensure Yugoslav withdrawal and complement the UN transitional authority, and most recently in Ivory Coast, where French troops and helicopter gunships were used to back up the UN force and force an end to the civil conflict. In Eastern Congo, with the gradual improvement of the security situation and increased capacity of the DRC Government and armed forces, the UN operation has taken on more of the characteristics of a stabilization mission since the renewal of its mandate in July 2010 and is now probably best characterized as a mixed peacekeeping/peace enforcement/peace-building operation with a mandate to protect civilians and support DRC Government efforts to re-establish effective control over its entire territory and assist in the disarmament and demobilization of armed groups operating in the eastern provinces. This modification of its mandate is a result of the improved security situation and ability of the DRC Government to exercise governmental authority and the cooperation of neighboring States such as Rwanda and Uganda in the efforts to neutralize armed groups operating in the region. This is a practical illustration of the fact that in contemporary operations the dividing line between peacekeeping and peace enforcement is often fluid and reflective of practical considerations, and also shows that the UN will usually only take on a more

[7] The current UN Operations being conducted by DPKO can be found on the UN Peacekeeping website at http://www.un.org/en/peacekeeping/operations/current.shtml.

enforcement-oriented mandate when the situation allows and it can operate in conjunction with other actors.

Peace operations are generally conducted directly by the UN, acting through the department of peacekeeping operations (DPKO), which falls under the responsibility of the UN Secretary-General and under the political authority of the Security Council. Peacekeeping forces are all made up of voluntary contributions of personnel and equipment by participating Member States which transfer elements of authority and control over the contingents to DPKO for the duration of the operation.[8]

2.3 Command and Control in UN (Mandated) Operations

2.3.1 Definition of Command and Control

Command and Control (C2 in military parlance) relate to the authority vested in certain individuals (or bodies) to direct the actions and exercise authority over (elements of) the armed forces. Command is normally exercised by a specific member of the armed forces acting under the responsibility and overall direction of the competent national or international governmental or administrative authority for the purpose of directing, coordinating, and controlling military forces. Control relates to the authority of a commander over part of the activities of subordinate organizations, or other organizations not normally under his command, which includes responsibility for implementing orders or directives for the achievement of specific purposes.[9] Most States and some international organizations, such as the UN and NATO, have developed sophisticated and quite intricate command and control structures and doctrines for the purpose of achieving specific objectives and ensuring that forces operate within designated legal and policy guidelines.

While there is a significant degree of convergence between the general principles and parlance relating to command and control between various States, there is no single all encompassing definition or designation of what degree of authority each level of command may involve and each State will have specific characteristic features and limitations relating to the modalities of command and the degree of authority exercised by commanders. There are, however, various generally recognized levels of command and control ranging from full or strategic command to tactical command.

---

[8] See *supra*, note 1. See also 'The Evolving Role of United Nations Peacekeeping Operations', in Capstone Doctrine, pp. 17–28.

[9] Cathcart 2010, pp. 237–238. See also NATO Glossary of Terms, which has been adopted by all NATO members. The US Department of Defense Joint Publication 1-02 Dictionary of Military and Associated Terms incorporates it along with the standard NATO list of abbreviations and can be found at http://www.bits.de/NRANEU/others/jp-doctrine/jp1_02(05).pdf.

2.3.2 Full Command

Full command implies the totality of command authority and covers all aspects of organization and direction of forces and is only possessed and exercised at the national level. No international or coalition commander or organization exercises full command over forces not forming part of his (its) national armed forces. Other levels or aspects of command or authority can be delegated.[10] Within the context of UN (mandated) operations, certain elements of command authority are normally delegated for specific purposes for the duration of the operation. The troop contributing country always retains full command. Full command always includes strategic level command that is to say the authority to determine whether a nation's armed forces will participate in a given (multinational) operation as a part of its overall foreign and defence policy and to withdraw from participation in accordance with any terms agreed to. Strategic level command is an attribute of national sovereignty and cannot be delegated. Strategic level command usually implies at least some degree of input in determining the overall strategic objectives of a given operation. This will vary according to circumstances and the degree of influence the State in question has in the formulation of those strategic level policy objectives.[11]

In cases where an international organization is involved in or has authority to determine the strategic objectives of an operation, the influence of any particular participating State will be influenced and limited by a number of factors, such as the degree of authority possessed by the organization, the relative weight of the State's contribution, and other considerations. The UN Security Council possesses primary responsibility in the maintenance and restoration of international peace and security and in any UN (mandated) operation will determine the overall objectives of the operation through the terms of the mandate. Obviously, the Council does not operate in a vacuum and the relative weight of its members and other key players, will have a corresponding influence upon the terms in which the mandate is formulated and its dependence upon voluntary contribution of troops and assets will, to some extent, shape the terms of the mandate.

2.3.3 Operational Command and Control

Operational command (OPCOM) is the authority vested in an individual or body to assign specific tasks or missions to subordinate commanders, to deploy units within the area of operations, to reassign forces, and to retain or delegate elements of operational or tactical level command (TACOM) or control. Operational level command deploys and employs forces to pursue and effectuate the overall strategic objectives of the operation as a whole and forms a bridge or link between strategy

[10] Cathcart 2010, pp. 235–238.

[11] Ibid., pp. 237–238.

and tactics. Operational control (OPCON) is the authority of a commander over part of the activities of subordinate level commanders or other persons placed temporarily under his control and is normally an attribute of operational level command. Part or all of OPCON can be delegated by the operational commander if necessary. Both OPCOM and/or control, or elements thereof, can be delegated by a troop contributing country (TCC) to a multinational commander or to an international body which will, in turn, designate an operational level commander to exercise such delegated authority, with the TCC retaining full command.[12]

In UN mandated enforcement and peace enforcement operations, the UN Security Council will determine the general objectives of the operation through the terms of the mandate and retain overall political authority and responsibility for the operation, but the operational level command will be normally designated to a specific participating State or regional organization or arrangement. In both of the full enforcement operations involving large-scale combat, Korea, and Desert Storm, operational level command was designated to a 'lead nation' (the USA) and in many of the post-Cold War peace enforcement operations mandated by the Security Council, OPCOM has been delegated to NATO and the national contingents participating in both of those categories of operations have been placed under the OPCOM and/or control of the operational commander designated by the 'lead nation', or by the organization acting under the Council's delegated authority. In the case of NATO, the North Atlantic Council acts on behalf of NATO's Member States as the Organization's highest political authority to enter into agreement with the UN to carry out the Security Council's mandate under the Council's overall authority, and military authority is exercised through the NATO military command structure, which will designate the operational level commander to lead NATO and associated forces in the mission area.[13]

In UN directed and controlled peace operations, the command structure generally is structured as follows. When the Security Council becomes involved in the process of considering whether to issue a mandate for a Peace Operation, without prejudice to its discretionary power to issue the mandate and determine its purpose and objectives, it will engage the advice and support of the UN Secretariat and enter into consultations with Member States to determine the necessity and prospects for success of the proposed mission and determine the scope of the mandate and the force composition for the mission. The Secretariat is directed by the UN Secretary-General (UNSG) who acts through the DPKO in conjunction with the Department of Field Support, each of which are headed by an Undersecretary General in charge of those respective departments acting under the overall authority of the UNSG.[14]

---

[12] Cathcart 2010, p. 238.

[13] Ibid., pp. 238–242.

[14] 'Planning a United Nations Peacekeeping Operation', in Capstone Doctrine, pp. 47–56. For a description and analysis of UN Operational Authority, see Cammaert and Klappe 2010, pp. 159–161.

Factors, which play a role in influencing the scope of the mandate and force composition, include the extent of consent and likely cooperation of the parties involved, the existence or lack of a ceasefire, the degree of relative safety for the peacekeeping personnel, whether the UN is the most appropriate body to conduct the operation or whether it can and should be delegated to a regional or subregional organization or arrangement, whether a reasonably precise mandate can be formulated and whether sufficient forces and assets will likely be forthcoming from Member States to execute the mandate. The Security Council always retains the discretionary power to determine whether a particular situation constitutes a threat to or breach of international peace and security and whether or not to issue a particular mandate and determine its overall scope and objectives. However, it will take due account of the advice of the UNSG and DPKO in shaping a mandate and it will often call upon the UNSG to conduct a Strategic Assessment involving all relevant UN actors and consultations with likely TCCs and with the Host Government and other key players to ascertain the requirements for the mission and the likelihood of its success.

This process will usually be assisted by the dispatch of a Technical Assessment Mission (TAM) to the proposed mission area as soon as conditions allow to assess conditions on the ground. Once a mandate has been formulated and issued by the Security Council, the process of mission start-up and deployment begins. While general policy guidelines on the process of force generation and deployment exist, there is no precise formula for how this will actually be carried out, since each mission poses specific challenges and requirements and the setting up of a mission will depend upon a number of factors; in particular the willingness of Member States to provide personnel and assets, the degree of resolve of the Security Council, the availability of financial resources, and the degree of cooperation from the Host Government. These will determine the force composition, available resources, and the speed of deployment of the mission in a practical sense. The TCCs participating in the mission will enter into agreement to place one or more contingents of military or police personnel at the disposal of the UNSG and transfer part of their authority over the personnel to the UN for the duration of the operation. In doing so, they may indicate certain restrictions upon the use of their personnel for the execution of particular tasks within the mission; these are generally referred to as 'caveats'. While it is UN policy to try to restrict such caveats as far as possible, they are an unavoidable consequence of the dependence of the UN upon Member States for voluntary contribution of personnel and the retention of full command by the TCC over its armed forces or police.[15]

Normally the level of authority transferred to the UN by the TCCs will be that of OPCOM and/or control. This is done either through a formal agreement (TOA) or through a Memorandum of Understanding (MOU), whereby all or part of operational level command or control is transferred to the UNSG acting through the Undersecretary General of Peacekeeping Operations who is in charge of DPKO. He/she will then designate a civilian Head of Mission (HOM) often

[15] 'Managing United Nations Peacekeeping Operations', in Capstone Doctrine, pp. 66–68.

designated as the Special Representative of the Secretary-General (SRSG) with the overall control of the mission and a Force Commander who will be vested with the delegated OPCOM and/or control over the military forces made available for the operation by the respective TCCs.[16]

The UN will also endeavor to enter into an agreement (Status of Forces Agreement or SOFA) with the Host Government at the earliest opportunity concerning the status of the mission and forces participating and ensuring free access into and throughout the mission area, respect for local law and the immunity of the personnel from the Host State's jurisdiction. In the absence of a formal agreement on status, the parties may agree to apply the Model UN SOFA as a matter of policy and the immunity of the UN and participating forces and other personnel is additionally provided for under customary international law. Force contingents and formed police units making up part of a UN peacekeeping force are always subject to the exclusive criminal and administrative jurisdiction of the Sending State.[17]

2.3.4 Tactical Command and Control

TACOM relates to the authority of a designated tactical level commander to exercise authority at the level of a single unit or combination of subunits and to assign specific tasks to subordinates within that unit and those subunits under his/her command to achieve specific tasks or missions assigned by higher authority. Tactical level control (TACON) relates to the detailed direction and control of movements and maneuvers at the local level in order to carry out specific tasks assigned by higher authority.

In both UN mandated (peace) enforcement operations which are conducted by a 'lead nation', or by a regional organization or arrangement, and in Peace Operations carried out directly by the UN under the direction of DPKO, TACOM, and control are normally retained by the TCC, which will designate a tactical level commander and one or more sublevel commanders with the level of authority appropriate at their particular level of command, although such tactical command and control must be exercised in conformity with the operational authority of the UN, NATO, or coalition operational commander. In UN directed Peace Operations, the normal practice is for the TCC to appoint a contingent commander who will exercise TACOM/TACON over the contingent made available for the operation and who will act as the representative in the field of the TCC in question. He/she will be assisted by one or more sublevel commanders who act under his/her direct authority. The TCC retains, as stated previously, exclusive criminal, disciplinary, and administrative authority and jurisdiction over its designated contingent commander and the personnel making up the contingent. In UN directed and

---

[16] Cammaert and Klappe 2010, pp. 159–60; 'Managing United Nations Peacekeeping Operations', in Capstone Doctrine, pp. 67–69.

[17] Fleck 2010, pp. 146–149.

conducted operations, the UN Force Commander exercises operational level command/control over the Force as a whole and can assign specific operational tasks and missions to the respective contingents making up the force for the fulfillment of the mission objectives. The Force Commander answers to the HOM/SRSG, who is in charge of the overall conducting of the mission, who in turn reports directly to the Undersecretary General for Peacekeeping Operations and he/she in turn to the UNSG.[18]

The Force Commander and the HOM have no direct authority over the internal functioning of a particular contingent, but can recommend the removal of a contingent commander and/or individual members of the contingent for serious failure to perform assigned tasks or missions or for breach of UN administrative codes of conduct. In cases of extreme misconduct, an entire contingent can be sent home and a TCC barred from further participation in that mission. While this is not always an effective full remedy for misconduct, much less for criminal behavior, it does act as a deterrent and the Force Commander can influence the functioning and performance of tactical level contingent commanders to some extent through this instrument and can at least ensure that a particular individual or group of individuals under his/her authority do not remain on station if their conduct threatens the performance of the mission.[19]

2.3.5 Summary

The command structure and arrangements set out above are not strictly uniform and certain variations can exist within the context of specific missions. However, the general structure set out above serves as a pattern and model for most missions and variations are usually minor in character. This structure and the corresponding levels of authority are crucial in understanding how UN (mandated) Peace (Enforcement) Operations function in a practical sense and should be borne in mind when determining and assessing questions of accountability and possible legal responsibility of either a criminal or more general nature, particularly in the realm of attributing specific acts or omissions to either the UN or other organization or to a TCC for failure to adhere to legal norms or policy directives.

---

[18] For definition of operational and tactical command and control, see Cathcart 2010, p. 238. For a description of how this functions in the field within the UN command structure, see Cammaert and Klappe 2010, pp. 160–163.

[19] Members of Military Contingents assigned to UN Operational Authority are bound by UN Codes of Conduct and Administrative Guidelines and the obligation to respect Host Nation Law. The TCCs which deploy them are bound to investigate and where evidence of criminal activity or misconduct exists, to prosecute members suspected of such misconduct or criminal activity. See Model MOU between the United Nations and Participating States, Article 7 bis-sexiens reproduced in Oswald et al. 2010, pp. 56–59. The authority of the UN to repatriate peacekeepers (or potentially entire contingents) is laid down in the Directives for Disciplinary Matters involving Members of National Contingents is reproduced in ibid., p. 387 *et seq.*

It should be remembered that the multilayered levels of authority range from the general to the specific and simply because a particular act or failure to act is carried out under UN Security Council mandate does not signify that it is an act attributable to the UN. Likewise, the fact that the UN (or relevant other organization) may exercise operational level command over contingents, does not always translate into actual authority or even responsibility for acts which are performed outside that purview. In short, an understanding of the levels of command and authority at the various levels they are exercised by different actors is crucial in determining which entity or individual can be held accountable for breaches of conduct or transgression of legal norms and for determining what the appropriate remedy might be. This will be explored in some more detail in the ensuing section.

2.4 Responsibility and Accountability Issues Related to Command and Transfer of Authority

2.4.1 Some Definitional Issues

While responsibility and accountability are, to some extent, terms of art they can have somewhat different meanings in different contexts and it may be useful to set out some definitions of how these terms will be used for the purposes of the remainder of this article. 'Accountability' will be used to denote oversight and scrutiny by political, administrative, and judicial bodies for the activities of an international organization, a State, or an individual acting under its authority and/or jurisdiction. It includes both political and legal oversight and scrutiny and pertains to both actions and omissions which constitute violations of legal obligations and those which do not violate any specific legal obligation. Accountability is a facet of the rule of law and is generally considered to be broader in scope than and inclusive of the principle of responsibility.[20] Legal accountability will always include responsibility *strictu* sensu, but can include judicial or quasi-judicial oversight related to legal questions not necessarily directly related to determining liability and questions of compensation, since (international) law is not exclusively concerned with determining liability and the consequences thereof. Political oversight would include oversight of a more general nature and possibly making policy changes and recommendations which may or may not have legal consequences.

'Responsibility' is a legal term of art and denotes the legal consequences of the breach of an international legal obligation, including liability for wrongful acts and

[20] There is no generally applicable definition of 'accountability'. The notion of accountability in the context of peace and peace enforcement operations was addressed by the International Law Association (ILA) within the broader context of accountability of international organizations. See International Law Association 2004, p. 164 *et seq.*

forms of reparation. It is a subset of the notion of accountability. Responsibility consists of two key elements: (i) the breach of an obligation under international law through an act or omission (ii) which is attributable or imputable to a State or an international organization possessing legal personality under international law.[21] The problem of attribution is of particular importance in the context of multinational UN (mandated) peace (enforcement) operations due to the complex layers of authority and control set out above.

2.4.2 Attribution Issues

The attribution of an act or omission to an international organization will depend upon a number of issues. Firstly, whether the organization in question possesses legal personality under international law which would enable it to bear rights and duties within the framework of international law. Secondly, whether the act or omission in question was under the effective control of the organization. Thirdly, whether the act or omission was carried out in an official capacity on behalf of the organization or was instead committed by an individual acting outside the scope of his/her official duties in a private capacity or acting under instructions of a State rather than on behalf of the organization.[22]

There is no doubt that the UN is an organization possessing legal personality under international law. This has been long recognized and also extends to subsidiary organs, which include specific UN Peacekeeping Missions. The North Atlantic Treaty Organization is likewise possessed of international legal personality within the scope of its activities, albeit somewhat more limited in scope than that pertaining to the UN, and is capable of entering into agreements with States and other international organizations and possessing legal capacity to bring and be subject to claims and enjoy and exercise immunities.[23]

---

[21] See Article 2 Articles on Responsibility of States (DARS) and Article 4 Draft Articles on the Responsibility of International Organizations (DARIO) respectively. Both documents can be found *inter alia* on the website of the International Law Commission, http://www.un.org/law/ilc/.

[22] Article 2 DARIO stipulates that responsibility applies to organizations established under international law and possessing international legal personality. Article 4 DARIO provides that responsibility of an organization results from acts and omissions in breach of an international obligation which are imputable to that organization. The standard of effective control has been widely recognized by both the ILC and ILA and is laid down in Article 6 DARIO. For further extensive analysis see e.g. Kondoch 2010, pp. 521–523.

[23] The legal personality of the UN was recognized as far back as the landmark *Reparations for Injuries* Advisory Opinion of 1949; *ICJ Reports* (1949) 174. Peacekeeping Operations are established as subsidiary organs of the mandating organ, i.e. the Security Council and possess legal personality within the scope of their activities. Likewise, NATO is an international organization possessed of international personality within the scope of its objectives and activities. See Zwanenburg 2004, pp. 66–67; Knoll 2008, p. 435.

The effective control test for the attribution of responsibility has been laid down in the case law of the International Court of Justice (ICJ) and is the approach followed by the International Law Commission (ILC) in its work on the international responsibility of both States and international organizations, as well as the approach favored by most authorities. It should be noted, however, that notwithstanding the broad support it enjoys, it has not been universally applied. Most notably, the European Court of Human Rights (ECtHR) has followed an 'ultimate control' approach in its decisions in the *Behrami* and *Saramati* cases, while the International Criminal Tribunal for the Former Yugoslavia employed an 'overall control' standard in its Appeals Chamber decision in the *Tadic* case, albeit in a somewhat different context. However, there are good reasons to conclude that the 'effective control' approach is the most logical and reasonable standard for the purposes of attribution of conduct in the context of multinational peace operations. In addition to the abovementioned overwhelming support it enjoys, it corresponds best to the realities of such operations and leaves less room for gaps in accountability.[24]

In the case of UN mandated peace (enforcement) operations which are conducted by regional organizations or coalitions of States acting under UN Security Council mandate such as those referred to earlier (see para 2.1 above), the link between the UN and the actual conduct of the mission is much too tenuous to generally attribute conduct of the mission to the UN. In such operations, the UN acts primarily as a legitimizing authority by providing a legal basis for the operation, determining the overall objectives through a broadly formulated mandate and delegating the actual conducting of the mission to a particular regional organization or arrangement, or group of States acting independently under its ultimate authority. Such authority is essentially political in nature and generally entails no more than the provision of information by the designated organization to the Council on a periodic (usually annual) basis in the context of determining whether the mandate should be adjusted and/or renewed. The actual conduct of the mission at both the operational and tactical level is in the hands of the regional organization and/or participating States, as set out above. Therefore, it does not correspond to the realities of decision-making or command and control to attribute conduct of either the designated regional organization or of participating States to the UN, simply on the basis of the provision of a legal basis for the operation in the form of a mandate. Moreover, the use of the 'ultimate control' standard can and has resulted in significant gaps in legal accountability and ensuring the provision of adequate remedies for possible breaches of obligations under international law

[24] For the general recognition of the 'effective control' standard see Kondoch 2010, p. 523. The ECtHR decision in the *Behrami v France* and *Saramati v France, Germany and Norway*, has received critical commentary from inter alia both Kondoch 2010 and Knoll 2008, respectively for applying a standard of 'ultimate control' instead of applying the 'effective control' standard consistently. See Kondoch 2010, pp. 525–528; Knoll 2008, pp. 443–444. See also Krieger 2009. The *Tadic* Appeals Chamber decision of the ICTY dealt with individual criminal responsibility, IT 94-I-A, 2 October 1995.

or injury as a result of liability not necessarily resulting from any breach of a legal obligation.[25]

Since the UN will not accept responsibility or provide compensation for acts not carried out under its direct authority and is not party to any human rights convention or subject to the jurisdiction of any regional or domestic court, the possibilities for providing a remedy for unlawful conduct or other injury arising within the context of a UN mandated operation which has been delegated to a regional organization or group of States are practically speaking, virtually non-existent insofar as they are viewed as being attributable to the UN rather than to Member States on the basis of an overall or ultimate control standard.

This is what happened in the abovementioned *Behrami/Saramati* cases where the ECtHR determined that acts allegedly in breach of the European Convention on Human Rights (ECHR) were not attributable to States party to the ECHR and that the UN was not subject to its jurisdiction. This frustrates the principle that legal rights should be accompanied by an effective remedy and ignores the reality of how such operations are conducted in practice.[26] While this gap is partly addressed by the practice of NATO and many troop contributing States of providing *ex gratia* financial compensation to individuals for injury or damage, this cannot be considered to be an adequate substitute for full legal accountability, nor does it always provide for an effective remedy. While, *ex gratia* financial compensation goes some way toward addressing the material damage caused within the context of a particular operation, it neither addresses the question of whether or not the operation was in breach of an obligation, nor does it provide any other form of compensation, other than monetary.

While UN mandated enforcement and peace enforcement operations are carried out under the 'ultimate' or perhaps the 'overall' control of the UN Security Council (depending on how one defines those terms), this has no relationship to the realities of how such missions are actually directed and conducted. This control is of a primarily political nature and neither the Security Council, nor any other body within the UN has any control, or even direct influence over how the mission is actually conducted, beyond the (theoretical) possibility of not renewing the mandate. For example, in the case of the UN mandated ISAF operation in Afghanistan, OPCOM is exercised by the NATO designated operational commander at ISAF Headquarters, who is appointed by the lead nation. TACOM is exercised by the commanders of each national contingent deployed within ISAF by the respective governments of the States participating in the mission, which also appoints or dismisses the contingent commander in question. In such cases, attribution of acts carried out pursuant to either NATO or TCC commanders to the UN would ignore the realities of how this and similar UN mandated (peace) enforcement missions are actually conducted.

---

[25] Krieger 2009, pp. 173–176.

[26] Ibid.

In the case of Peace Operations carried out directly by the UN under the DPKO command structure outlined above, the situation is significantly different. In such operations, the UN is not only the authority providing the mandate for the operation, but at least in principle exercises *de jure* OPCOM and/or control over the operation. Whether this will actually translate into effective control in relation to a specific act or omission is another matter and would depend upon the nature of the act and a number of other considerations. These could include whether it was carried out in an operational context in official capacity, whether the actor was in fact, acting under UN direction, at the instructions of (the agent of) a particular State, or whether it was an *ultra vires* act carried out in violation of UN rules, directives, or procedures. For example, if the UN Force Commander in one of the Peace Operations referred to previously (see para 2.2 above) gave contingents under his command the order to not forcibly oppose a group threatening civilians, such an order would be attributable to the UN in the event the order resulted in civilians being killed or raped as a result of such an order. If the Force Commander ordered the contingent to use all necessary means to prevent harm occurring to the civilians and the contingent commander either ignored the order (perhaps at the instruction of his own government) or used force in a manifestly disproportionate and indiscriminate manner in violation of UN Rules of Engagement, resulting in large-scale civilian casualties, that act would not be attributable to the UN, but rather to the TCC in question, since it would be *ultra vires* in character.

This would also partially apply to operations conducted under UN mandate, whereby the operation is under dual authority. For example, in both the Kosovo and Eastern Timor operations, the UN was directly involved and charged with political and administrative aspects of the mission acting directly through a UN subsidiary organ, while the military aspects of the operation had been delegated to a regional organization or group of States acting through a separate chain of command under a Security Council mandate.

In such cases, it would only be realistic to attribute conduct carried out either directly by a UN organ or agents or by other actors who were acting under UN instructions and/or were under its effective control at the time the act or omission occurred to the UN, rather than to the regional organization or State which committed the act or omission. In operations carried out directly by the UN under the DPKO command structure there is a (refutable) presumption that operational aspects of the mission can be attributed to the UN, but it would be necessary to examine whether the act in question was in fact carried out under UN control and additionally was not carried out in wilful disregard of UN orders or directives or was the result of gross negligence. If any of those possibilities were relevant, the act would not pertain to the UN, but rather to the Sending State.[27] For example, if troops opened fire upon unarmed peaceful demonstrators under the orders of their

[27] Kondoch 2010, p. 524, pointing out that Article 9 of the Model UN MOU excludes UN responsibility for injury resulting from gross negligence or wilful misconduct. See also Oswald et al. 2010, p. 60.

contingent commander or a subcommander under his direct authority in wilful disregard of UN operational rules and procedures, the act would not be attributable to the UN, but to the Sending State.

There is also the possibility that an act was carried out in an 'off-duty' capacity. The UN considers an act to be of an 'off-duty' nature whenever it is not conducted in an official or operational context and not whether the individual concerned was located in an operational area or was in or out of uniform when the act took place.[28] Consequently, acts of an 'off-duty' character, such as most allegations of sexual abuse committed by UN peacekeeping troops, would not be carried out in an official or operational capacity and would therefore not be imputable to the UN, but rather to the Sending State. Additionally acts arising under 'operational necessity' are not eligible for compensation.[29]

There is also the possibility that responsibility could be shared by more than one actor, i.e., by both an international organization and by one or more Sending States. This could be the case, if the act was jointly planned and conducted by two or more actors and there was clear evidence of breach of conduct or failure to act on the part of these actors within their respective spheres of authority. The notion of joint or several responsibility is, however, somewhat undeveloped in international law and is to be considered exceptional.[30]

In sum, the complexities of multinational peace operations require a careful case-by-case assessment regarding the nature of the operation, the command structure employed, the nature of the act, and other relevant considerations for the purposes of attribution of conduct to a specific actor or actors.

---

[28] Kondoch 2010, p. 524, citing a 1986 Memorandum of the UN Office of Legal Affairs, which is reproduced in the *United Nations Juridical Yearbook* 1986, p. 300.

[29] A general description of the problem of sexual abuse in the context of (UN) Peace Operations is given by Klappe 2010, pp. 497–499. 'Operational Necessity' is discussed by Zwanenburg 2004, pp. 305–306. See also Kondoch 2010, p. 525, where he cites the (then) UN Secretary-General 'the UN's liability for property loss and damage caused by its forces in the ordinary operation of the Force is subject to the exception of operational necessity' which is defined 'as a situation in which damage results from the necessary actions taken by a peace-keeping force in pursuing its mandate. The determination of such necessity remains at the discretion of the force commander.'

[30] Kondoch 2010, p. 530 citing the lack of any court decision and the relative lack of State practice to date in relation to joint or several responsibility. See also Report of the International Law Commission 2001, Commentaries, Article 46, para 3, p. 124, where it is stated that 'notions of joint responsibility derive from internal law and analogies must be applied with care. The principle of independent responsibility reflects the position under general international law in the absence of agreement to the contrary by the States concerned.' A transfer of authority agreement does not normally include any provision relating to joint or several responsibility.

2.4.3 The United Nations' Primacy in the Maintenance of Peace in Relation to Issues of Accountability

In addition to the complexities of command and control relationships in UN (mandated) Peace Operations and the problems this poses for attribution of conduct, there would also seem to be a degree of confusion relating to the primacy of the UN in matters relating to peace and security and the implications this might have for purposes of ensuring accountability. The UN has as one of its primary objectives the maintenance of international peace and security and has considerable powers vested in it by the Member States through various provisions of the Charter for the execution of this task.[31] The Charter provides the Security Council with primary responsibility in this area and the Council makes abundant use of its discretionary authority and powers which are both explicit and implicit in nature. There is no doubt that the Security Council has both the power to set up specific peace (enforcement) operations and to determine whether these should be conducted directly by the UN through the DPKO command structure outlined above, or whether to delegate the actual conducting of such operations to regional organizations or *ad hoc* coalitions of Member States.[32]

In all cases, the Security Council retains ultimate authority in the sense that the operation is conducted under a mandate which provides a legal basis for the operation and sets out the overall objectives and parameters of the mission. Likewise, the Council has the power to alter or terminate the mandate in accordance with its provisions. However, this ultimate authority is by no means necessarily synonymous with effective control and must be seen in its proper context. The Council's authority and its attendant mandate is a necessary legal condition for the deployment of troops onto any State's territory without its full consent and for the conducting of many kinds of activities, including the use of force beyond self-defence and the exercise of any degree of public authority over persons or territory, which is normally exercised by the State exercising sovereignty over that territory. It is also authority of a political nature in that it signals the resolve of the Council to carry out the tasks set out in the mandate and the backing of Member States for the operation.

If the UN retains direct control over the conduct of the operation through its own command structure, the UN will also have authority over those aspects of the operation which it effectively controls and which are carried out under its authority and auspices, primarily as we have seen at the level of OPCON. This is the normal situation in relation to Peace Operations carried out by the UN acting through the DPKO command structure set out above. In operations conducted under other command structures, the ultimate authority of the UN Security Council does not translate into more than nominal authority over how the operation is conducted

[31] Wolfrum 2002; Goodrich et al. 1969, pp. 25–29.

[32] Simma et al. 2002, pp. 445–449; Goodrich et al. 1969, pp. 202–207.

and does not approach what is generally understood as the exercise of effective control. This applies to the (Peace) Enforcement operations carried out by regional organizations or (coalitions of) Member State(s) acting under UN Security Council mandate.

The Council's primary responsibility and ultimate authority should be seen for what they are, namely an instrument for the maintenance of peace and security and not as an indication of how such operations are conducted in actual practice or as synonymous with effective control for the purpose of attributing conduct and determining the consequences of possible breaches of international law. This is where the distinction between accountability and responsibility, as defined above, becomes particularly relevant. The former implies in the case of a body like the Council, the ability to exercise political oversight of a general nature and to initiate, alter or terminate a mandate for a particular operation. The latter deals with the legal consequences for allegations of conduct which allegedly breaches international law.

2.4.4 The Precedence of Obligations Under the Charter Over Other International Obligations

Article 103 of the Charter provides in the event of a conflict between an obligation arising under the Charter and those under any other international agreement that those under the Charter will take precedence. This provision, notwithstanding its seeming simplicity, has caused a significant amount of comment and given rise to diverging opinions and approaches. On the one end of the spectrum, it is taken to mean that any obligation (or right) which could potentially stand in the way of the effectiveness of the UN in carrying out its tasks and realizing its objectives would be trumped by the Charter. On the other end of the scale of opinion it is argued that the obligations of Member States under international treaties will only be affected to the extent they are directly incompatible with a specific provision of the Charter or a binding decision of the Council which is not considered to be *ultra vires*. To the extent these conflicting interpretations impact upon the question under discussion in this article, the legal implications of transfer of authority in UN (mandated) peace operations, they require some attention without pretending to resolve the issue in its entirety.[33]

The UN Collective Security System is a political and legal instrument consisting of a complex set of obligations, attributions of authority, and interlocking responsibilities, and which provides a framework for cooperation between Member States and other bodies, such as regional arrangements and the Organization.

[33] For authoritative commentary on Article 103, see *inter alia* Bernhardt 2002, p. 1292 *et seq*. The broad interpretation of Article 103 by the ECtHR in the *Behrami* and *Saramati* decisions is (rightly) criticized by Krieger 2009, pp. 177–178; Knoll 2008, pp. 445–448.

This system is partly codified in the Charter and is partly a product of practice and of pragmatism resulting from lack of feasible alternatives. This system is the instrument through which the Organization, acting through the Security Council in conjunction with other organs, with Member States and with regional arrangements, is reliant upon for the fulfillment of one of the primary objectives of the Charter; the restoration and maintenance of international peace and security. Indeed, this objective, although only one of the primary objectives underlying the Charter, is arguably the most important of the purposes laid down in the Charter.

On the other hand, the UN and with it, the Council and the UN Collective Security System are legal constructs and the products of an international agreement of a particular nature and do not operate outside the framework of international law. The Charter further provides that the Council, while possessing primary responsibility for the maintenance of peace and security and a very wide measure of discretionary authority in determining which situations call for the implementation of the collective security system, is nevertheless bound by the fundamental principles underlying the Charter. It is generally agreed that these include, in addition to those explicitly named in Articles 1 and 2 of the Charter, those rules and norms of international law which constitute peremptory rights and obligations of a *jus cogens* nature, although there is less than universal agreement as to which obligations this includes.

If one were to view the Charter as simply 'trumping' any other obligation which might potentially affect the functioning of the Council and its responsibilities in relation to the maintenance of peace and security, this could lead to the consequence that the Council had virtually unlimited authority to set aside international law in view of its wide discretionary powers to determine the existence of a situation requiring the implementation of the collective security system. This would neither reflect the actual provisions of the Charter itself, nor the way the Organization sees itself and its members see it as being bound by (fundamental) rules of international law. This is evident from Article 24 of the Charter, which *inter alia* provides that the Council will act in conformity with the purposes and principles of the Charter in carrying out its primary responsibility in the maintenance and restoration of international peace and security. This provision is widely considered to include adherence to fundamental legal principles and the UN has consistently acknowledged that it is bound by fundamental rules of international law, including humanitarian and applicable human rights law in the conducting of UN operations.[34]

---

[34] See *infra*, note 36. For the UN's acknowledgment of the duty to comply with fundamental legal norms in the conduct of operations, see 'The Normative Framework for United Nations Peacekeeping Operations', Capstone Doctrine, pp. 13–15. See also Secretary General's Bulletin on the Observance by United Nations Forces of International Humanitarian Law of 6 August 1999 (ST/SGB/1999/13). In addition, the countries participating in a UN Peace Operation (or UN mandated (peace) enforcement operation) are bound by the human rights and humanitarian law conventions to which they are party in so fat as those are applicable in the context of the mission and will often instruct their troops to observe their principles, regardless whether the conventions are applicable as a matter of law.

To be sure, it is clear that the implementation of enforcement measures will inevitably impact upon the rights and obligations that States enjoy and are bound by under international law. Indeed this is inherent in the system itself, since the imposition of any type of enforcement measures, particularly those involving the use of force, will inevitably restrict and even set aside a whole range of rights that States normally enjoy under both treaties and customary law.[35] However, this inherent power to affect, restrict, and temporarily set aside many of the rights and obligations that States enjoy and are bound by does not mean the Council acts outside the framework of international law, much less give it a *carte blanche* to violate fundamental rights of either States or of individuals.[36] Still less does it give Member States or regional organizations a legal excuse to ignore other obligations under international law, simply on the basis that they are acting pursuant to a Charter mandate and the fact that Charter obligations in principle override conflicting obligations arising from other international agreements. To the extent the rights or obligations of States or other relevant actors inherently or incidentally conflict with or are curtailed by the execution of a Council measure taken within the context of the collective security system and the Council's measures are not in violation of a peremptory norm or otherwise conflict with the Purposes and Principles of the Charter, the affected or conflicting rights and obligations will be suspended or overridden to the extent necessary to ensure the effective discharge of the Council's task in accordance with the Charter.[37]

Moreover, it is also clear that while neither Member States nor regional organizations are under an obligation to actively participate in enforcement measures involving the use of force, they are under an obligation to carry out binding decisions of the Council and to not interfere with or otherwise obstruct any measures the Council has agreed to undertake or implement within the context of the maintenance or restoration of international peace and security. This obligation flows from the entire system of the Charter itself, including (but not necessarily limited to) Articles 1, 2, 24, 25, 29, and the relevant provisions of Chapters VI and VII, in addition to Article 103 itself.

Likewise since the Charter system of collective security is dependent upon voluntary cooperation of Member States and regional arrangements insofar as it involves the use of military force, the general duty of cooperation and ensuring that this system is as effective as possible which rests upon all Members, implies that such voluntary cooperation is not unnecessarily or unduly hindered as long as the actors involved are acting within the terms of the mandate and the overall Charter legal framework.

---

[35] Goodrich et al. 1969, p. 290 *et seq;* Simma et al. 2002, pp. 754–755.

[36] Simma et al. 2002, pp. 1295–1302; de Wet 2004, pp. 191–215; Gill 1995, pp. 74–79.

[37] The key word here is *conflict*. Only in the case of an actual conflict between an obligation under the Charter and another obligation under international law of a non-peremptory nature does Article 103 set aside the conflicting obligation. In addition to the sources cited above see *inter alia* Kleffner 2010, pp. 76–77.

Taken together, the network of mutual obligations and responsibilities built into the entire system should be taken to mean that all relevant actors including the Council, the other organs of the organization, the Member States, and regional agencies and organizations are mutually under a duty to respect the rights and prerogatives afforded to each respective participant in the system and to faithfully carry out obligations agreed to within the Charter legal framework. At the same time, all participants in the system are likewise under an obligation to ensure that such measures are in conformity with the principles and purposes of the Charter and do not conflict with peremptory norms of international law.

To the extent that a particular measure was perceived as being (potentially) in violation of such a peremptory norm, the reasons for such objection should be brought to the attention of the Council and other relevant actors and possible remedial measures could be proposed and if the objections were found to be well founded by a majority in the Council, the measures could be amended or suspended. In the event no remedial action was undertaken, the matter could be brought to the attention of the General Assembly and if a majority in that organ were of the opinion that a particular measure undertaken or authorized by the Council was incompatible with a peremptory norm or was otherwise *ultra vires*, it could recommend a remedial amendment of the measure, or request an advisory opinion on the question from the ICJ of Justice as a means of clarifying the situation.

Only in the unlikely event that a recommendation of the Court which had determined that a particular measure or action of the Council was (potentially) in violation of such a peremptory norm whereby the Council ignored the General Assembly's recommendation and the Court's decision and abstained from taking the necessary remedial action to bring it into conformity with that norm, would there be a legal basis for a Member State or other relevant actor, to suspend compliance with the execution of the measure in question in accordance with the Court's recommendation until such time as the measure had been brought into such conformity. This is the most appropriate and legally and politically acceptable means for ensuring that the Council's effectiveness would not be impaired while at the same time providing a safeguard and potential remedy for actions or measures of the Council which were not in conformity with the Purposes and Principles of the Charter.[38] However, such a possible remedy would only be relevant or likely to be forthcoming in the event that the measure or action in question was attributable to the Council itself and if it were considered by both a majority of the General Assembly and the Court to be a (potential) violation of an obligation of a fundamental nature which required such an extraordinary signal to the Council. The alternative of individual States deciding for themselves whether a

[38] For a more detailed discussion of the remedies open to other organs of the UN and Member States in the event of a perceived *ultra vires* decision by the Council, see Gill 1995, pp. 113–126.

particular measure of the Council was or was not in conformity with the purposes and principles of the Charter would be subject to abuse and *ex parte* interpretation on the part of each Member State and could potentially lead to the unravelling of the entire UN Collective Security System itself. Likewise, the use of the advisory procedure of the Court makes sure that there would be a sufficient body of States which were concerned that a Council measure was potentially *ultra vires* to justify questioning the validity of the measure and the primary authority of the Council in the maintenance of peace and security under the Charter. Moreover, use of the advisory procedure circumvents the problem of whether the Court could exercise jurisdiction *vis-à-vis* a subject of international law like the UN which is not subject to its contentious jurisdiction.

This obviously leaves the possibility open that other actions taken pursuant to a decision of the Council in the execution of a mandate could potentially be in breach of an international obligation. The following paragraph will examine some of the questions and potential gaps in accountability which could arise in that context and more in general in connection with the complex structure of authority and attribution of conduct relating to peace operations examined above.

2.4.5 Gaps and Limitations in Ensuring Full Accountability

The intricacies of command and attribution of conduct resulting from the way UN (mandated) operations are authorized and executed give rise to a number of real and potential gaps in ensuring full accountability for breaches of international obligations and full compliance with international and national legal standards on the part of the UN, of regional organizations, and the Member States involved. Only some of these will be highlighted here.

Firstly, it is clear that in the case of UN mandated operations, whatever their specific classification, the fact that the operation is carried out under UN authority in the form of a mandate designating one or more States or a particular regional organization to lead and conduct the operation should not be seen as synonymous with anything approaching effective control by the UN over the operation. This has long been accepted for 'pure' enforcement operations of the Korea and Desert Storm variety, but has not always been as well understood in the case of peace enforcement missions such as those in Kosovo, Iraq and elsewhere.

This seems to be particularly the case in operations whereby the UN conducts part of the mission itself in the realm of peace-building and may even exercise transitional authority over a territory, while the military and stabilization role is delegated to a regional organization or one or more Member States. Only those actions which are directly carried out under effective UN control are realistically attributable to the UN itself. Nevertheless, on the evidence of a number of court decisions at both the regional and the national level, it seems clear that confusion persists and that standards of attribution vary and do not always follow the effective control test.[39] This leads to unfortunate results and is an issue that requires further clarification and attention. In some cases, it may be necessary where there is joint or shared responsibility for the conduct of the operation, to further clarify the degree of delegation of authority and the respective areas of responsibility and respective tasks in legal or quasi-legal agreements between the mandating organization and the regional organization to a much greater degree than hitherto has been the general practice. This could partly be achieved by general acceptance and application in practice of the 'effective control' standard for purposes of attribution and further improved by clearer allocation of authority and responsibility setting out which actor is responsible for particular areas of activity when operations are planned, subject to amendment in the light of changing circumstances. In two recent decisions, the ECtHR has reaffirmed the effective control standard and rejected arguments by the Respondent State (in those cases the United Kingdom) that the fact that the UN Security Council had issued resolutions acknowledging the role of the Multi-National Security Force in Iraq in the relevant period translated into either ultimate authority, or effective control for purposes of determining attribution of conduct or determining whether the acts in question were within the jurisdiction of the European Convention. This is a welcome development and a sign that the effective control standard is in fact the correct one to follow in such cases. Nevertheless, it remains to be seen how well it will be followed in situations which are less clear-cut than the situation in post-conflict Iraq.[40]

Secondly, when an operation is conducted directly by the UN within the framework of the DPKO command structure and national contingents are transferred to the OPCOM/control of the Organization, it will be necessary to examine the level of OPCOM/control that has been transferred, whether the act in question falls within the ambit of such transferred authority, whether in fact such authority is being or has been exercised and whether a particular act can be attributed to the UN or to the Troop Contributing State, for example, because the contingent is acting under conflicting instructions from its home State. Moreover, acts which are considered to be of an 'off-duty' character, or which the UN views as being

---

[39] In addition to the *Behrami* and *Saramati* decisions of the ECtHR referred to above, the decisions of national courts have also received attention in the literature. For a discussion of the UK House of Lords decision in *Al Jeddah v Secretary of State for Defence* (2007), see *inter alia* Kondoch 2010, pp. 525–528; Sari 2009. For a discussion of the Hague District Court's decision in relation to a decision by a national court in the Netherlands, see Spijkers 2009.

[40] The ECtHR decisions referred to are those in the *Al Skeini* and *Al Jedda* cases of 7 July 2011. Especially in the latter case, the issues of attribution of conduct and the application of the effective control standard were squarely before the Court and it determined that notwithstanding the recognition and endorsement of the multinational security force in SC Resolutions 1483 (2003) and 1511 (2003) this did not result in the United Nations exercising any degree of authority or control over the operation. In doing so, the Court accepted the reasoning of the UK House of Lords in 2007 (UKHL 58, 12 December 2007) which had distinguished the factual and legal situation in post-conflict Iraq from that pertaining to Kosovo in relation to the abovementioned *Behrami* and *Saramati* cases.

committed in flagrant disregard of UN instructions or are the result of gross negligence, should always be attributed to the State in question rather than to the UN in recognition of the UN's refusal to accept responsibility for such acts.

A separate problem from the lack of a uniform agreement concerning the question of attribution is the lack of effective remedies in many cases of alleged breach of an international obligation or other forms of misconduct. It is clear that the remedies available at present do not always cover all possible situations where breaches of obligation have occurred or are likely to occur, for example, because a court lacks jurisdiction over a particular matter or actor or because of the simple lack of an available effective remedy. There are unfortunately many (potential) gaps in effective remedies at present. If an act is attributed to the UN, it will automatically fall outside the jurisdiction of and/or enjoy immunity from procedure before any regional or national court. This is one reason why a realistic assessment of the command structure and application of the 'effective control' standard is imperative.

A proper understanding of the command structure in place for a particular (type of) operation and application of the effective control standard for purposes of attribution could potentially bring more chance of an effective remedy than hitherto has been the case. To be sure, action which falls under 'operational necessity' or is not attributable to a particular actor over which jurisdiction may be exercised may not be amenable to a particular remedy. Such operational necessity would include actions directly related to the execution of the mandate, including the movement of troop, the use of force and operational detentions conducted within the parameters of the mandate and the operational instructions which are based upon it. But insofar as an action potentially or in fact leads to a breach of an international obligation, attention should be given to ensurie that only genuine operational necessity and other circumstances precluding wrongfulness stand in the way of an effective remedy.

However, the problem does not end there. If an act is attributed to the UN or to another organization exercising OPCOM/control and in fact should be so attributed on the basis of the effective control standard, there is at present no guarantee of an effective remedy. While the UN will accept responsibility for acts which fall under its authority and provide some level of compensation, there is no redress or appeals procedure and the nature of the compensation is limited to personal damages for injury or material damage, rather than assumption of responsibility at the international level. While this will cover many types of incidental damage, it is not a substitute for full legal accountability and is carried out on an *ad hoc* basis. This is because there is neither a standing UN Claims Tribunal, despite this being a longstanding provision in the UN Model SOFA, nor any other international judicial or quasi-judicial body which has the power to exercise any form of judicial review or oversight over either existing claims procedures or regarding any other matter connected with the conduct of UN Peace Operations. While the Council has overall authority to issue, amend, and terminate mandates implying some power of review, it does not generally address issues of legal responsibility or specific allegations of wrongful conduct and its control in connection with operations carried out under its mandate and its oversight of missions is essentially political in character. Nor does the ICJ have much of a role to play in this respect, barring the rather remote possibility it were requested to issue an advisory opinion on a matter of responsibility connected with a UN Peace Operation. The same holds largely true with regard to operations carried out by regional organizations under UN mandate. There are likewise no standing claims tribunals or other forms of judicial or quasi-judicial oversight of either existing claims procedures used in such operations or in relation to any other aspect affecting the (potential) responsibility of such regional organizations in the conduct of UN (mandated) operations. Moreover, to the extent an action were attributable to a particular regional organization or arrangement, there would be little or no scope of addressing questions relating to responsibility before a national court as the organization would either likely fall outside its jurisdiction or be able to claim immunity as a separate international legal person.[41] These considerations are good arguments in favor of instituting such a standing UN Claims Tribunal with jurisdiction to consider questions of breach of obligation committed within the context of UN Peace Operations and determine whether the act in question was attributable to the UN itself, to the TCC, or both and order appropriate forms of redress including, but not limited to financial compensation.

There is, moreover another broad area which is inadequately enforced under the existing procedures, namely acts which the UN considers to be of an unofficial or 'off-duty' character. These include the numerous acts of sexual and personal abuse committed by UN peacekeepers. While the UN has taken strenuous efforts to impose high standards of conduct among peacekeepers and has initiated a number of measures to prevent such abuse, or where this fails, to induce the TCC responsible to effectively exercise its exclusive criminal and disciplinary jurisdiction, much room for improvement remains.[42] The UN has no remedy for actual abuse at its disposal other than repatriation of the person(s) allegedly responsible for a particular act of such abuse and the debarring of the contingent in question from further participation in the mission. This means it is largely dependent upon the TCC's willingness to carry out its responsibilities faithfully and effectively. Unfortunately, not all States contributing troops to UN Peace Operations are willing to do so for a variety of reasons the discussion of which goes beyond the scope of this article.

2.5 Conclusions

The command structure for UN (mandated) peace and peace enforcement operations is highly complex and raises a range of legal and operational questions, a number of which have been discussed and analyzed in the preceding paragraphs of

---

[41] The gaps in available remedies and proposals for improvement in accountability have been set out by *inter alia* Zwanenburg 2004, p. 303 *et seq.* and Kondoch 2010, pp. 531–533.

[42] See e.g. Klappe 2010, pp. 495–499.

this article. On the basis thereof, we can, hopefully, give some answers to some of the most pertinent questions.

Firstly, it is important to have a good understanding of the various types of UN (mandated) operations and their respective command structures. This is imperative both for understanding how such operations function in practice, as well as for purposes of attribution of conduct and determining the legal consequences of acts which (potentially) involve breach of international obligations which can occur in the conduct of those missions. It is important to grasp what transfer of operational level command and/or control entails as well as what it does not include and in what kind of context it occurs, both in a generic sense as part of the collective security system and for the purposes of attributing specific acts or omissions to a particular actor within the context of a specific operation.

Secondly, it is necessary to understand what the Council's overall authority and primacy in the maintenance and restoration of international peace and security actually mean in terms of both the functioning of the collective security system as a whole and for the purpose of determining how responsibility should be apportioned. The Council's primacy and overall or ultimate authority should be seen in context and not confused with effective control for purposes of attribution of conduct in relation to allegations of a specific breach. Moreover, it is clear that the 'effective control' standard is the most appropriate and realistic standard to employ in determining attribution issues, because it corresponds best to the realities of how the system and command structure actually function, as well as better reflecting accepted legal doctrine as set out in the ILC's work on international responsibility and the case law of the International Court of Justice.

Finally, we have determined that, notwithstanding the United Nations' commitment to adherence to relevant international obligations in the conduct of its operations, there are nevertheless a number of real and potential gaps in the remedies currently available and in ensuring full accountability of the UN, of regional organizations, and of participating Member States for their conduct in the execution of this primary task and flagship activity of the United Nations Collective Security System. This could be at least partially addressed and remedied by a combination of applying realistic assessment relating to attribution of conduct so that existing tribunals can more effectively exercise jurisdiction when this is possible and through the establishment of a UN Claims Commission with adequate authority to adjudicate claims when the UN itself is the responsible agent thereby avoiding the possibility that no judicial body has competence to provide a remedy when this is called for.

In any case it is clear that the present situation is less than satisfactory and requires further attention and remedial measures of some nature. It should be equally clear that this is also in the interest of all actors concerned, from the United Nations itself to the Member States which contribute troops, assets, and other support for this task. It is undoubtedly imperative for ensuring the legitimacy of such operations and promoting the rule of law, which lies at the heart of the United Nations' purposes and principles.

References

Bernhardt R (2002) Article 103. In: Simma B et al (eds) The Charter of the United Nations: A commentary, vol 2, 2nd edn. Oxford University Press, Oxford, pp 1295–1302
Bowett DW (1964) United Nations forces. Frederick A. Praeger, New York
Cammaert P, Klappe B (2010) Authority, command and control in United Nations—led peace operations. In: Gill TD, Fleck D (eds) The handbook of the international law of military operations. Oxford University Press, Oxford, pp 159–163
Capstone Doctrine (2008) Department of Peacekeeping Operations, Department of Field Support United Nations Peacekeeping Operations: principles and guidelines
Cathcart B (2010) Command and control. In: Gill TD, Fleck D (eds) The handbook of the International law of military operations. Oxford University Press, Oxford, pp 235–244
de Wet E (2004) The Chapter VII powers of the United Nations Security Council. Hart Publishing, Oxford
Findlay T (2002) The use of force in UN peace operations. Oxford University Press, Oxford
Fleck D (2010) Status of forces in peace operations. In: Gill TD, Fleck D (eds) The handbook of the international law of military operations. Oxford University Press, Oxford, pp 199–200
Franck T (2002) Recourse to force. Cambridge University Press, Cambridge
Gill TD (1995) Legal and some political limitations on the power of the UN Security Council to exercise its enforcement powers under Chapter VII of the Charter. Netherlands Yearbook of International Law 26:33–138
Gill TD, Fleck D (eds) (2010) The handbook of the international law of military operations. Oxford University Press, Oxford
Gill T et al (2010) Enforcement and peace enforcement operations. In: Gill TD, Fleck D (eds) The handbook of the international law of military operations. Oxford University Press, Oxford, pp 81–135
Goodrich LM, Hambro E, Simons AP (eds) (1969) Charter of the United Nations. 3rd rev.ed. Columbia University Press, New York
International Law Commission (2001) Report of the International Law Commission on its fifty third session at Geneva, Switzerland, from 23 April to 1 June and 2 July to 10 Aug 2001
International Law Association (2004) Final report of the committee on accountability of international organizations. Report of the seventy-first Conference held in Berlin 16–21 Aug 2004
Klappe B (2010) Prevention and repression of (sexual) violence, exploitation and abuse in the context of peace operations. In: Gill TD, Fleck D (eds) The handbook of the international law of military operations. Oxford University Press, Oxford, pp 495–500
Kleffner J (2010) Human rights and international humanitarian law. In: Gill TD, Fleck D (eds) The handbook of the international law of military operations. Oxford University Press, Oxford, pp 51–77
Knoll B (2008) Rights without remedies: The European Court's failure to close the human rights gap in Kosovo. Zeitschrift für ausländisches öffentliches Recht und Völkerrecht 68:431–451
Kondoch B (2010) The responsibility of peacekeepers, their sending states and international organizations. In: Gill TD, Fleck D (eds) The handbook of the international law of military operations. Oxford University Press, Oxford, pp 515–534
Krieger H (2009) A credibility gap: the Behrami and Saramati decisions of the European Court of Human Rights. J Int Peacekeeping 13:159–180
Oswald B, Durham H, Bates A (2010) Documents on the Law of UN Peace Operations. Oxford University Press, Oxford
Sari A (2009) The *Al Jeddah* case before the House of Lords. J Int Peacekeeping 13:181–196
Simma B, Mosler H, Paulus A, Chaitidou E (eds) (2002) The Charter of the United Nations: a commentary, 2nd edn. 2 vol. Oxford University Press, Oxford
Spijkers O (2009) The immunity of the United Nations in relation to the genocide in Srebrenica in the eyes of a Dutch Court. J Int Peacekeeping 13:197–219

White ND (1993) Keeping the peace: the United Nations and the maintenance of international peace and security. Manchester University Press, Manchester

Wolfrum R (2002) Preamble. In: Simma B et al (eds) The Charter of the United Nations: a commentary, vol 1, 2nd edn. Oxford University Press, Oxford, pp 33–44

Zwanenburg M (2004) Accountability under international humanitarian law for United Nations and North Atlantic Treaty Organization Peace Support Operations. Martinus Nijhoff, Dordrecht

Part II
Agora: The Case of Iraq: International Law and Politics

Chapter 3
After 'Iraq': Back to the International Rule of Law? An Introduction to the NYIL 2011 Agora

Janne Nijman

Abstract This chapter introduces the fundamental question which is addressed from different perspectives by the authors in this Agora: what does the 2003 Iraq intervention teach us about the relation between international law and politics? This chapter briefly discusses the relevance of the work by Martti Koskenniemi to that question and it treats the different points of view put forward in the contributions. It also notes that one possible position on the intervention in Iraq is not considered in this Agora, nor in the debate more generally—viz. that an intervention would be *legal but illegitimate*. However, if this position were examined, it could serve discussion about the political preferences which sometimes explain the choice of international legal arguments. This chapter concludes that from the contributions in this Agora a complex image emerges of the relation between international law and politics: beyond the relative indeterminacy of the law and beyond the collapse of the separation between international law and politics, an international *rule of law* re-emerges as a specific way of doing politics.

Keywords International rule of law · Legality · Legitimacy · 2003 Iraq intervention · Koskenniemi · (Social) constructivism · Use of force · Davids Committee

---

Associate Professor of International Law and Senior Research Fellow. The author would like to thank Ellen Hey, Wouter Werner and Catherine Brölmann for their valuable comments.

J. Nijman (✉)
Amsterdam Center for International Law, University of Amsterdam,
Amsterdam, The Netherlands
e-mail: J.E.Nijman@uva.nl

I. F. Dekker and E. Hey (eds.), *Netherlands Yearbook of International Law 2011*,
Netherlands Yearbook of International Law 42, DOI: 10.1007/978-90-6704-849-1_3,

Contents

3.1 Introduction

The 2003 Iraq war was illegal and yet it took place. Arguably, this plunged international law into crisis. A crisis which was debated in international law scholarship as well as in the public media. On November 18, 2004, *The Economist* wrote:

> [t]he United Nations and the rule of international law are in crisis. Their relevance is being questioned as never before. The criticism reached such a pitch after last year's Iraq war that many wondered whether a body increasingly seen as ineffective and anachronistic could, or indeed should, survive.[1]

Again, political leaders had sidelined international law—recall the outcry attributed to President Bush, 'I don't care what the international lawyers say, we are going to kick some ass.'[2] Again, international law had failed to be the legal framework constraining illegal political and military actions. Indeed, the Iraq war may have plunged international law in crisis, but as Douzinas observed, in the months prior to the intervention, international law also experienced a short period of 'glory'.[3] The attention it received in the media and public debate was probably unprecedented. Be this as it may, the fact that the intervention in Iraq took place, raised fundamental questions: does international law really matter in international politics, other than in an 'instrumental' way? Does international law exist separately from international politics, to the extent that it can fulfill a normative function? In other words, is politics subordinated to the international rule of law? Or is it the other way around? In short, what does the 2003 Iraq intervention teach us about the relation between international law and politics?

---

[1] *The Economist*, November 18, 2004. See on how determination of a world 'crisis' is a Western-dominated process, Charlesworth 2002.

[2] Clarke 2004, p. 24.

[3] Douzinas 2007, pp. 198–235.

These are not new questions. On the contrary, they are among the ever-returning theoretical questions of our discipline[4] and it is the perennial responsibility of scholars, both those versed in international law and in other disciplines, to dissect the decisions-making processes and discourses that result in the side-stepping of international law. While history teaches us that there are no definitive answers to the questions posed, analysis is vital if we are to foster understanding about the relation between international law and politics. It is the aim of the NYIL to contribute to this endeavor with an Agora dedicated to 'Iraq' as a case for examining the ever-perplexing relation between international law and politics. What does the fact that the Iraq war was illegal and yet took place teach us about that relation? Authors from both the disciplines of international relations (IR) and international law have been asked to analyse the military intervention in Iraq with this question in mind. The Agora as a whole illustrates how various understandings of the relation between law and politics operate in theory and in practice—'in practice' here refers to the arguments forwarded by governments either to support militarily (UK, Italy) or politically (The Netherlands) the US led intervention or to abstain from any support (Germany, France). The Agora moreover shows that actors have mobilized and conceptualized 'law' and 'politics' differently. As these are both indeterminate terms, different ways of framing them may partly explain different findings on their interrelationship. The contributions, to which we will return below, approach the question posed from various perspectives. Here it suffices to mention that Kenneth Manusama deals with the role played by governmental legal advice regarding Iraq during the decision-making processes in the UK and the Netherlands. Thomas Mertens and Janine van Dinther address the justifications employed by the Dutch government for politically supporting the war from a constitutional history as well as an international legal theory perspective. Thereafter, Philip Liste moves away from the purely governmental discourse to include the role of public discourse in the decision-making processes of two democracies, Germany and the US. Tanja Aalberts also takes a discourse-oriented approach to the topic and deconstructs the different lines of argumentation put forward by the Davids Committee and the Dutch government so as to disclose how the Dutch legality argument rested on legitimacy claims and political visions of 'international society' and 'international community'. Bertjan Verbeek uses the Iraq case to explain four different IR perspectives on the role of international law in political decision making, and vice versa the four IR perspectives serve to explain the choices made by France, Italy, the Netherlands, the United Kingdom, and the United States. Verbeek, like Liste, includes the domestic political

[4] See e.g. for these questions in context of 'crisis' after WWI, Alvarez 1936, p. 5; de Louter 1919, p. 77: 'une crise pathologique'; Brierly 1958 (Inaugural lecture 1924), p. 68; more extensively on this time's search for renewal and reconstruction, or in Brierly's words 'rehabilitation', Nijman 2004, pp. 85–91. For a similar sense of crisis after WWII see, ibid., Chap. 4. Current literature on the 'crisis of international law' is substantial. See e.g. Domingo 2010; for a different voice, see Michael Sharf's response to Goldsmith and Posner 2005, in Sharf 2005.

dimension in his analysis; ultimately, it is one of the explanatory factors for the choices made. Lastly, Nigel White points at a shift in the *problematique* of authorization. In the case of Libya authorization was secured by a United Nations Security Council (UNSC) Resolution, but then questions emerged about the legitimate interpretation of that resolution. White thus points to the limits of the legality scheme of the United Nations' collective security system even when initially well applied.

3.2 Background

In international law scholarship, many consider the Iraq war to have brought another crisis onto international law. Others claim that when international law scholarship keeps talking about 'crisis', it uses these crises as a vehicle for 'development'[5] and 'renewal'.[6] Still others qualify the current crisis by observing that international law is actually 'in a permanent state of crisis'.[7] Without intending to detract from these observations, it is true that during the first few years of the twenty-first century many perceive international law as challenged to its core. In the decades after WWII, international law and international institutions developed and increased to the extent that the normative force of 'international law' was ever less contested among mainstream international lawyers, to the point that in 1995 many would have agreed with Thomas Franck that 'international law has entered its 'post-ontological era'.[8] International law's independent existence needed no further defence. Rather, Frank argued, new challenges needed to be faced: is international law fair? With 'Iraq', questions regarding international law's existence as something independent from, and prevalent over, politics were back on the table. Does not the intervention in Iraq prove what the Realists and, from a different perspective, the Crits have said all along: international law has no identity separate from politics; it is not strong enough to bend the conduct of states.

At this point it is worth recalling an important presupposition held by many international lawyers.[9] This presupposition is that international law is independent from politics to the extent that it is able to constrain action based on power; that in

---

[5] Charlesworth 2002, p. 377; *infra*, Liste 2011.

[6] Kennedy 2000, p. 335.

[7] Douzinas 2007, p. 234.

[8] Franck 1995, p. 6.

[9] Cf. Judith Shklar as quoted in Tamanaha 2004, p. 59. 'Legalism is, above all, the operative outlook of the legal profession. ... The tendency to think of law as "there" as a discrete entity, discernibly different from morals and politics, has its deepest roots in the legal profession's views of its own functions, and forms the very basis of most of our judicial institutions and procedures.' Legalism as an operational outlook consists of 'the ethical attitude that holds moral conduct to be a matter of rule following, and moral relationships to consist of duties and rights determined by rules.' Shklar 1964, p. 1.

its relationship with politics, international law exists separate from, and is prevalent over, politics: sovereign power as limited by the 'international rule of law'.[10] It is this opposition between law and politics that collapsed in many governmental justifications of the Iraq war.

The collapse of that opposition also finds reflection in contemporary international law theory, for example, in the work of 'rationalists' like Goldsmith and Posner. In their 2005 *The Limits of International Law* they argue a rationalist and realist position in which international law is not only meaningless, but also is not a self-standing value and goal in itself; it is just one aspect of politics.[11] And so it *should* be, according to the authors. In their view, international law cannot and should not develop in such a way that it would actually limit the powerful. At the other side of the spectrum is the Kantian philosopher Jurgen Habermas. He too finds the international rule of law in crisis after the March 2003 intervention. He defends the international rule of law and opts for a constitutionalist future.[12]

But the Iraq crisis was not just a cause, it was also a symptom. Anthony Carty—with a focus on the interaction between the Western and the non-Western world—understands the relation between international law and politics in the context of the deeper crisis of international society:

> [b]oth major internationalist projects, the United Nations (UN) and the World Trade Organization (WTO) are in deep enough crisis, where it is apparent to the mildest observer, that egotistical, or subjective power considerations dominate the Western treatment of the non-Western world, as they have since the foundation of the rapacious modernity so well described by Richard Tuck.[13]

The international law theorist who has arguably challenged and impacted our thinking on the relation between international law and politics most in the past two decades, and who indeed is quoted in almost all contributions to this Agora, is Martti Koskenniemi. He has convincingly argued that the collapse of the opposition between international law and politics is *inherent* to international law. His argument is different from traditional analyses in our discipline, which would attribute the crisis of international law, for example, to the politics of sovereignty, to international politics more generally, or to another external factor, thus upholding the separation of law and politics. Moreover, in traditional analysis the prevalence of the former over the latter is assumed, often implicitly and

---

[10] Tamanaha 2004, p. 129; also Fitzmaurice 1957, p. 6. Fitzmaurice explains his standpoint: 'the important principle of the subordination of the sovereignty of each State to the supremacy of international law—in short, of the sovereignty or rule of law in the international field, which might indeed be called the first and the greatest principle of international law. From it all the rest follows: without it, there may be customs, practices, habits, courtesies—what anyone will—but there is no law.' This assumption is also held by some legal institutions, which claim to offer legal constraints to power. For an example see Nouwen and Werner 2011.

[11] Goldsmith and Posner 2005.

[12] Habermas 2006.

[13] Carty 2006, p. 321.

unquestioningly. Koskenniemi on the other hand finds international law to be inherently political.[14]

Koskenniemi has pointed to the connection between the rule of law and the principles of Enlightenment and how—transposed to the international level—'[t]he fight for an international Rule of Law is a fight against politics, understood as a matter of furthering subjective desires and leading into an international anarchy. Though some measure of politics is inevitable, it should be constrained by non-political rules: "...the health of the political realm is maintained by conscientious objection to the political."'[15] So, the fight for an international rule of law is a liberal project about saving the law's independence and primacy over politics. In the same article, which sums up the argument made in *From Apology to Utopia*,[16] Koskenniemi claims 'that our inherited ideal of a World Order based on the Rule of Law thinly hides from sight the fact that social conflict must still be solved by political means and that even though there may exist a common legal rhetoric among international lawyers, that rhetoric must, *for reasons internal to the ideal itself,* rely on essentially contested—political—principles to justify outcomes to international disputes.'[17] The (liberal) view on the relation between international law and politics is founded on the 'objectivity' of (international) law in contrast to the subjectivity of politics. Koskenniemi argues that, however, such objectivity does not exist. His 'politics' is the politics that comes with law as a relatively indeterminate language used by lawyers to justify substantive outcomes. One is reminded of Tony Blair's complaint in his March 2003 Sedgefield Speech: '[t]he lawyers continue to divide over it—with their legal opinions bearing a remarkable similarity to their political view of the war.'[18]

Given the aforementioned sense of crisis in international law, it is unsurprising that the relation between law and politics is a *real* topic also in contemporary international legal theory.[19] Traditionally, views oscillate between a Realist, instrumentalist position on the one hand and a 'Kantian', Legalist position on the other. Koskenniemi's understanding of the oscillation between apologetic and

---

[14] The meaning of 'politics' and 'political' in the context of Koskenniemi's argument may be described as the under-determinacy of the law which makes choices possible and necessary; in the Preface to Koskenniemi 2011, p. v. 'The "politics of international law" refers to no jurisprudential thesis about the *real nature* of politics or (international) law. Instead, it points to the experience of a certain fluidity and contestability that most people—lawyers and non-lawyers—have when they enter the world of international law and find themselves in the presence of alternative and often conflicting rules, principles or institutional avenues between which they are expected to choose and realise that it is by no means self-evident how to justify that choice.'

[15] Koskenniemi 1990, p. 5. This quote ends with a citation of Martin Wight.

[16] Koskenniemi 1989.

[17] Koskenniemi 1990, p. 7.

[18] See for full text of Tony Blair's 5 March 2004 Speech at Sledgefield, *The Guardian* 5 March 2004, http://www.guardian.co.uk/politics/2004/mar/05/iraq.iraq. Please note the similarity with the following words by Koskenniemi in the Epilogue to Koskenniemi 2005, pp. 568–569. '*From Apology to Utopia* assumes that there is no access to legal rules or the legal meaning of international behaviour that is independent from the way competent lawyers see those things.'

[19] See also the discussion on 'lawfare'; Werner 2011.

utopian international legal arguments and his critique of the liberal, legalist approach have shaken up the discipline considerably. Ever since, many feel they cannot approach international law as they did before. It then comes as no surprise that—apart from the contributions by Verbeek and White—all contributions to some degree engage with Koskenniemi's claims. Indeed for some, 'Iraq' is a case in point of precisely those claims. Meanwhile, all contributions offer clues for a view on the relation between international law and politics which recognizes Koskenniemi's claim on the relative indeterminacy—and thus the politics—of international law, while leaving room for a more social constructivist understanding of international law. This understanding holds that international law—though inherently marked by the oscillation between concreteness and normativity, between instrumentalism and formalism—impacts and influences its subjects nonetheless. The old separation between law and politics may have collapsed with the revelation of 'the politics of international law', in spite of its ultimate underdeterminacy international law in the end has a shaping influence on international political actors. That too becomes visible in this Agora.

3.3 The Eclipse of International Law by Political Decision Making on 'the Case of Iraq'

The case of Iraq is an excellent case to study the relation between international law and politics, since so much material on the various political decision-making processes is publicly available today. In most participating states an enquiry of some sort has been conducted into the causes of the Iraq war and into the way choices about involvement were made. Thus in the United States a number of commissions enquired different aspects of 'Iraq'.[20] At the time of writing (November 2011), the final report of the public inquiry by the Chilcot Committee in the United Kingdom had not been published. The Committee held public

[20] See, e.g. Report by the US Senate Intelligence Committee (2006) showed that there had not been sufficient intelligence on WMD to justify the Iraq war. Earlier, in 2005, the Silberman-Robb Commission reported: '[w]e conclude that the Intelligence Community was dead wrong in almost all of its pre-war judgments about Iraq's weapons of mass destruction.' Among other recommendations, the Commission advises to rethink the daily intelligence briefings to the US President: '[t]he daily intelligence briefings given to you before the Iraq war were flawed. Through attention-grabbing headlines and repetition of questionable data, these briefings overstated the case that Iraq was rebuilding its WMD programs.' The Commission on the Intelligence Capabilities of the United States Regarding Weapons of Mass Destruction Report to the President of the United States March 31, 2005. The Baker-Hamilton Iraq Study Group Report (2006) had more of a future—exit—focus.

hearings in 2010 and early 2011.[21] In the Netherlands, the Davids Committee published its final report on January 12, 2010.[22]

The publication of the Davids Report on the Dutch decision-making process leading to political support for the 2003 military intervention in Iraq was the immediate reason for the NYIL to dedicate an Agora to the examination of the relation between international law and politics. The Report concluded that in the absence of a second UNSC resolution the Netherlands had supported an *illegal* war. What was the nature of the decision-making process that could result in political support for an illegal war? After the presentation of the Report to Prime Minister Balkenende,[23] much of the political and public debate focussed on the role played by *legal* advice—or: the Legal Advisor—in the decision-making process.[24] The initial defence of the Prime Minister—that only in hindsight the mandate could be judged as 'inadequate'—was rejected promptly by Committee Member, Nico Schrijver. Schrijver stated that 'one knew enough at the time' to conclude that the legal basis for the intervention was insufficient.[25] If the availability of legal knowledge and advice was not the issue, as the Report determined, then the question remains how politics handled the law. What perception of the role of international law in political decision-making prevailed in The Hague at the time, resulting in the counsel of the Legal Advisor remaining unrevealed and thus put aside when Parliament was informed?[26]

One finds at least three different understandings of the relation between law and politics at work in the Dutch decision-making process. The first one is that an international rule of law exists which prevails over and constrains politics. This is the understanding of the Dutch Legal Advisor (DJZ/IR) in her 'independent role' and the majority of the Davids Committee. Such an understanding of the relation between law and politics would require the Netherlands to act in conformity with positive international law—which after all stipulates clearly the best course of

---

[21] http://www.iraqinquiry.org.uk/

[22] Davids Committee 2010. See http://www.rijksoverheid.nl/onderwerpen/irak/commissie-davids. The report was published in Dutch, but the conclusions and a summary are available in English on the official website. Chapter 8, on the legal foundation, was translated and published in the Netherlands International Law Review (NILR 2010, pp. 81–137).

[23] January 12, 2010.

[24] Another important issue was the Committee's observations about the information given by the Government to Parliament, the lack of full disclosure of information.

[25] *NRC Handelsblad*, January 19, 2010.

[26] Davids Committee 2010, p. 247; NILR 2010, p. 111. 'In a note in the dossier for the minister of foreign affairs for the emergency debate the next day, DAM/GO indicated that the qualification 'wafer-thin' by DLA/IL shared the position that UN resolution 678 was unlimited in time and pursued an almost unlimited objective. The legal basis could thus be found in the existing resolutions.' The qualification 'wafer-thin' was not just given to the legal basis in case of regime change, the Legal Advisor (DJZ/IR) used the qualification in a broader sense also to included the US 'revival doctrine.' The wording used with respect to the possibility of justifying intervention aimed at regime change as 'ronduit onjuist' / 'completely incorrect'. Davids Committee 2010, pp. 244–245; NILR 2010, p. 109.

action based on 'objective interpretation' of the law. The idea of the objectivity of law in relation to politics is, for example, reflected in this quote:

> [a]n *objective interpretation* of the text of resolution 1441 in the context of the Iraq debate in the autumn of 2002 and in the light of its object and purpose can only lead to the conclusion that this resolution did not give any authority to individual member states to use force without further deliberation by the Council.[27]

This understanding assumes that the objectivity and determinacy of international law make it possible to judge an action as legal or illegal. It assumes that it was clear from the beginning that without a second UNSC authorising the military intervention, the war was illegal.

Arguably, both the Legal Advisor and the Davids Committee operate on the basis of the modern, legalist understanding of the relation between law and politics. This classic international rule of law understanding may indeed be read in Memorandum DJZ/IR/2003/158. It is a good example of the ideological commitment to 'legalism' which in Shklar's view characterises the legal profession[28]:

> [t]he Directorate of Legal Affairs (DLA) considers it her task to provide you, whenever necessary, with information in the most objective and authoritative way possible. Naturally DLA also addresses policy considerations and does take into account the margins of appreciation allowed *vel non* by public international law. *This said, public international law, in the same way as all legal systems, sets boundaries to policy-making which cannot be crossed.* In cases of risk this will happen nonetheless, DLA has a monitoring and admonitory function, which in her opinion serves your interest and that of the Ministry.[29]

Another understanding of the relation between international law and politics is one in which there is no primacy of law, in which political considerations are *internal* to international law. The establishment of a *legal* basis for military intervention then is considered to be partly a political affair. This seems to be the view of the political advisors at the Dutch Ministry of Foreign Affairs. The quest for a 'legal basis' for intervention involved as much political as legal analysis:

> DAM/GO wrote a memo … which took as a starting point that the existing UN resolutions provided a 'sufficient (although not undisputed) legal basis' for military action. *The assessment was*, however, *not only legal, 'but just as much (…) political'*. A new UN resolution would be politically desirable although legally 'not absolutely necessary'.[30]

---

[27] Davids Committee 2010, p. 241; NILR 2010, p. 105.

[28] See *supra*, note 9.

[29] Memorandum of DJZ to the Minister via the SG, 'Irak—rechtsbasis militair ingrijpen', 29 April 2003, DJZ/IR/2003/158 (unauthorized translation by the author). See also, *NRC Handelsblad*, January 26, 2009, 'Memorandum DJZ/IR/2003/158: Juristen van Buitenlandse Zaken achtten Irakoorlog van meet af aan onwettig', para 3 of the memo, p. 2 (emphasis added). See also, Davids Committee 2010, p. 245; NILR 2010, p. 109. 'Furthermore, DLA/IL warned of a number of consequences in the event of passing over the Security Council. Less legitimisation of the use of force, the setting of precedents and, in the long term, an undermining of the principle of the rule of law would have to be taken into account.'

[30] Davids Committee 2010, p. 246; NILR 2010, p. 110 (emphasis added).

A third understanding of the relation between international law and politics is adopted by for example former diplomat Peter van Walsum, also a member of the Davids Committee. In this perspective compliance with international law is understood as one interest among many, each to be taken into account. Van Walsum has argued that a conscientious or responsible government does not only take its lead from international law but also from international politics.[31] In this view, the Dutch government should have been clear from the start: the war might have been illegal but it was politically justifiable because a vital political interest—'prevention of nuclear proliferation'—was in play. This understanding of the relation between international law and politics also appears from the following statement before the Davids Committee by the 2003 Minister for Foreign Affairs Jaap de Hoop Scheffer:

> I find that a government, a minister, should regard international law as an important part of his considerations when formulating policy but not as the exclusive and only part of his considerations.[32]

The second and third understandings seem to have impacted Dutch decision making on Iraq more than the first one. Meanwhile, the Davids Committee in its Report recommends adjustments[33] in the decision-making procedure of the Dutch government with a view to fortify the rule of law over politics. This is not to say that the hampered reception of the Legal Advisor's counsel on the matter was a matter of institutional obstacles only. An observation by de Hoop Scheffer shows that he was well aware of the opinion of the Dutch Legal Advisor (DJZ/IR):

> [y]ou can assume that when I took office, I was aware of the opinions within the legal parts of the ministry on the principle of discretionary powers on the appropriateness and legitimacy or the lack thereof. That wasn't new for me.[34]

In other words, much depends on how legal advice is weighed and this is related to how one perceives the relation between law and politics. Besides the institutional structure, the issue of political culture is at least as important, as also Kenneth Manusama shows in his contribution.

3.4 Different Points of View

Kenneth Manusama analyses the role of legal advice and legal advisors in the governmental decision-making processes on Iraq 2003 in the UK and the Netherlands. In both cases, the Legal Advisors indicated the Iraq War to be

---

[31] Davids Committee 2010, p. 270; NILR 2010, p. 133. '... a responsible government should allow itself to be led not only by the rules of international law but also by the demands of international politics. If the two considerations conflict, the government is faced with a dilemma but no government will accept that its vital political objectives should defer to international law under all circumstances.'

[32] Davids Committee 2010, p. 251; NILR 2010, p. 115.

[33] Davids Committee 2010, conclusion no. 22, p. 427.

[34] De Hoop Scheffer, 21 September 2009. Davids Committee 2010, p. 246; NILR 2010, p. 109.

unlawful. And yet, both states supported the Iraq war, even if in different ways. The comparative element of Manusama's analysis is especially useful since the two states have very different institutional structures for providing legal advice on international matters. The article thus brings to light that the institutional structure is only part of the 'problem'; more important is how politicians and policy-makers deal with the advice given to them, i.e., political culture. The pervasive political culture at the time, according to Manusama, was 'obstructionist' in which it was acceptable for political advisors to marginalize, obstruct, and push aside international law advice. Thereby illustrating the difficult position that legal advisors find themselves in, which Manusama, with reference to Koskenniemi characterises as 'between commitment and cynicism.' Manusama thereby shows how the legal advisor is 'caught in a dialectic of commitment to [upholding the international rule of law] and cynicism about its practical impact on decision-making in a highly political environment.'[35] Manusama's analysis also points out that the reshuffling of the organizational chart in the Netherlands is unlikely to make a difference to the role of international law in future decision making, ultimately it is political culture which counts. Manusama's contribution invites international lawyers, politicians, and citizens in the Netherlands to rethink 'Iraq' as a *political* crisis rather than a legal crisis.

It seems that a change of political culture is something of an urgent challenge. In the current Dutch political culture, according to Manusama, international law is dealt with as if 'a choice must be made between legal arguments on the one hand and political arguments on the other.' It is noteworthy that the *actual* understanding of the relation between international law and politics among political decision makers does not correspond to the popular, general perception that the Government of the Netherlands of old pursues its constitutional duty to promote international legality, or: the cherished image of the so-called Dutch Grotian tradition of promoting the international rule of law.[36] After all, in the currently prevailing conception of the relation between law and politics, international law is not defining, constraining, or trumping political power, it serves merely as a source of argumentation.

Manusama's conclusions, which are based on practice, tie in readily with the sharp observations by Mertens and van Dinther, which come from a more theoretical perspective. They too demystify the Dutch Grotian tradition by showing how policy-makers accept deviation of *lex lata* in favor of *lex ferenda*. The authors disclose how the Netherlands in reality has a tradition in opting for a particular, more subjective, if you like: future-oriented and thus *political*, interpretation of international law and international legal order.

Dutch political support for the illegal Iraq war has often been explained on the basis of political interests such as transatlantic loyalty; or a genuine fear and

---

35 See *infra*, Manusama 2012.

36 Schrijver 2010.

concern among the members of government for the weapons of mass destruction inside Iraq; or by human rights violations by Saddam Hussein against his own people; or other reasons 'external' in nature. Mertens and van Dinther take a different approach. They examine the 'intellectual underpinning of the Dutch support of the Iraq war' and trace the support in the case of the Iraq War both to the Dutch constitutional tradition on international law and politics and to the currently much debated 'turn to ethics' (another Koskenniemian phrase) in international law, which had surfaced forcefully with the legitimacy question of the Kosovo intervention (see, e.g., Cassese, Simma, and Habermas). The authors demonstrate how the reasoning on which political support for Iraq intervention was based fits well into an older legal and intellectual trend existing long before the 2003 decision. The latter decision should be understood as part of the Dutch—so-called—'ethical' tradition on international law and international legal order dating back to the early twentieth century.

Their brief survey of Dutch constitutional history shows how the governmental duty to promote the international legal order as stipulated in the Dutch constitution has been read consistently so as to mean that a deviation from positive international law is appropriate when necessary to develop and promote the international legal order, that is: when necessary to promote a number of policy objectives (e.g., human rights, fair international economic order, and world peace). The constitutional duty to promote the international legal order understood as such includes a major margin of appreciation—some would call it subjectivism—that can go as far as allowing for a violation of positive international law, a deviation of *lex lata* in favor of compliance with envisioned *lex ferenda*. In the case at hand, the Dutch tradition to accept—occasionally even order[37]—non-compliance with positive international law has facilitated Dutch political support of the Coalition of the Willing: the war was legal, but even if it was illegal it was in any case legitimate. Moreover, the authors show how in the case of Iraq the Dutch 'ethical tradition' on international law tied in neatly with the current shift in international law theory and practice from the legal to the ethical. The domestic and international legal culture together provided a context which was favorable to the relativization of the lack of legal basis for Iraq intervention. Finally, the authors take issue with precisely this culture of ethics in defence of a return to strict compliance with positive international law. With their critical assessment of the Iraq case, the authors offer profound insights into the relation between international law and politics as it was understood in The Hague in the context of the Iraq war.

Coming from two different perspectives, the two contributions seem to concur that the political support for an illegal war can be best explained by the Netherlands' own constitutional tradition—accommodated by the 'turn to ethics' in international relations—which accepts marginalisation of positive international law in favor of the ethical, which is political. According to Mertens and van Dinther, the Davids Report can be read as an attempt to halt this shift from legality

[37] Leaving aside whether this is at all allowed according to international law.

to legitimacy and to return to a stricter reading of the law. Ultimately, the authors seem to suggest what could be called a Kantian reading of the Davids Report: the Report is a plea for a break with the Dutch 'ethical' tradition in favor of a turn to a Kantian view on international law, a return to legal formalism.

Albeit from a different angle than Mertens and van Dinther, Tanja Aalberts' confirms the focus of the Davids Report on the government's *legality* claim—the so-called 'corpus theory' of Security Council authorization—while leaving aside two *legitimacy* claims which are made by the Dutch government and which, as Aalberts rightly points out, interacted with the legality claim. While Mertens and van Dinther concur with the legal and political consequences of what they read as a return to a Kantian understanding of international relations and international law, Aalberts is unsatisfied by the Davids Report and goes on to (de)construct both the legality and the legitimacy arguments. Her analysis of the Dutch legal justifications is grounded in an understanding of law as 'a scheme of interpretation'; or more specifically—and in Koskenniemi's words—'legal arguments do not produce substantive outcomes but seek to justify them.'

Once international legal argumentation is understood as thriving on international law's indeterminacy and thus as inherently political, one may discern the particular vision of international society and its legal order operating in the background. What Aalberts calls the 'legitimacy by synergy' argument justifies the invasion by a synergy between the UN Charter law on the use of force and the extra-Charter values of the international society (in whatever ideological version). This argument reveals a conception of international society and international law in which the principle of sovereign equality is qualified: rather than a society of equal sovereign states, international society consists of 'good sovereigns' and 'bad states'. States are equal provided that they behave in accordance with the law and values of the international society. If they do not, they cannot count on being protected by the same law and values. In this vision on international society, the bad can be disciplined by the good to forge the international rule of law and to protect the international order. A less inclusive international society lays in wait with such liberal antipluralism. Furthermore, Aalberts points to a legitimacy argument made by the Dutch government which she identifies as 'legitimacy by defiance'. When politics hamper international law procedures and processes and the UN Security Council fails to authorize enforcement of peace and security, it is legitimate according to the Dutch Government to disobey the Security Council and its formal authority. The legality position of the Dutch government is unmistakeably influenced by the two aforementioned legitimacy claims.

Aalberts concurs with Mertens' and van Dinther's conclusion that the Dutch support of the Iraq war is best explained by the idea that the international legal order includes more than only positive international law, and that the latter can be deviated from if the promotion of the international legal order as a whole—including its policy objectives—so requires. Aalberts' analysis also shows that with these policy objectives comes a particular—let us say liberal, anti-pluralist—vision on international society and the ways to safeguard the international legal order through disobeying the Security Council. The various justifications interact and Aalberts' analysis shows how legal arguments are interpretations of the law influenced by (political) visions on international society, international legal order, and political interests.

While the focus of Aalberts and of Mertens and van Dinther is mainly on the Dutch governmental discourse of justification, Philip Liste further expands our view in two ways. Firstly, his focus is on the discourses of international law in Germany and the United States. Secondly, he adds the societal dimension of the politics of international law to the discourse analysis of governmental justifications of the Iraq war—that is to say, the public discourse on Iraq in which a variety of social actors participate. Both the governmental and the public discourse differ significantly depending on the two states considered. Liste confronts the 'governmental politics of international law' with the 'common sense politics of international law' of the public discourse. In short, Liste's aim is not

> to discover the 'real' interrelationship between international law and politics but to describe how the nexus of [politics and law] is socially constructed within [these] diverse discourses.[38]

In his view, the construction of this nexus determines the meaning of international law. In Liste's discourse-oriented perspective, the public is engaged in the construction of the meaning of international law: it is created through inter-relation between 'politics', 'democracy' and 'international law'.

Since the nexus of international law and politics is socially constructed through processes in which—at least within democracies—society takes part, 'state politics of international law are not without constraints.' The constraints then depend on what value and status international law has in society, on how important it is in the evaluation of arguments made, whether a certain course of action is appropriate.

In the US, the governmental justification is grounded on the enforcement of international law. As long as the United Nations and international law were able to authorize and thus legitimize the Iraq Intervention both were accepted as relevant and meaningful. However when both failed in their task to justify the intervention as the legitimate enforcement of international law, which was perceived as a vital national interest, they lost relevance and meaning in the US. Liste shows how both the governmental and public discourse with respect to the Iraq war share this instrumentalist approach to international law. In other words, in both the governmental and the public discourse the nexus of law and politics is constructed as 'a clear-cut subordination of law to politics.' This is rooted in the fact that democratic values are understood as privileged in relation to international law. So, if democracy demands it, deviation from international law is required. In the US, democratically produced domestic law trumps international law as a source of legitimacy since international law is perceived as being created without a democratic process. Democracy may thus legitimise deviation from international law.

[38] Liste 2012, p. 179.

Germany, contrary to for example the Netherlands, from the outset spoke-out against the Iraq war and opted against political support—not to speak of military support—for the US led coalition. Liste points out how for the German government 'Iraq' was mainly about the dilemma of whether or not to support its major ally. How to deal with this transatlantic conflict on world order? More than a legal problem, for Germany this was a truly *political* issue. Traditional German international legalism clearly prescribed the required course of action in the Iraq crisis: no military intervention nor support thereof. However, this approach was complicated by its major ally's course of action. How to keep Americanism and International Legalism reconciled? This dilemma impacted the discursive representation of the nexus of law and politics in both the governmental and public discourse. Liste notes there is no structural subordination of law to politics or vice versa. He finds 'discursive ambivalence' and thus two types of signification of international law. Two constructions also of the nexus of international law and politics: either, law is accepted as a value in itself and confirmed as a 'monument' of world order; as such it is then able to constitute politics. Or, law is simply part of the factual presence of power. That is: 'the foundations of international law are basically seen in power politics.' The former cannot function without the latter, a real separation of the two so that politics can be constrained by law is rejected as utopian. Liste also illustrates that in Germany, contrary to the United States, international law and democracy are an inseparable pair: it is democratic to comply with international law. The discourses regarding the Iraq War in Germany thus do not illustrate a clear-cut subordination of politics to international law. Liste shows us something important about the relation between international law and politics: this relation may be conceptualized differently in the states even if in both states that conceptualization is based on democratic politics.

Bertjan Verbeek argues how an approach combining international relations and international law can be helpful in explaining the different role of international law in the different choices (regarding, for example, the legal basis *vel non* to be found in Security Council Resolution 1441) made by rather similar states such as France, Italy, the Netherlands, the United Kingdom, and the United States in the build up to the 2003 war against Iraq. Verbeek shows whether and how these states have taken international law into account when deciding on the 2003 intervention. Ultimately, Verbeek presents his major conclusion as a modest outcome: 'there is no clear-cut answer to the question of how international law and international politics are related.'[39] This is not quite justified, as his contribution clearly illustrates how the two major IR debates help to explain 'the precise nature of the relationship' and in particular how in the case of Iraq there is more than a mere instrumental use of international law. States actions were influenced by international law standards, and the US and UK for example sought to secure a second UNSC resolution precisely because international law played a role in their policies. When they ultimately went ahead without such a resolution this significantly undermined their position.

[39] Verbeek 2012, p. 211.

In other words, international law can only be ignored at a cost: '[f]or IR theory, this means that international law restricts the range of legitimate options available to states.' In the legal discourse, international law holds political power to account notwithstanding the fact that 'international law remains open to competing interpretations' and '[t]he specific choices states make thus remain difficult to predict.' IR theory may help to explain these choices.

This Agora concludes with a contribution by Nigel White, which convincingly argues that '[t]he main protagonists in favor of the use of military force against Libya, France and the UK, were mindful of the lessons from Iraq, both in terms of the legality of the 2003 invasion (when the main protagonists were the UK and the US) and its state-building consequences.'[40] Indeed, in relation to the situation in Libya, authorization by the proper authority was sought and secured with UNSC Resolution 1973. However, as demonstrated by White, while in the case of Libya the legal basis for the use of force may have been adequate, legal problems were not absent. In this case, problems hinged on the interpretation of the terms of the resolution—to take all necessary measures, 'to protect civilians and civilian populated areas under threat of attack' in Libya—indicating the level of force. White concludes on a not-so-optimistic note: '[t]he response to the crisis moved from an immediate and necessary protection of civilians toward regime change, illustrating that the UN collective security system does not appear to be capable of governing or regulating the use of force, even force which was initially taken under its authority.'[41] On the other hand, with respect to the 'state-building consequences' there is room for a little more optimism. At the time of writing (November 2011) it is really too early to tell, but it is well possible that it will pay off that in relation to Libya the 'state-building consequences' were taken into account right from the start; and it is likely that the long-term consequences of the military assistance to Libyan resistance will differ from the violence and chaos which came about in the aftermath of the Iraq war. Ultimately, White seems to confirm that even when properly applied, the legality scheme does not answer all questions. The interpretation of the SC authorization, the probability of success, and the question of proportionality of force and possible consequences have to be taken into account. In other words, to wage a war the criteria of both legality and legitimacy have to be fulfilled.

3.5 Legal, but Illegitimate?

To many legal thinkers and commentators the turn from formal legality to legitimacy as a *prime* basis for the condemnation of the 2003 military intervention in Iraq is utterly problematic as legitimacy is so much more subjective and political than the

[40] White 2012, p. 216.

[41] White 2012, p. 228.

realm of positive international law. To be sure, legitimacy is a factor—witness the number of treatments of the Iraq operation as illegal-but-legitimate—,[42] but it cannot be the prime factor or decisive point of reference.[43] This probably explains the fact that a fourth possible position is not considered by any of the authors in this Agora, nor by the lawyers participating in the debate more generally—viz. that an intervention would be *legal but illegitimate*. Note in this respect that also legal philosophers Mertens and van Dinther deal with the Iraq crisis as a crisis of legality and conclude with a plea for a return to formal legality by the Dutch government.

At least three argumentative patterns feature both in international law theory and in practice: (i) the war in Iraq was illegal full stop, and if illegal, war cannot be legitimate; (ii) the war in Iraq was illegal, but it was legitimate; and (iii) the war in Iraq was legal and legitimate. However, once one accepts Koskenniemi's claim that 'legal arguments do not *produce* substantive outcomes but seek to *justify* them'[44] and subsequently applies the relative indeterminacy of international law in the context of the present case, the absence of the fourth argumentative position 'legal but illegitimate' is not self-evident. After all, one needs to recognize that both 'legal' and 'illegal' can be the outcome of legal reasoning on the 2003 intervention in Iraq, since the substance of international law itself does not lead to a decisive outcome.[45] Moreover, the outcome is determined by political preferences which operate within international law as a scheme of interpretation. Formal legality alone then turns out as insufficiently determinative in decision making on the use of force, which is informed in the end by legitimacy reasoning.[46] The fourth argumentative position 'legal but illegitimate' would direct the legal debate into transparency about political preferences which through legitimacy reasoning influence decision-making. In 2003, those who supported the war initially won the debate by taking it beyond the questions of formal legality; ultimately, the idea that the war was legitimate, albeit illegal, became an acceptable one and gave a legal guise to the military intervention. The converse position that the Iraq war was 'legal, but illegitimate' is for many international lawyers perhaps a difficult course to take. Yet, arguably the question of legitimacy-illegitimacy should not have been left to politicians while lawyers—understandably—stayed in the comfort-zone of formal legality; such precisely because to serve the international rule of law as well as law's promise of justice requires international lawyers to move beyond legal formalism when necessary.

---

42 See e.g. Anne-Marie Slaughter, Good Reasons for Going Around the U.N., *New York Times*, March 18, 2003, p. A33.

43 Cf. e.g. Aalberts' contribution which demonstrates how legitimacy considerations influenced Dutch decision-making but were not made explicit by the Government as it simply stuck to the position of legality. Aalberts 2012.

44 Koskenniemi 2005, p. 570.

45 Or, as Koskenniemi observed '[w]ere the lawyers defending the lawfulness of the Iraq war of 2003 simply incompetent lawyers? Surely the problem was elsewhere.' Koskenniemi 2005, p. 569.

46 Cf. e.g. Aalberts 2012; Mertens and van Dinther 2012.

In her much discussed 2003 article in the New York Times, Anne-Marie Slaughter basically took the 'illegal, but legitimate' position and concludes: '[t]hat is the lesson that the United Nations and all of us should draw from this crisis. Overall, everyone involved is still playing by the rules. But depending on what we find in Iraq, the rules may have to evolve, so that what is legitimate is also legal.'[47] Slaughter has been criticized for her stance, but she needs to be credited for something she writes in an earlier paragraph:

> [t]he United States will now claim authorization under Resolution 1441. Most international lawyers will probably reject this claim and find the use of force illegal under the terms of the Charter. *But even for international lawyers, insisting on formal legality in this case may be counterproductive*. The better way to understand what has happened is that neither side can command a majority without a veto. By leaving well enough alone, both sides can continue to claim to have the better of the argument over how best to disarm Iraq.[48]

I read the italicized sentence in Slaughter's quote so as to mean that arguing about the legality of the war is not enough for international lawyers. This is—as we may now conclude—a valuable point. Rather than to stick to the level of formal legality and the relative indeterminacy of the law as a scheme of interpretation, international lawyers participating in the debate must engage with moral and political arguments regarding the use of force. This should not be left to politicians, political and/or moral philosophers, and theologians alone.[49] Just war doctrine is one of the doctrines which may serve as a model for deciding whether in a given case military intervention is prudent and advisable, as it can test Governments' arguments against standards of both legality and legitimacy.

Most international lawyers understand the contemporary *jus ad bellum*—grounded in the UN Charter as well as in customary international law—as having replaced the just war doctrine of the sixteenth-seventeenth century.[50] The use of force then is addressed *within* the framework of positive international law, which is the realm of legality, hinging entirely on (a) the duty that has been violated and (b) the authorization by the competent authority. However, once the debate starts (inevitably) moving outside the formal legality realm, a revisit of the tradition would be very helpful. After all, the just war doctrine offers a decision-making model on the use of force that has been developed by political leaders, their advisors, and critics in over 2000 years.[51] A brief revisit provides the lawyer with

---

[47] See e.g. Anne-Marie Slaughter, Good Reasons for Going Around the U.N., *New York Times*, March 18, 2003, p. A33.

[48] Ibid. (emphasis added).

[49] Indeed, the political philosopher, Michael Walzer, used just war doctrine when condemning the invasion in Iraq. Earlier however in the case of the war on terror the traditionally restrictive, just war doctrine re-emerged in order to justify possible illegal interventions as legitimate. See, Falk 2004.

[50] Haggenmacher 1983; Tuck 1999.

[51] See supra note 50; also, e.g. Russell 1975. See for the famous argument by Thomas Aquinas on just war Dyson 2002, p. 239 *et seq.*

considerations which in hindsight faded into the background of the debate. For a war to be waged legitimately, not only the aforementioned criteria (a) just cause and (b) legitimate authority, but *all six* criteria need to be fulfilled: war is waged (c) for the right reasons, (d) in last resort (*ultima ratio*), (e) with a serious chance of success, and thus (f) without risking to bring greater evil and chaos (proportionality).[52] The application of these criteria of justice in the legal-political process of decision making on Iraq would have contested on their own ground governments who argued the war to be (perhaps-) illegal-but-legitimate. If applied conscientiously the just war criteria would have challenged the legitimacy claim by showing that a well-developed 'state-building' plan for the post-war period was lacking and that hence the risk of bringing greater evil—viz. violent anarchy—to the Iraqi was not proportionate. Governments of states such as the UK, Italy, and the Netherlands would have had to account for the probable chance of success and clarify their motives, for example, not serving oil or other corporate interests. The just war doctrine could have served to start off a discussion about the political preferences which sometimes explain the choice of international legal arguments.

In other words, against the backdrop of Martti Koskenniemi's important insights about the structure of international legal argument and the nature of international law, this is a plea which complements Koskenniemi's plea for the 'culture of formalism'. International law oscillates between formalism and instrumentalism but a plea to strengthen the culture of formalism does not suffice, as is clear from the case of Iraq. The instrumentalist arguments should be embedded in a culture of accountability for the political preferences that determine instrumentalist positions, the reasons *why* a particular international law language is used.[53] Where we are dealing with military intervention, the just war doctrine could be a helpful model for decision making and testing the international legal arguments made. By accounting for political preferences that determine the interpretation which justifies a certain legal outcome, a distancing between politics and law re-emerges.

---

[52] See e.g. Childress 1978.

[53] On this 'why' in the context of interpretation of political and legal theory, see Quentin Skinner's methodology as discussed in Nijman 2004, p. 20–21. 'A linguistic act is thus considered to include a social or political act which either challenges or confirms the actual practice of contemporary national and/or international political life. We have to consider a historic text in relation to the appropriate 'practical context in which the argument it contains was made in order to understand what is *done*. What is done could be, for example, providing legitimisation for certain practices, or conversely, challenging them. Certain terms may be used to either support or undermine social, political, moral or legal practices and when they are successful, they cease to be merely descriptive, but in addition obtain an 'evaluative dimension', which influences conventions and awareness. These 'evaluative-descriptive terms' evidently play an important role in language as they are the *locus* of change. 'It is essentially by manipulating this set of terms that any society succeeds in establishing and altering its moral identity.' To understand such manipulation one has to have some clue about the practical context in which these social and political acts are carried out.' (Footnotes omitted.)

3.6 Conclusion: Toward a Reconstruction of the International Rule of Law

The present chapter introducing this Agora's study of 'Iraq' as a case from which to learn more about the relationship between international law and politics bears a question mark in its title. Has the case of Iraq been a final blow to the international rule of law or has it merely once more highlighted the complexity of the interrelationship between international law and politics? On the basis of the contributions to this Agora it is fair to conclude the latter. The concept of the international rule of law which subordinates politics to an international law that is objective and determinate and that, as such, can provide political leaders with substantive outcomes and applicable answers cannot be upheld. The strict separation between objectivity and subjectivity, between agents or actors and norms, has been replaced by an image of interpretative processes through which actors, that is States, 'come to define not only their objectives but perhaps even their identity by principles offered by international law.'[54] The calls for strengthening legal formalism recognize the inherent politics of international law and the fact that international law and politics are thus interwoven. However, this is not the same thing as concluding that international law *is* politics in the sense that law has no separate identity or specific normative function. The fact that international law and politics are interwoven does not preclude the existence of an international rule of law—which is that law constrains politics—altogether. Rather, the international rule of law is a specific way of doing politics. Ultimately, relative undeterminacy does not erase international law's functioning as a constraint or guidance of politics, nor the possibility of a more constructivist view on the role of international law. So the Agora confirms.

The constraining power of international law is represented in what Koskenniemi calls 'the formalist logic' of international law, i.e., international law as a standard to evaluate and criticize 'behaviour, including the behaviour of those in dominant positions.'[55] It exists in oscillation with the instrumentalist logic of international law, i.e., the objectives and political preferences of actors. The formalist logic is able to fulfill the task to 'constrain those in powerful positions', because it 'refuses to engage with the question of its objectives.'[56] It offers a language to advance claims and policies as well as to criticizes such international actions and uphold law so as to constrain power. The latter being among the prime needs of the international community.

To understand the objectives of international law, one has to understand the objectives of the actors who use international law to reach these goals. Arguably, however, the use of the instrumentalist logic of international law invites in turn the

54 Koskenniemi 2003, p. 94.

55 Koskenniemi 2003, p. 102.

56 Koskenniemi 2003, p. 96.

use of the formalist logic of international law. In a way, the two professional 'cultures' or 'sensibilities' depend on and reinforce each other in the work of the international lawyer. Formalism challenges the international lawyer to face questions of legality, instrumentalism makes facing questions of legitimacy unavoidable since instrumentalism is aimed at (political) transformation and thus by definition seeks the limits of formal legality. The oscillation between the logic of instrumentalism and the logic of formalism defines international law theory and practice. As Koskenniemi has put it: 'international law operates-and should operate-as a relatively autonomous formal technique *as well as* an instrument for advancing particular claims and agendas in the context of political struggle.'[57] In the latter guise it is used by decision makers, but the former could be used by those affected by the instrumentalist claims. This is important when taking Schmitt's argument serious, which Koskenniemi recalls, that 'there is a dark side to such anti-formalism' related to its politics-dependency.[58] In the previous section, the case was made for an explanatory culture of accountability for the political preferences shaping the instrumentalist positions. Such openness about the reasons (objectives) behind a chosen policy alternative should not undermine but support, complement, and qualify the 'cultivation of the culture of formalism.'[59]

International law thus is useful for cooperation and conflict resolution because it offers 'an interpretative scheme' relied on by a weak actor for protection against the politically powerful.[60] One could add that international law might be relied on just as well by powerful actors who seek legitimation of its actions. 'There is a constant push and pull in the international world between a *culture of instrumentalism* and a *culture of formalism*.'[61] The international lawyer operates this dialectic between the instrumentalist logic and the formalist logic, both of which are indeterminate and thus neither is 'fully constraining'.[62] And yet, together they sustain what could be called the international rule of law:

> '[p]ower' and 'law' are entangled in such complex ways that it is difficult to interpret particular events as manifesting either one or the other: power works through 'formal rules'—just like instead of 'naked power', we see everywhere power defined, delimited, and directed by rules.[63]

---

[57] Koskenniemi 2003, p. 96.

[58] Koskenniemi 2003, p. 98.

[59] This may come close to Koskenniemi's observation: '[w]hile the culture of formalism is a necessary though often misunderstood aspect of the legal craft, as a historical matter, it has often provided a recipe for indifference and needs to be accompanied by a live sense of its political justification.' Ibid., p. 107.

[60] Koskenniemi 2003, p. 102.

[61] Koskenniemi 2003, p. 102–103.

[62] Koskenniemi 2003, p. 104.

[63] Koskenniemi 2003, p. 103.

The instrumentalist and formalist logic—together at play in the international rule of law—are under-determined and inconclusive, and so the international lawyer becomes center stage: she has to make choices which are inherently political. International law is (also) a political project. If that is lost from sight 'formalism loses political direction, [and] formalism itself is lost.'[64] This paradox complicates the relationship between international law and politics. When we apply this to 'the case of Iraq' we may conclude, as elucidated from various perspectives in this Agora, that rather than causing a crisis of the international rule of law, Iraq has put international law *qua political project* into a state of crisis. If international law is to live up to its 'expectations about international law's autonomy'[65] from the political realm, it must recognize the political nature of the aspirations of the international community: peace, equality, and freedom. Then we will be able to see when indeed international law is living up to its 'promise of justice'[66] as it puts political questions on the international agenda and is open and accountable about the politics of international law, which is different from, yet connected to, international politics *tout court.*

Consequently, when we recognize that 'politics of international law is what competent international lawyers do' and that '*competence is the ability to use grammar in order to generate meaning by doing things in argument,*'[67] it follows that while legal meaning is contingent, and highly contextual, it *exists*. International law is a specific language for doing politics, the international rule of law stands for a specific way of doing politics. Legal meaning is constructed when international law language is used and thus while being used it shapes and is shaped in each specific case. Through the use of legal language states (re)construct their identity and set a standard for their conduct in the next case (or, so White shows for the UK in relation to the 2011 situation in Libya).

From the contributions in this Agora emerges a complex image of the relation between international law and politics: beyond the relative indeterminacy of the law and beyond the collapse of the separation between international law and politics, an international rule of law re-emerges in the gap between law and political objectives, in the realm of the interpretative processes that international law is.

---

64 Koskenniemi 2003, p. 107.

65 Koskenniemi 2003, p. 107.

66 Koskenniemi 2003, p. 111. 'A return to morality—in contrast to 'moralization'—is not available (Koskenniemi 2002). As a promise of justice, international law describes the international world as a political community in which questions of just distribution and entitlement are constantly on the agenda.'

67 Koskenniemi 2005, p. 571.

References

Aalberts TE (2012) Forging international order: inquiring the Dutch support of the Iraq invasion. 42 Netherlands Yearbook of International Law, pp 139–175

Alvarez A (1936) Exposé de motifs et déclaration des grands principes du droit moderne. Editons internationales, Paris

Brierly JL (1958) The basis of international law, Inaugural Lecture, 1924, Oxford University. In: Brierly, Lauterpacht, Waldock (eds) The basis of obligation in international law and other papers. Clarendon Press, Oxford, pp 68–80

Carty A (2006) New philosophical foundations for international law: from an order of fear to one of respect. Camb Rev Int Aff 19:311–330

Charlesworth H (2002) International law: a discipline of crisis. Modern Law Rev 65:377–392

Childress JF (1978) Just-war theories: the bases, interrelations, priorities, and functions of their criteria. Theologic Stud 39:427–445

Clarke RA (2004) Against all enemies: inside America's war on terror. Free Press, New York

Committee Davids (2010) Rapport: commissie van onderzoek besluitvorming Irak. Boom, Amsterdam

de Louter J (1919) La crise de droit international. 26 Revue Générale de Droit International Public

Domingo R (2010) The crisis of international law. Vanderbilt J Trans Law 42:1543–1593

Douzinas C (2007) Human rights and empire: the political philosophy of cosmopolitanism. Routledge-Cavendish, Abingdon

Dyson RW (ed) (2002) Aquinas political writings. Cambridge University Press, Cambridge

Falk R (2004) Legality to legitimacy: the revival of the just war framework. Harv Int Rev 26:40–44

Fitzmaurice G (1957) The general principles of international law considered from the standpoint of the rule of law. Recueil des cours 92:1–227

Franck T (1995) Fairness in international law and institutions. Clarendon Press, Oxford

Goldsmith JL, Posner EA (2005) The limits of international law. Oxford University Press, New York

Habermas J (2006) The divided west. Polity Press, Cambridge

Haggenmacher P (1983) Grotius et la doctrine de la guerre juste. Presses Universitaires de France, Paris

Kennedy D (2000) When renewal repeats: thinking against the box. Int Law Politics 32:335–500

Koskenniemi M (1989) From apology to utopia. The structure of international legal argument. Lakimiesliiton Kustannus, Helsinki

Koskenniemi M (1990) The politics of international law. Eur J Int Law 1:4–32

Koskenniemi M (2003) What is international law for? In: Evans MD (ed) International law. Oxford University Press, Oxford, pp 89–114

Koskenniemi M (2005) From apology to Utopia. The structure of international legal argument, 2nd edn. Cambridge University Press, Cambridge

Koskenniemi M (2011) The politics of international law. Hart Publishing, Oxford

Liste P (2012) 'Public' international law? Democracy and discourses of legal reality. 42 Netherlands Yearbook of International Law, pp 177–191

Manusama KM (2012) Between a rock and a hard place: providing legal advice on military action against Iraq. 42 Netherlands Yearbook of International Law, pp 95–121

Mertens T, van Dinther J (2012) Whose international order? Which law? 42 Netherlands Yearbook of International Law, pp 123–138

Nijman JE (2004) The concept of international legal personality: an inquiry into the history and theory of international law. T.M.C. Asser Press, The Hague

NILR (2010) Report of the Dutch committee of inquiry on the war in Iraq, Chap. 8: the basis in international law for the military intervention in Iraq. Neth Int Law Rev 57:81–137

Nouwen S, Werner W (2011) Doing justice to the political. The international criminal court in Uganda and Sudan. Eur J Int Law 21:941–965

Russell FH (1975) The just war in the middle ages. Cambridge University Press, Cambridge

Schrijver N (2010) A missionary burden or enlightened self-interest? International law in Dutch foreign policy. Neth Int Law Rev 57:209–244

Sharf M (2005) International law in crisis: a qualitative empirical contribution to the compliance debate. Cardozo Law Rev 31:45–97

Shklar J (1964) Legalism: law, morals, and political trials, 2nd edn. Harvard University Press, Cambridge

Tamanaha B (2004) On the rule of law: history, politics, theory. Cambridge University Press, Cambridge

Tuck R (1999) The rights of war and peace: political thought and the international order from Grotius to Kant. Oxford University Press, New York

Verbeek B (2012) Does might still make right? International relations theory and the use of international law regarding the 2003 Iraq war. 42 Netherlands Yearbook of International Law, pp 193–214

Werner W (2011) The curious career of lawfare. Case West Reserv J Int Law 43:61–74

White ND (2012) Libya and lessons from Iraq: international law and the use of force by the United Kingdom. 42 Netherlands Yearbook of International Law, pp 215–229

Chapter 4
Between a Rock and a Hard Place: Providing Legal Advice on Military Action Against Iraq

Kenneth M. Manusama

Abstract This article describes the role of legal advice and legal advisers in the policy-making process toward the 2003 invasion of Iraq, on the basis of the report of the Davids Committee in the Netherlands and the documents declassified in the course of the UK's Chilcot Inquiry. The controversial nature and seemingly weak legal basis for the 2003 invasion of Iraq prompted much public and academic discussion, even leading to the leaking of otherwise confidential legal memoranda from government lawyers to the media. Unprecedented and (semi)public inquiries were carried out into the policy-making processes and motives for resorting to the use of armed force, including the role of legal advice and legal advisers. In the Netherlands, legal advisers were at a disadvantage because of the hierarchical structure in which they are placed, and because the basic policy was set at a very early stage. The legal advice rendered in the United Kingdom was given far more consideration and prominence. Yet, when advice and policy started to diverge, the

Assistant Professor of International Law at the Department of Transnational Legal Studies at the Faculty of Law of the Vrije Universiteit Amsterdam, and Executive Director of the Vitoria Institute for International Law and Policy. The author was also an interim legal counsel at the Ministry of Foreign Affairs of the Netherlands in 2009. This research topic was in great part inspired by that experience. The author gives thanks to Prof. Wouter Werner and Dr. Erik Denters for reviewing first drafts of this article. Any opinions expressed in this article are the sole responsibility of the author.

K. M. Manusama (✉)
Department of Transnational Legal Studies, Faculty of Law, Vrije Universiteit Amsterdam, Amsterdam, The Netherlands
e-mail: k.m.manusama@vu.nl

K. M. Manusama
Vitoria Institute for International Law and Policy, Amsterdam, The Netherlands
e-mail: manusama@victoriainstitute.org

I. F. Dekker and E. Hey (eds.), *Netherlands Yearbook of International Law 2011*,
Netherlands Yearbook of International Law 42, DOI: 10.1007/978-90-6704-849-1_4,

formal structure in which legal advice had to be requested from the Attorney General became subject to manipulation as to timing and, perhaps, substance. This description and analysis reveal common and familiar themes regarding the role, responsibilities, and perceptions of legal advice in foreign policy.

Keywords Iraq · Legal adviser · United Kingdom · The Netherlands · Use of force · Resolution 1441 (2002) · Revival argument · Security Council · Davids Committee · Chilcot Inquiry

Contents

4.1 Introduction

In recent times, the position and work of the government legal adviser, particularly with respect to issues of international law, have become more transparent—or exposed if you will. From the drafters of the now infamous "Torture Memos" to the leaked legal memo from the Legal Adviser of the Netherlands and the public testimony of Legal Advisers from the Foreign and Commonwealth Office (FCO) before a British Iraq Inquiry, the work of government lawyers now stands front and center. The invasion of Iraq in 2003 and the resulting legal outcries culminated in (semi-) public investigations into the governmental decision-making processes in the Netherlands and the United Kingdom. These investigations provide a unique insight into the inner workings of national decision-making processes, the use of legal advice and the position of legal advisers in that process in two vastly different institutional structures. This contribution, based on these investigations, aims to describe—to the extent possible[1]—in a historical-narrative approach[2] the use of legal advice and the role of legal advisers in the decision-making process concerning the Iraq invasion. It examines to what extent the institutional structure negatively influences the process of providing effective legal advice and how that legal advice is received and used by policy makers at the Ministry and by their political masters.

By way of preliminaries, this contribution first briefly sets out the role of Legal Advisers and the legal controversies involved in the Iraq invasion in Sects. 4.2 and 4.3. Secondly, the core of this contribution examines the process of providing legal advice in the Netherlands and the United Kingdom as part of the decision-making process towards invading Iraq in Sects. 4.4 and 4.5, followed, thirdly, by concluding remarks in Sect. 4.6.

4.2 Legal Advisers in International Law

Since 1990, the Legal Advisers of UN Member States come together for informal meetings at the UN around the meetings of the Sixth Committee of the General Assembly.[3] As was noted in the first meeting, the Legal Advisers considered such consultations of great value, not in the least because as practitioners of international law 'Legal Advisers often work in a certain solitude and might have the need to share their concerns with someone in a similar position.'[4] Invited to these meetings are Legal Advisers, generally defined as

> 'Head of the Office responsible for International Legal Services'. By this is meant the person who is responsible for international legal matters within the Ministry of Foreign Affairs (MFA) and for formulating instructions to the representatives of his or her country in the Sixth Committee of the General Assembly or for supervising this activity.[5]

How this person, who provides authoritative legal opinion within the government, is institutionally embedded may differ greatly. Roughly, three models

---

[1] The Iraq Inquiry in the United Kingdom has not concluded or published any preliminary findings at the time of writing. The analysis here is based on the public oral and written statements from relevant witnesses, as well as numerous declassified documents. Many documents on which the Dutch inquiry was based have not been publicly released. The discussion of these documents relies, therefore, solely on their rendition in the report.

[2] A historical narrative approach places the legal advice in the context of historical events and policy-making in order to be able to assess the impact of that advice on the decision-making process. See e.g. Carty and Smith 2000, pp. 2–3.

[3] The Sixth Committee of the UN General Assembly is the Legal Committee and deals with international legal matters. The International Law Commission also reports to the Sixth Committee.

[4] Corell 1991, p. 372.

[5] United Nations Office of the Legal Counsel, Background information to the Informal Meetings of Legal Advisers of Ministries of Foreign Affairs, available at http://www.un.org/law/counsel/meetings.htm.

by way of which advice on international law is provided to governments may be distinguished, namely: (1) through integration in the diplomatic service, (2) through integration with other legal services, or (3) through an autonomous entity within the foreign ministry.[6] As discussed briefly below, the Dutch Legal Adviser used to function as a separate entity within the Ministry, but was later integrated into a broader legal department. In the case of the UK, there is an independent Legal Adviser within the Foreign Office, but the official and authoritative advice for the entire UK Government is rendered by the Attorney General (AG).[7] Established by statute, the Legal Adviser in the US Department of State is a political appointee. He or she holds the rank of Assistant Secretary of State and has direct access to the Secretary of State.[8] In all three cases, the Legal Adviser acts externally as 'agent' for their respective governments, for instance, before the International Court of Justice.

Yet, in whatever institutional setting such a person finds him- or herself, Legal Advisers are confronted with the same problems regarding the relationship between their chosen field of practice, the power of politics, and their institutional role. First, as the participants in the second Legal Advisers meeting stressed, in the practice of law of Legal Advisers, law and policy are intertwined.[9] This unavoidable entanglement is for many government lawyers, especially in Foreign Affairs, a source of fascination and commitment, but also presents a real and enduring professional problem. Secondly, the position of legal adviser within a MFA forces him or her to oscillate between the role of independent legal adviser and advocate for the client.

4.3 Legal Controversies Surrounding the Invasion of Iraq

Many opinions about the legal case for armed intervention in Iraq circulate and have circulated, with conventional wisdom being that the use of armed force against Iraq was illegal, although the grounds for such a finding may differ.[10] As background to the main topic of this article, this section briefly outlines the purported legal case for the invasion of Iraq—including criticism.

UN Security Council resolutions 678 (1990)[11] and 687 (1991)[12] have been the two legal pillars of the so-called revival theory upon which the uses of force

---

[6] Cf. Merillat 1964, pp. 1–8; Berman 1994, p. 82.

[7] See Sect. 4.5.1.

[8] See e.g. Scharf and Williams 2010, pp. 15–18; Bilder 1962.

[9] Corell 1992, p. 4. See also generally on the meetings of the Legal Advisers, Corell 1999.

[10] See e.g. for a compact yet comprehensive discussion of the legal issues regarding the Iraq War, Gray 2004, pp. 270–281. See also the transcript public hearing of Sir Michael Wood, 26 January 2010, pp. 48–54, available at www.iraqinquiry.org.uk.

[11] UN Doc. S/RES/678, 29 November 1990.

[12] UN Doc. S/RES/687, 3 April 1991.

against Iraq have been predicated since 1991, including the 2003 invasion.[13] Resolution 678 authorized UN Member States to forcefully evict Iraqi troops from Kuwait in August 1990 and 'to restore international peace and security in the area.' The US, and to a lesser extent the UK,[14] advanced the revival theory and argued as follows. First, the infamous resolution 687 outlined what was required for the restoration of peace and security, i.e. complete disarmament of Iraq with respect to its weapons of mass destruction (WMD) and WMD programs. Secondly, it was argued that with the acceptance by Iraq of its obligations under resolution 687 a ceasefire may have come into effect, but that the authorization to use force was only suspended, and that the ceasefire was conditional on the fulfillment of these obligations. Thus, thirdly, a material breach of Iraq's obligations would lift the suspension of the authorization to use force, as was purportedly the case in January 1993 and December 1998 when force was used to induce compliance. The US and others concluded, therefore, that the original authorization in resolution 678 was automatically revived, or perhaps had never even gone into hibernation from which it had to be revived. Resolution 1441 (2002), in their view, did not alter this situation. On that legal basis, and despite efforts to obtain a new and explicit authorization in a second resolution, the US and partners invaded Iraq and changed its regime.

Although this purported legal basis was little debated at the time, serious criticism can and has been offered, mostly after the invasion. The criticism relates to all three steps in the argument.[15] In the public arena, next to large demonstrations in the streets of many European cities, perhaps the most unusual step was taken by several well-known international jurists who came out against the war for being illegal.[16] Thus, whilst the world publicly and hotly debated the legitimacy of the invasion, hidden from view the legal debate raged (or not) within the British Government and the MFA of the Netherlands.

4.4 The Netherlands: The Davids Report

In the Netherlands, the controversy surrounding the 2003 invasion of Iraq was sparked anew in January 2009, when a memo from the Office of the Legal Adviser of the Dutch MFA was leaked to the press.[17] This memo, written days after the invasion, once again outlined the legal objections to and commensurate legal risks

---

13 For a more elaborate discussion of the meaning and interpretation of resolution 678 (1990) and 687 (1991), and the revival theory see Manusama 2006.

14 See the letters to the Security Council by the UK, US and Australia, UN Docs. S/2003/350, 20 March 2003; S/2003/351, 20 March 2003; S/2003/351, 20 March 2003.

15 See e.g. Murphy 2004, pp. 173–257.

16 Crawford et al. 2003.

17 Joost Oranje, 'Memorandum DJZ/IR/2003/158–Juristen van Buitenlandse Zaken achtten Irak oorlog van meet af aan onwettig' [Memorandum DJZ/IR/2003/158–Lawyers from Foreign Affairs considered Iraq War illegal from beginning], *NRC Handelsblad*, 17 January 2009.

of the use of force against Iraq. After its publication, the Government succumbed to longtime public and political pressure and installed the 'Committee of Inquiry on Decision-making Iraq', subsequently dubbed the Davids Committee after its chair, the former President of the Supreme Court Davids. The Davids Committee released its report on 12 January 2010.[18] The following subsections discuss the role of the Legal Adviser as it emanates from the report.

4.4.1 The Office of the Legal Adviser and Iraq Between 1990 and 2002

Until 1998, matters of international law were dealt with by the Office of the Legal Adviser, as an independent entity within the Ministry. As such, the Legal Adviser, known as JURA, was 'directly responsible to the Minister through his Secretary-General (SG)'[19] and had more or less direct access to the Minister.[20] After a restructuring of the Ministry, the Legal Adviser's Office was subsumed under a general Directorate for Legal Affairs (DLA), and the Legal Adviser was internally 'merely' the Head of the International Law Department within that Directorate. Moreover, legal advice now had to also pass through the Office of the Director-General for Political Affairs (DGPA) before reaching the SG and the Minister. The Head of the International Law Department is still known as the Legal Adviser of the Ministry, and of the Netherlands in its relations with other states. The tasks of the Legal Adviser do not seem to have changed much, as a result of this restructuring of the MFA. Generally, the Legal Adviser (i) advises the Minister on all matters of international law—whether solicited or not—and (ii) represents the Netherlands (a) in international affairs, and (b) in international legal proceedings.[21]

In the period between 1991 and 2002, the US and coalition partners took military action against Iraq on several occasions related to Iraq's disarmament obligations. The Dutch legal position on these actions was relatively consistent, and consistently supported in Parliament. Regarding the 1993 bombings of Iraq, then Foreign Minister and later Judge of the International Court of Justice, Peter Kooijmans, argued that there was a 'direct causal relationship' between resolutions 678 and 687 and that they could therefore serve as the legal basis for this military action.[22] This stance appears to be contrary to the advice offered by the Office of the Legal Adviser in 1992, which submitted that the authorization of resolution

---

[18] Davids Committee 2010. Chapter 8 of the report on legal issues was translated in English and published in its entirety in the *Netherlands International Law Review* (NILR 2010, pp. 81–137).

[19] Riphagen 1964, p. 79.

[20] Davids Committee 2010, note 48, p. 243; NILR 2010, note 48, p. 107.

[21] Cf. Riphagen 1964, pp. 80–83 and Lammers 2009.

[22] Davids Committee 2010, p. 47 and sources cited therein.

678 only extended to the liberation of Kuwait.[23] As tensions slowly rose once more in the beginning of 1998, the Legal Adviser advised the Minister on 12 January 1998 that any lawful intervention had to be preceded by a United Nations Security Council (UNSC) resolution authorizing the use of force after determining a material breach and issuing an ultimatum.[24] The next day, however, a joint letter from the Ministers of Defence and Foreign Affairs to Parliament stated that complete compliance by Iraq with UNSC resolutions was and remained the goal. Moreover, this letter noted that it would almost certainly be impossible to obtain an in itself desirable update of the already established legal basis for the use of force provided by preceding resolutions. In other words, the Government thought that a new resolution authorizing the use of force was desirable, but not legally necessary. Upon questioning by members of Parliament on 19 February 1998, the Minister confirmed this position, contrary to the legal advice of 12 January 1998 as well as to the advice sent to him a couple of days earlier, although it is unclear whether the memo that contained this latter advice reached him.[25] In the more immediate run-up to the military operations by the US and UK in February 1999, the new Minister for Foreign Affairs reiterated that the relevant UNSC resolutions, as well as Iraq's non-compliance constituted a sufficient legal basis for unilateral military action, not in the least because the UNSC had determined in resolution 1205 (1998)[26] the existence of a material breach of Iraq's obligations.[27] Indeed, any military intervention would be legitimized by the entirety of UNSC resolutions,[28] although the Davids Report does not accurately reflect this position.[29] Only a few days before military action started, the Legal Adviser appears to have been involved in reviewing a memo by another directorate. In a handwritten note attached to the memo, the Legal Adviser opined that it would be

---

[23] Davids Committee 2010, p. 243; NILR 2010, p. 107.

[24] Davids Committee 2010, p. 244; NILR 2010, p. 108.

[25] Davids Committee 2010, note 28, p. 50.

[26] UN Doc. S/RES/1205, 5 November 1998.

[27] Letter of the Minister of Foreign Affairs, 13 December 1998, *Kamerstukken II*, 1998/99, 21 664, nr. 100; Cf. Davids Report 2010, p. 52. In the report, the relevant passage from the letter is paraphrased as if the question was whether Iraq's noncompliance with the relevant resolutions offered a sufficient legal basis. In the view of this author this is an incorrect reflection of the letter and the Government's position.

[28] Letter of the Minister of Foreign Affairs, 17 December 1998, *Kamerstukken II*, 1998/99, 21 664, nr. 102; Cf. Davids Committee 2010, p. 53.

[29] In the report, the relevant passage from the letter of 13 December is paraphrased as if the question was whether Iraq's non-compliance with the relevant resolutions offered a sufficient legal basis. In the view of this author, this is an incorrect reflection of the letter and the Government's position. The Government was of the opinion that Iraq's non-compliance justified military action on the basis of the preceding resolutions, not solely on the basis of non-compliance. As is widely accepted, there exists no unilateral right to enforce UNSC resolutions when these resolutions do not contain an authorization to use force. The Dutch Government, with the US and UK, considered that the original authorization in resolution 678 (1990) was revived due to Iraq's non-compliance.

inadvisable to state that the entirety of UNSC resolutions formed the legal basis for the use of force. Rather, the Legal Adviser cryptically 'proposed to recognise that this basis was admittedly "thin" but nevertheless "can be substantiated".'[30] Yet, this perceived difference may just be an unsuccessful legal hair-splitting by the legal adviser.

4.4.2 Desirable, but Not Necessary

As the Davids Report reflects, force was frequently used in the context of the no-fly zones over Northern and Southern Iraq, but not with respect to Iraq's disarmament obligations.[31] Consequently, the Committee was unable to unearth any relevant documents in which any further legal advice or legal opinion was offered. Not until the nature of international relations profoundly changed in the aftermath of the attacks of 11 September 2001 did the Iraq conundrum and additional eagerness to use force against it, come to the fore again. In this context, different departments within the Ministry contributed to a general policy document (a 'rolling document') in the first half of 2002. The Legal Adviser provided its own analysis of the international law in force on 27 May 2002. Interestingly, it acknowledged the unlimited temporal and substantive scope of resolution 678. However, according to the advice any interpretation of this resolution that would allow a unilateral military action was not supported by legal developments since 1991, state practice, or legal doctrine. Regime change was plainly illegal and the Legal Adviser concluded, therefore, that even if existing UNSC resolutions would provide a legal basis for any future US military action against Iraq it would be very thin. In addition, the Legal Adviser rather sweepingly warned about the consequences of bypassing the UNSC in terms of legitimacy, precedent, and the undermining of the rule of law.[32] The 'rolling document' on Iraq reflected the Legal Adviser's views and referred to its memo, which was attached to the document. The 'rolling document' was presented to the Minister prior to a brainstorm session on Iraq policy on 9 August 2002, which would prove to be pivotal in determining the Government's position in the months before the invasion of Iraq.[33] The Committee characterized this meeting, at which the Deputy Legal Adviser (now Legal Adviser) was present, as 'careless', because no record was kept.[34] From the basic policy that came out of the meeting, three points stand out for present purposes. First, disarmament was the first priority of the Government, not regime change; second, existing resolutions provided a legal

---

[30] Davids Committee 2010, p. 244; NILR 2010, p. 108.

[31] Davids Committee 2010, p. 56.

[32] Davids Committee 2010, p. 245; NILR 2010, p. 109.

[33] Ibid.

[34] Davids Committee 2010, p. 84.

basis for that purpose, albeit a controversial and tenuous one; third, an additional resolution explicitly authorizing the use of force would be politically desirable, but not legally necessary.[35] These, and other points, were laid down in a letter to Parliament in the preparation of which the Legal Adviser was not involved. Consequently, its position was not correctly reflected in either the letter or the dossier prepared for the Minister for the debate with Parliament.[36] A substantial part of Parliament did not accept the Government's legal position.

From September 2002 to March 2003, the Office of the Legal Adviser did not provide any recorded legal advice. The Minister did request a reaction to an article by former Ambassador van Walsum (and later member of the Davids Committee), in which the Legal Adviser countered *inter alia* the assertion that the mere possession of WMD constituted an imminent threat against which self-defense under Article 51 UN Charter could be used.[37] As the then Deputy Legal Adviser explained to the Committee, the silence on the part of the Legal Adviser in the period mentioned was due to the risk of being repetitive and of being left out of the discussion.[38]

4.4.3 Interpreting Resolution 1441 (2003) and Bureaucratic Infighting

While the Office of the Legal Adviser did not have any legal advice on record, the Government continued defending its stated legal position since 1998 before Parliament: that an additional resolution was not legally necessary, but would be politically desirable.[39] The US initiated a last-ditch effort within the UN to ensure complete inspection and verification of Iraq's disarmament, but, more importantly, sought additional (political) authorization for the use of force against Iraq. With the primary political and legal standpoints set, the Dutch Government continued to support efforts within the UN towards an authorizing resolution. The arduous negotiations at the UNSC resulted in resolution 1441, but arguably accomplished little, except offering Iraq a renewed opportunity to comply with its obligations. Both the text itself, as well as the Council debate, appear inconclusive as to whether it authorizes the use of force, suspends the revived authorization of

---

35 Davids Committee 2010, p. 85.

36 Davids Committee 2010, pp. 247, 251; NILR 2010, pp. 111, 114. Contrary to the actual position of the Legal Adviser, the dossier noted that the Legal Adviser was of the opinion that the legal basis for regime change was very thin, and that resolution 678 (1990) was temporally unlimited and unlimited in purpose.

37 Davids Committee 2010, p. 246; NILR 2010, p. 110.

38 Davids Committee 2010, p. 251; NILR 2010, p. 114.

39 Davids Committee 2010, p. 247; NILR 2010, p. 111. The Davids Report only acknowledges similarities between the legal standpoints in 1998 and 2002. In the view of this author, the two views do not merely share similarities, but share the core standpoint that a new authorization would not be legally necessary.

resolution 678, or does neither. In any case, both sides maintained their own interpretation of the resolution.[40] The Dutch Minister of Foreign Affairs in a letter to Parliament acknowledged that the resolution did not answer the question whether any possible use of force would need to be confirmed by a new UNSC resolution.[41] As the resort to armed force seemed inevitable in early 2003, the Legal Adviser was requested by the DGPA to provide a legal argument in support of the use of force without a second resolution after resolution 1441. While the first part of the resulting memo of 13 March 2003 of the Legal Adviser obliged the DGPA, the second part included the by now well-known objections to the long stated Government position. Moreover, the Legal Adviser stated that it was not out of the realms of possibility that the Netherlands would lose if a legal procedure would be started against it before the International Court of Justice.[42] Nevertheless, this clear and strongly worded (op)position was not reflected in the letter to Parliament of 18 March 2003. This letter explained the Government's position according to which it had become clear that a second resolution was not going to materialize, and stated explicitly in so many words for the first time that 'a second resolution is desirable, but not necessary.'[43]

The Legal Adviser's memo did elicit an equally strongly worded memo from the DGPA to the Minister on 14 April 2003, illustrating perhaps the general attitude towards international law and the role of law versus politics. The DGPA's memo criticized the Legal Adviser for deviating from its standpoint since 1992 when the legal basis for military action was acknowledged—albeit very tenuously—and without solid legal substantiation.[44] More importantly, however, the DGPA argued that the legal argument was formalistic and that the decision-making process in the Security Council 'was of a political and not a legal nature' and that therefore the issue had to be argued on the basis of political arguments. In addition, the legal advice did not provide an alternative legal cover for the politically legitimate use of force against Iraq.[45]

In another round of bureaucratic infighting, the Legal Adviser authored a follow up memo that was later leaked to the press.[46] The Legal Adviser, *inter alia* out of professional integrity and for the sake of posterity, refuted that its position had

---

[40] For a more elaborate analysis of resolution 1441 (2002) see Manusama 2006, pp. 214–217. The Davids Report concludes that resolution 1441 does not contain any authorization to use force without further UNSC decision making. Davids Committee 2010, p. 241.

[41] Letter of the Minister of Foreign Affairs, 11 November 2002, *Kamerstukken II*, 2002/03, 23 432, nr. 63.

[42] Davids Committee 2010, pp. 247–248; NILR 2010, pp. 111–112.

[43] Letter of the Minister of Foreign Affairs, 18 March 2003, *Kamerstukken II*, 2002/03, 23 432, nr. 94.

[44] Davids Committee 2010, pp. 248–249, 261; NILR 2010, p. 112.

[45] Davids Committee 2010, p. 249; NILR 2010, pp. 111–112.

[46] Foreign Affairs, DJZ/IR/NA/00195, memorandum from DLA to minister via the SG, 'Iraq—Legal basis for military action', 29 April 2003, Memorandum DJZ/IR/2003/158. See also Oranje 2009.

changed, outlining again its objections to the official policy, and criticized that policy for being both materially and procedurally at fault. In addition, the Legal Adviser outlined the fundamental nature of the law on the use of force and the need to preserve that body of law for the future. Famously, this memo never reached the Minister, but was sent back by the Ministry's SG. The Legal Adviser was requested to file the memo in the archives for posterity, and informed that the discussion was closed for now.

4.4.4 Findings

It may be noted that during the entire period, in which four different Ministers of Foreign Affairs from three different political parties spearheaded the official position on Iraq, they all argued the same political position, contrary to the same legal advice. Yet, it is clear from the examination above that from the outset, the Office of the Legal Adviser was balancing its objective legal advice with the prevailing political opinions and established policy on the desirability and legitimacy of military action against Iraq to ensure Iraq's compliance with its obligations. The Legal Adviser argued that resolution 678 could not be relied upon as a legal basis for the use of force, as it only related to the liberation of Kuwait. It appears from the report, however, that other directorates and departments within the Ministry seized on the tiniest of openings that the Legal Adviser offered. In a handwritten note attached to a memo from a different department in 1998, the Legal Adviser conceded that existing resolutions could provide a 'wafer-thin' legal basis. That position was gradually inflated by the political departments as to mean a 'sufficient' legal basis. Over time, the official stance of the Government that no additional authorizing resolution would be necessary also de facto bound the Legal Adviser, although this stance was incorrectly reflected by the Davids Committee. As the Committee notes, '[t]he Committee was not able to ascertain how this legal advice in the 1990s was assessed within the Ministry of Foreign Affairs. However, it is evident from the communication with [Parliament] that the arguments of the [Legal Adviser] and later the [Directorate for Legal Affairs] had not been adopted.'[47] Nevertheless, a sense of urgency in the wording of the Legal Adviser's memos can be discerned as of 2002, when the threat of a full-scale invasion of Iraq by the US became apparent. At the last hour, the Legal Adviser even provided a coherent legal argument for the legality of military action without an explicit, additional authorization, although stating its objections in equal measure. When the Legal Adviser's Office felt that its professionalism and integrity was being questioned,[48] the Legal Adviser attempted to put the record straight regarding its legal analysis since 1991 by writing the memo that was leaked later.

---

[47] NILR 2010, p. 108.

[48] See paragraph 1 of the leaked memo, Ibid.

Given the volume of legal advice available, and the persistent tug of war between the Office of the Legal Adviser and the rest of the Ministry, it is curious that the Committee concluded that '[t]he interpretation of international law adopted within the Ministry of Foreign Affairs was not based on a thorough, up-to-date legal analysis.'[49] Although the original memoranda on which the Committee based this conclusion could not be examined for present purposes, it is abundantly clear that the analysis of the Legal Adviser was just not accepted by the policy makers, as it did not accord with their political preferences. Thus, while '[t]he difference of opinion that existed (…) was extremely unfortunate,'[50] that difference did not exist because the legal analysis was not thorough or up-to-date. Another explanation for the lack of acceptance of the legal advice at the top level may be related to the Committee's recommendation that the Ministry's organizational structure should be changed 'to ensure that advice on international law is properly considered in the decision-making process within the Ministry of Foreign Affairs.'[51] Apparently, the Committee considered that this was not the case. This rationale could be explained by the fact that as of 1998, the Legal Adviser was cut off from direct access to the Minister. When the Legal Adviser was integrated into a larger DLA and access to the Minister was through the office of the DGPA, any legal advice brought before the Minister has already been subject to political evaluation. In such a structure, the Minister cannot sufficiently weigh legal advice on its own merits. Notably, the former Minister for Foreign Affairs De Hoop Scheffer stated before the Committee that in his view 'a government, a minister, should regard international law as an important part of his considerations when formulating policy but not as the exclusive and only part of his considerations.'[52] Realistically, international law is indeed 'only' one factor in the formulation of foreign policy. Yet, as the 2003 memo from DGPA reflects, international law is sometimes regarded (incorrectly) as an 'either/or' proposition in which a choice must be made between legal arguments on the one hand and political arguments on the other. The 'obstructionist' view of international law was also reflected by the DGPA when he lamented that the Legal Adviser did not offer any alternative legal arguments that could support the political view and stated policy.

4.5 The United Kingdom: The Chilcot Inquiry

At the time of writing, the Iraq Inquiry in the United Kingdom, chaired by Sir Chilcot (hereafter Chilcot Inquiry) and launched in July 2009, is still in the process of conducting a thorough and unprecedented investigation into the UK

---

[49] Davids Committee 2010, p. 531 (conclusions in English).

[50] Ibid.

[51] Ibid.

[52] Davids Committee 2010, p. 251; NILR 2010, p. 115.

Government's participation in the Iraq War. The Chilcot Inquiry focused even more so on the legality of the issue than the Dutch investigation, although both were triggered initially by a leaked legal memo. The leaked British memo contained formal legal advice that contravened or at least stood on tense footing with established policy goals. The following subsections detail how legal advice from different legal advisers was created and received within the UK Government, on the basis of the available declassified documents, as well as statements and testimonies available at the time of writing.[53]

4.5.1 UK Legal Advice on Iraq Before Resolution 1441 (2002)

Historically, legal advice for the UK Government was centralized into one single source, the Law Officers of the Crown, the AG, and the Solicitor General. As became clear in the Suez-Canal crisis, the Lord Chancellor may also play a significant role in providing legal advice, although he is only, *inter alia*, the head of the judiciary.[54] It is the AG, however, who is the Chief Legal Adviser to the UK Government and is a 'Minister and Member of Government'. As such, the AG is a political appointee, but is supposed to render advice independently of the Government, and its formal legal opinions are, in principle, not publicly available.[55] Despite its formal, central position, the AG stands in a complex relationship with the legal services of governmental departments, including the Legal Adviser of the FCO. With the emergence of the FCO legal service, however, the dominant source for the substance of the legal advice in international affairs is now the FCO, although leaving intact the formal position of the AG as the legal adviser of Her Majesty's Government (HMG).[56] Until legal advice is formally requested from the AG, all other legal opinions by the AG or the FCO expressed before such a request is made are not official and considered provisional. In practice, the AG and the FCO Legal Adviser work closely together,[57] although it may be presumed that in this relationship, the FCO provides most of the substance and the AG holds most

[53] All documents, statements and testimonies are publically available on the website of the Inquiry, www.iraqinquiry.org.uk. Unless considered necessary for the sake of clarity, the titles of the documents as used by the Chilcot Inquiry on the website are maintained, although the titles do not seem to reflect a concise and consistent system of referencing.

[54] See the outstanding article on how legal advice was rendered, weighed, and used in the Suez-Canal crisis by Watson 1988. The British Government in that case bypassed the negative legal opinions of the AG, as well as the Legal Adviser from the Foreign and Commonwealth Office, and instead relied on the unofficial views of the Lord Chancellor.

[55] House of Lords and House of Commons, Joint Committee on the Draft Constitutional Renewal Bill, *Draft Constitutional Renewal Bill—Volume I: Report*, HL Paper 166-I/HC Paper 551-I, 31 July 2008, para 77; Butler Report 2004, para 372; see also the excellent statement by David Brummell (Legal Secretariat to the Law Officers) to the Inquiry, 14 January 2010.

[56] Parry 1964, pp. 122–123. Butler Report 2004, paras 368–373.

[57] Statement by Sir Michael Wood, 15 January 2010, para 8. See also Weller 2010, p. 191.

of the responsibility. Indeed, as AG Lord Goldsmith would testify, the AG is considered to be the counterpart of the Legal Adviser from the US Department of State.[58]

As testified by key UK officials, the basic UK policy framework for Iraq consisted of containing Saddam Hussein with respect to the development of WMD through sanctions and no-fly zones.[59] Yet, the international consensus on that policy as well as the sanctions themselves was falling apart before 9/11, however, leading to a thorough policy review.[60] After 9/11, the perception of Iraq and the threat that it posed to the international community changed dramatically. As UK Prime Minister Tony Blair argued in his testimony, 'the calculus of risk changed.'[61] The basic policy framework, therefore, first moved to more intrusive inspection and subsequently towards necessary regime change to remove the threat from Iraq's alleged WMD programs, with a sound basis in international law, i.e., a UNSC resolution.[62]

In the years before 9/11, the UK based its arguments for the use of force against Iraq squarely on the revival argument. As Sir Michael Wood—FCO Legal Adviser at the relevant time—stated, resolution 678 (1990) had been revived, for instance, in the case of Operation *Desert Fox* in 1998 because the UNSC had made a determination in resolution 1205 (1998) that Iraq had been in material breach of its obligations.[63] However, it was uncontroversial among FCO lawyers, according to Wood, that this determination could not continue to serve as a legal basis for the use of force—a position that was consistently maintained over time.[64] Other legal implications of the paradigm shift caused by 9/11 were also quickly apparent. In a memo to Blair on 25 March 2002, Foreign Secretary (FS) Straw outlined 'two potential [legal] elephant traps,' namely that regime change is not a basis for the use of force in and of itself and that a new UNSC resolution 'may well be

58 Transcript public hearing of Rt Hon. Lord Goldsmith QC, 27 January 2010, p. 20.

59 See e.g. transcript public hearing of Simon Webb, Sir Peter Ricketts, William Patey, 24 November 2009, pp. 12–26. Transcript public hearing of Rt Hon. Jack Straw MP, 21 January 2010, p. 39.

60 Ibid. See also e.g. Letter from Tom McKane (Cabinet Office) to Alan Goulty (FCO) on Iraq Future Strategy, 20 October 2000; Letter from John Sawers (Prime Minister's Private Secretary) to Sherard Cowper-Coles (FCO) on a new Iraq policy framework, 7 March 2001; Memorandum by the Rt Hon. Jack Straw MP to the Inquiry, 21 January 2010, paras 1–23.

61 Transcript public hearing of Rt Hon Tony Blair, 29 January 2010, p. 7.

62 See e.g. Note from PM Tony Blair to Jonathan Powell (PM Chief of Staff), 17 March 2002; Transcript public hearing of Sir Peter Rickets and Edward Chaplin, 1 December 2009, pp. 6–8. See also the earlier leaked so-called 'Iraq Options Paper', Memorandum from the Overseas and Defence Secretariat Cabinet Office, 8 March 2002. This memo was part of the so-called 'Downingstreet Memos' that were published on 18 September 2004 in *The Observer* newspaper. These memoranda are available in transcribed form on www.downingstreetmemo.com.

63 Statement by Sir Michael Wood, 15 January 2010, para 8; Transcript public hearing of Sir Michael Wood, 26 January 2010, pp. 14–15.

64 Ibid. See also Letter from Simon McDonald (FCO) to Michael Tatham Esq. (Cabinet Office) on Iraq: Options, 3 December 2001, p. 1; Weller 2010, pp. 232, 244.

required.'[65] Despite this latter memo, Wood had issued a note to Straw's Private Secretary a day later, expressing concern about the FS' comments to his US colleague about being comfortable to make the case for military action. Wood had issued the note to ensure that everybody was clear and consistent about the legal position, as his office would do throughout.[66] He was also glad to see that the FS was not discussing the legal issues in public because '[t]he [AG's] advice will need to be sought at the appropriate stage before Ministerial decisions on actions or public statements.'[67]

Similar concerns were expressed by the AG himself on 28 March 2002 with respect to public comments made by the Defence Secretary. He basically reprimanded the Defence Secretary for stating a legal position while the AG had not been asked, or had given any definitive advice on the matter, which had put him in a difficult position.[68] The AG was apprised of the substantive legal situation in April 2002. However, by his own admission, although he was kept informed of developments by the FCO and aware—through the press—of discussion of the legal issue, he was not yet asked to provide legal advice or invited to Cabinet meetings to discuss the issue during the first half of 2002.[69] Nevertheless, he was asked to participate in the well publicized meeting with the most senior government officials, including Prime Minister Tony Blair on 23 July 2002.[70] In that meeting, as well as in unsolicited (and apparently unwelcome) advice of 30 July 2002, the AG expressed his view that self-defense could not provide a legal basis for the removal of Saddam Hussein to ensure compliance with Iraq's disarmament obligations. For existing resolutions to provide such legal cover, a new UNSC resolution was needed to determine that Iraq was in material breach of its obligations.[71] In August, Wood similarly outlined for his FCO colleagues once more in clear terms what he thought the legal position was, adding the political implications of not complying with international law, as well as the

---

65 Memorandum from Jack Straw (Foreign Secretary) to Tony Blair (PM), 25 March 2003, para 9. See also the Memorandum by the Rt Hon. Jack Straw MP to the Inquiry, paras 24–25. Straw also seemed adamant that he unequivocally supported the position that a second resolution was never, but that for political and strategic reasons, he publicly left room to maneuver. Transcript public hearing of Rt Hon. Jack Straw MP, 8 February 2010, pp. 3–4.

66 Transcript public hearing of Sir Michael Wood, 26 January 2010, pp. 16–17, 19–20.

67 Letter from Sir Michael Wood (FCO Legal Adviser) to the Foreign Secretary's Private Secretary on Iraq, 26 March 2002, para 5.

68 Letter from Lord Goldsmith (Attorney General) to Geoff Hoon (Defence Secretary), 28 March 2002.

69 Transcript public hearing of Rt Hon. Lord Goldsmith QC, 27 January 2010, pp. 16–18. The AG met with William Howard Taft IV, Legal Adviser of the US State Department on 22 May 2002, but apparently did not discuss the legal issue in depth.

70 Memorandum from Matthew Rycroft to David Manning, 23 July 2002 on Iraq: Prime Minister's Meeting, 23 July, available at http://www.timesonline.co.uk/tol/news/uk/article387374.ece.

71 Ibid, pp. 21–23; Advice from Lord Goldsmith QC (Attorney General) to Tony Blair (Prime Minister), 30 July 2002, para 13.

international and individual criminal responsibilities that may arise from unlawful military action.[72]

4.5.2 Towards Resolution 1441 (2002)

Despite on-going military planning, the US embarked on the so-called UN-route for a new UNSC resolution in the summer of 2002, in part at the urging of the UK. For the UK, the immediate objective for the resolution was in line with its legal perspective: the UK needed to provide sufficient ground for the lawful use of force by finding a material breach by Iraq, if force was eventually needed.[73] A draft was first of all negotiated and drafted within the US Administration, but with UK involvement, including FCO legal advisers. After the UN speech by US President Bush, and as negotiations were initiated with other Security Council members at the highest levels, the issues of 'material breach' and whether the text contained any triggers that would authorize the use of force dominated the discussions. Indeed, in an update report from FCO Legal Adviser Wood to the AG's Office on 24 September, Wood outlined the scenarios that could result from the negotiations on a first draft that was about to be circulated to other UNSC permanent members. Apparently, the draft contained: (1) a determination that there was a material breach by Iraq of its obligations, and (2) that further non-compliance with obligations set out in the new resolution would authorize UN members to 'use all necessary means', i.e., the magic UN-words for the use of armed force.[74] Should the latter provision be excluded, or be replaced by more ambiguous language, force would still be lawful according to the UK on the basis, inter alia, of the Desert Fox precedent. Should both provisions be left out, Wood argued, force would not be authorized. Indeed, FCO officials, including Wood, took pains at different times to remind the FS that in such a case, the military actions in Kosovo could not serve as a precedent, because in that case no authorizing resolution had even been sought.[75] Moreover, Wood cautioned—almost reprimanded—the FS about public comments made to the parliamentary Foreign Affairs Committee to

---

[72] Letter from Sir Michael Wood (FCO Legal Adviser) to Stephen Wright (FCO) re Iraq, Legality of the use of force, 15 August 2002.

[73] See e.g. Letter from Simon McDonald (FCO) to Sir David Manning (Cabinet Office), 27 August 2002, p. 2; Transcript from public hearing of Rt Hon. Lord Goldsmith QC, 27 January 2010, pp. 25–26.

[74] Note from Michael Wood (FCO Legal Adviser) to Catherine Adams (Legal Secretariat Law Officers), 24 September 2002, para 2.

[75] Minute from Peter Rickets (FCO) to Foreign Secretary's Private Secretary re Iraq Resolutions, 'The Kosovo Option', 3 October 2002; Note from Michael Wood (FCO Legal Adviser) to Edward Chaplin (Foreign Secretary's Private Secretary) re Iraq and authorization to use force, 17 October 2002.

the effect that he considered existing resolutions to be sufficient.[76] Such statements 'might box in the Attorney and others, the more one said in public, without having—or following the full proper legal advice.'[77] As the pressure mounted to agree on a text, the FCO Legal Adviser was requested by the FS to shortly outline the consequences in domestic and international law of military action without international authority.[78] In another update of the AG's Office on 18 October, Wood appraised the AG of the fact that the draft resolution as it stood did not contain, in his view, a revival of the earlier authorization, because it stated that any decision on further action would be for the UNSC to take, albeit implicitly.[79]

Although being kept abreast of and consulted about the negotiations and the legal issues discussed, the AG was never directly involved.[80] During negotiations, the AG's Office was sent some, but not all of the reports on how negotiations were progressing. The updates of 24 September and 18 October were both concluded with the words that '[w]e would be grateful for any advice which the Attorney General may wish to give on the resolution as currently drafted (…)', but this apparently did not amount to a formal request for determining the legal opinion of HMG. AG Lord Goldsmith himself characterized these updates as 'we are telling you but we are not asking you to do anything about it', in part because 'it didn't seem the practice to do that.'[81] Nevertheless, the AG did express his views, partly because of the informal requests in the FCO updates. On several occasions when he met and/or spoke with FCO officials, the FS, as well as the Prime Minister and officials in his office, the AG expressed his concern that the draft texts did not authorize the use of force.[82] Yet, some 2 weeks before the resolution was to be adopted, he 'was no longer actively consulted'.[83] Significantly, the AG was persuaded during this period not to put his concerns in writing, although he did give advice in various meetings and did feel the desire to put his views on record, e.g. in a report of a meeting with the Prime Minister.[84] On the eve of the adoption of the resolution, the AG met with FS Straw and 'warned' him that he 'shouldn't take it

[76] Note from Michael Wood (FCO Legal Adviser) to Edward Chaplin (Foreign Secretary's Private Secretary) on Iraq: International Law, 4 October 2002.

[77] Transcript public hearing of Sir Michael Wood, 26 January 2010, p. 18.

[78] Note from the Simone McDonald (Foreign Secretary's Private Secretary) to Michael Wood (FCO Legal Adviser) re Iraq. 15 October 2010.

[79] Note from Michael Wood (FCO Legal Adviser) to Cathy Adams (Legal Secretariat of the Law Officers—Attorney General's Chambers), 18 October 2002, para 4.

[80] See e.g. Transcript public hearing of Cathy Adams, 30 June 2010, pp. 9–11.

[81] Transcript public hearing of the Rt Hon Lord Goldsmith QC, 27 January 2010, p. 36.

[82] Statement by the Rt Hon Lord Goldsmith QC, 17 January 2011, paras 1.3, 1.15–1.17.

[83] Ibid., para 1.3.

[84] Ibid., paras 2.7, 2.8 and 3. The record of the meeting with the Prime Minister on 22 October, in which the AG's advice was noted, was laid down in a note to the Prime Minister on 23 October. This record has not been published by the Inquiry at the time of writing.

for granted that, when it came to it and definitive legal advice was given, that it was going to be that we were in a position to take military action.'[85]

4.5.3 On the Necessity of a Second Resolution

Resolution 1441 (2002) was adopted unanimously on 8 November.[86] It determined that Iraq 'has been and remains in material breach of its obligations'[87] and that it is given 'a final opportunity' to comply with such obligations.[88] 'Any failure to comply with, and cooperate fully in the implementation of this resolution' would constitute a further material breach to be reported to the UNSC for assessment,[89] at which time the Council will convene 'to consider the situation and the need for full compliance (...).'[90] The UNSC warned that Iraq 'will face serious consequences as a result of its continued violations of its obligations.'[91] These paragraphs and phrases would become the flashpoints for heated debate within HMG in a short period of time.

4.5.3.1 The Day After Resolution 1441 (2002)

Days after the resolution had been adopted, the AG contacted the PM's Chief of Staff, as well as FS Straw, in order to express his concern about 'Chinese whispers' that he allegedly had an optimistic view of the legal effects of resolution 1441, while in fact he did not. Moreover, the AG suggested—again—that he should put his advice in writing, yet, was advised that such a step would not be necessary at that time.[92] The AG explained that, in his view, in the event of non-compliance by Iraq, it was for the UNSC to determine whether a material breach had occurred. Straw countered mainly with political arguments and the need for compromise texts. Moreover, he stated the argument of both the UK and US that a second resolution in which a further material breach would be determined is preferable, but not essential. Furthermore, when the AG persisted in his reading of the

85 Transcript public hearing of the Rt Hon Lord Goldsmith QC, 27 January 2010, p. 32.

86 UN Doc. S/RES/1441, 8 November 2002; UN Doc. S/PV.4644, 8 November 2002.

87 Ibid., operative para 1.

88 Ibid., operative para 2.

89 Ibid., operative para 4.

90 Ibid., operative para 12.

91 Ibid., operative para 13.

92 Iraq: Note of telephone conversation between the Attorney General and Jonathan Powell—Monday, 11th November 2002, by David Brummell; Iraq: Note of telephone conversation between the Foreign Secretary and the Attorney General on Tuesday, 12 November 2002, by David Brummell.

resolution, Straw urged and persuaded the AG to look at the full negotiating history, and that there was a danger in trying to obtain a second resolution.[93]

Before and after the adoption of the resolution, both the AG and the FCO Legal Adviser supported the revival argument and shared the interpretation after resolution 1441 (2002) that a further determination by the UNSC was necessary. While the former came to this conclusion despite the lack of clarity in the text, the latter considered the text crystal clear.[94] As the AG embarked on further investigations of, *inter alia*, the negotiating history, Wood sent the AG a detailed letter, ostensibly a request for advice at the behest of the FS on 9 December 2002,[95] although it is unclear from the statements and testimonies before the Inquiry that it indeed was a formal request.[96] In this letter, Wood set out the different possible interpretations of resolution 1441 (2002), although the AG was fully aware of Wood's own views.

After comments made by FS Jack Straw to the US Vice President, Wood felt it necessary on 24 January to remind him that the UK could not lawfully use force without a further decision by the UNSC.[97] The following days, Straw personally told Wood that he 'was being very dogmatic and that international law was pretty vague and that he wasn't used to people taking such a firm position.'[98] The sharp rebuke was put on record on 29 January: 'I note your advice, but I do not accept it.'[99] Straw then proceeded to compare the uncertainties of international law and the absence of an international court, and offered an alternative view on the issue. The AG, who was copied on this written exchange, felt the need to confirm to Straw the right, duty and importance of government lawyers to 'give advice which they honestly consider to be correct', while being positive and constructive at the same time.[100] During his testimony before the Chilcot Inquiry, Straw was questioned at length about this episode, where he repeated the firm stance that while legal advisers may have a duty to offer their legal advice as they see it, unsolicited or not, he did not have to accept it.[101] Both the AG and Straw acknowledged the

[93] Iraq: Note of telephone conversation between the Foreign Secretary and the Attorney General on Tuesday, 12 November 2002, by David Brummell.

[94] See e.g. respectively, the transcript public of the Rt Hon Lord Goldsmith QC, 27 January 2010, p. 47.

[95] Note from Michael Wood (FCO Legal Adviser) to Catherine Adams (Legal Secretariat of the Law Officers—Attorney General's Chambers), 9 December 2002.

[96] The Chilcot Inquiry heard Cathy Adams, legal counselor to the Attorney General, on 30 June 2010, at which time it was still trying to 'clarify the point at which Lord Goldsmith was formally instructed to advise.' Transcript public hearing of Cathy Adams, 30 June 2010, p. 17.

[97] Note from Michael Wood (FCO Legal Adviser) to the Foreign Secretary's Private Secretary re Iraq: legal basis for the use of force, 24 January 2003.

[98] Transcript public hearing of Michael Wood, 26 January 2010, p. 31.

[99] Note from Foreign Secretary Jack Straw to Michael Wood (FCO Legal Adviser) re Iraq: legal basis for use of force, 29 January 2003.

[100] Note from Attorney General Lord Goldsmith to Foreign Secretary Jack Straw re legal advice and law officers, 3 February 2003, para 2.

[101] Transcript public hearing of the Rt Hon Jack Straw MP, 8 February 2010, pp. 5–6.

'established mechanism' that is applicable in case of such a conflict, namely to seek an opinion from the Law Officers.[102]

4.5.3.2 Endgame: Toward Final Legal Advice

As per the suggestion of Straw, the AG poured over the FCO arguments and many sources regarding the negotiating history, while the UK considered tabling a draft resolution. He was invited on 19 December 2002, not to offer specific and/or formal legal advice, but to offer his views to the Prime Minister in a draft legal memo on several issues and scenarios,[103] which he did on 14 January. In this advice, the AG followed the FCO view that the revival argument is indeed valid, but that in the case of resolution 1441 (2002) the UNSC had instituted a 'firebreak' by giving Iraq a final opportunity to comply. Operative para 4 posed that any non-compliance 'shall constitute a material breach' and 'will be reported to the Council for assessment'. According to the official UK position, a material breach had to be of a significant nature, leading to a necessary assessment of whether the non-compliance was significant. 'The question then arises as to who is to make that assessment.'[104] The AG concluded that it was for the UNSC to decide whether a material breach was present, and thereby reviving the original authorization to use force. In any case, the Council had to have another discussion. The AG repeated this stance in a cautionary note to the Prime Minister, despite the fact, as the AG himself pointed out, that he had spoken with Sir Jeremy Greenstock, the UK's ambassador to the United Nations, who had made a persuasive case in favor of military action.[105] On 6 February, the FS wrote to the AG regarding his provisional, draft advice. At first, he agreed with the AG that

> a unanimous and express [UNSC] authorisation would be the safest legal basis, yet, he vehemently disagreed with the AG's analysis that a further Security Council decision was a necessity. Straw then proceeded to detail how negotiations on certain terms had gone, and argued that the better interpretation was that resolution 678 (1990) was revived by the fact of a material breach, a report by the inspectors, and a mere UNSC discussion or consideration.[106]

A further draft of 12 February signified a subtle, yet significant shift along the lines of the FS' comments. The AG mentioned his further discussions with Straw, Greenstock, as well as US colleagues, and appeared at first glance to maintain his position. However, he now referred to the uncertainty of the text and different views on the meaning of operative paragraph 12, but 'in these circumstances,

[102] Ibid., p. 6; Note from Attorney General Lord Goldsmith to Foreign Secretary Jack Straw re legal advice and law officers, 3 February 2003, para 3.

[103] Note from the Attorney General's Office of meeting at No. 10, 19 December 2002, para 10.

[104] Attorney General's draft advice to Prime Minister, 14 January 2003, para 4.

[105] Note from Lord Goldsmith to Prime Minister, 30 January 2003.

[106] Letter from Foreign Secretary Jack Straw (signed by Simon McDonald) to Attorney General Lord Goldsmith re Iraq: Second Resolution, 6 February 2003.

I remain of the opinion that *the safest legal course* would be to secure the adoption of a further Council decision.'[107] Not only did the AG waver on the clarity of the text and the proper view on it, but also now adopted the FS' language, giving room for the implication that a further decision would not be a legal necessity. Moreover, the AG was now 'prepared to accept that a reasonable case can be made that resolution 1441 revives the authorization to use force.'[108] The well-known leaked memo of 7 March 2003 explained in even further detail this legal position and elaborated on some legal and political consequences.[109] At the same time, it also included all the doubts and possible contrary views to this standpoint, and was thus 'very equivocal.'[110] In a recorded meeting, however, the AG and the FS agreed that publicly, the case needed to be explained as strongly and unambiguously as possible.[111] The AG now clearly switched roles, from independent legal adviser to advocate for the government. Consequently, shorter and unequivocal legal advice was presented to the parliamentary Foreign Affairs Committee on 17 March,[112] at which time the UK also withdrew its draft texts for a second UNSC resolution. Many lawyers, including FCO Legal Adviser Wood, were present at the drafting meeting of this latest advice. The next day, FCO Deputy Legal Adviser, Elizabeth Wilmshurst, handed in her resignation to her boss, Michael Wood, citing the clear illegality of the pending use of force against Iraq as had been the consistent view of the FCO Legal Adviser's Office.[113] US, UK and other coalition forces started the military campaign to oust the regime of Saddam Hussein on 20 March 2003.

4.5.4 Findings

Contrary to the Netherlands, the legal advice on Iraq in the UK actually coincided with and even instructed policy. From the outset, the UK argued that another UNSC determination of the occurrence of a material breach was necessary in order to have a sufficient legal basis for the use of force. Both the FCO Legal Adviser and the AG were consistent and in agreement regarding their legal opinions and voiced them on different occasions. To a certain extent, the legal opinion of the

[107] Attorney General Lord Goldsmith's draft advice, 'Iraq: Interpretation of Resolution 1441', 12 February 2003, para 12 (emphasis added).

[108] Ibid., para 13.

[109] Attorney General Lord Goldsmith's legal advice, 'Iraq: Resolution 1441', 7 March 2003, available at http://news.bbc.co.uk/2/shared/bsp/hi/pdfs/28_04_05_attorney_general.pdf.

[110] Sands 2005, p. 197.

[111] Note from Simon McDonald (FCO) about the meeting between Foreign Secretary Jack Straw and the Attorney General on 13 March 2003, 'Iraq: Meeting with the Attorney General', 17 March 2003, para 1.

[112] Reproduced in Warbrick and McGoldrick 2003, pp. 811–814.

[113] Letter from Elizabeth Wilmshurst (FCO Deputy Legal Adviser) to Michael Wood (FCO Legal Adviser) on early retirement/resignation, 18 March 2003.

UK came back to haunt it. Because the UK insisted, on legal grounds, on a new UNSC decision, it succeeded in persuading the US to go to the United Nations, but once there, lost control of the process. The UK did get what it wanted in resolution 1441 (2002), namely a determination of a material breach, which would have revived the original authorization. Yet, the other UNSC members succeeded in introducing the final opportunity for Iraq to comply and injected great ambiguity as to what was to follow next. During the negotiations, the two most relevant UK legal advisers repeatedly warned that the draft resolutions included this obstacle to the revival argument. Moreover, they had to deal with public political statements designed to keep all options open. Thus, already before resolution 1441 (2002), law and policy started to diverge.

Departmental legal adviser, Michael Wood, was able to remain consistent in his advice, not in the least because the AG is the Chief Legal Adviser who must issue the formal legal opinion for the entire government in matters of such high importance. In the final analysis, the AG came down on the side of a sufficient legal basis because of the vagueness of resolution 1441 (2002) where that vagueness can easily be argued to be grounds for finding an insufficient legal basis. The difference between the two opinions, so it can be argued, is not a legal judgment, but rather a political one. The AG has both legal and political functions, is a political appointee, yet he is supposed to work independently from the government in a client–attorney relationship leaving the AG, arguably, exposed to too much political pressure. Given the constitutional and institutional position of the AG it is not surprising that the AG had to, in effect, bridge the gap between legal interpretation and stated policy goals, a role that is inherently vulnerable to great political pressure. As Weller notes, however, the AG to a large extent brought such pressure on himself, by exposing himself 'to such a one-sided argument from the very strongest advocates of the use of force', although he was free to also consult with others.[114]

Furthermore, it could be argued that the procedure for providing advice also serves as an important obstacle for ensuring that political decisions fall within the legal parameters. The AG has to be formally asked to provide his advice by a (Prime) Minister, in order for that advice to be formal and definitive. Consequently, in the Iraq case, the FCO Legal Adviser and the AG himself repeatedly had to point to the fact that all legal advice is provisional until a formal request for definitive advice is made. This leads to the obvious conclusion that the timing of the formal legal advice can be manipulated, and that it is even more exposed to political pressures to produce desired end results.

From the testimonies and statements of many of the UK legal advisers involved, it may be surmised that they agree on the basis of the Iraq experience that legal advice should not only be structurally encased in the decision-making processes, but also that the AG must be involved and asked to provide his official advice at different stages in the process. However, one might also argue that such reforms

[114] Weller 2010, p. 249.

would not address the fact that the institutional structure, in which the AG is the Chief Legal Adviser on all legal matters, not only on international law, seems outdated, unnecessary, and undesirable. The AG's Office constitutes a bureaucracy that duplicates the work of, in this case, the FCO Legal Adviser's Office.

4.6 Conclusions: Between a Rock and a Hard Place

In the final analysis, the legal advice that was offered in both the UK and the Netherlands cases concluded that the use of armed force against Iraq in March 2003, after resolution 1441, was unlawful, albeit that the arguments for that conclusion differed clearly, most notably on the acceptability of the revival argument and the role of the UNSC in the decision-making process. The examination of the process through which legal advice was given, received, and weighed in both countries in the Iraq case illustrates clearly the familiar, universal and persistent problems and obstacles with which legal advisers are confronted, most pressingly in crisis situations.

First and foremost, direct access of legal advisers to their political masters and ultimate decision-makers, i.e., the Minister of Foreign Affairs, President or Prime Minister is paramount.[115] The Dutch example shows that the formal hierarchical structure can be a serious impediment, while the formal position of the AG in the UK with full access to the political decision makers does not guarantee that legal advice is sufficiently heard or considered. In any case, it is agreed that it is desirable that legal advice is folded into and integrated in policy-making processes.[116] Secondly, regardless of formal position, much depends on whether the legal adviser is active in offering advice instead of waiting until advice is solicited.[117] Whether a government lawyer is active or passive depends not only on the personality of the particular lawyer, but also on the perception of his own role and responsibilities *vis-à-vis* the law, political masters, and who the ultimate 'client' is. Thirdly, even more is needed. The position of a legal adviser and rendered legal advice will not 'improve', should such be deemed necessary, by only modifying organizational charts. The desire of the international lawyer to make legal advice an integral part of the foreign policy decision-making process will not materialize if all those involved in that process do not view the advice as integral to this process. The materialization of this desire is crucially dependent on the political culture among the policy makers and their perception of the role of the legal adviser and legal considerations. While it is a valid point of policy makers that international law is but one factor to be considered in the policy-making process, there is no need for a fundamental choice to be made between law and politics. The initial proposals by

[115] Corell 1999, p. 105.

[116] See e.g. Corell, ibid.; Statement by Sir Michael Wood, 15 January 2010, para 32.

[117] Corell, ibid.

the Dutch Minister of Foreign Affairs in response to the recommendations of the Davids Committee to grant direct access to the (Deputy) Legal Adviser[118] were not sufficient either. When legal advice is made an integral part of the process at the highest levels and offered actively by the Legal Adviser's Office, that advice must still be properly accepted and weighed by policy makers.

When looking closer at the role and functioning of the Legal Adviser, the Davids Report posed the essential question whether legal advisers are supposed to be an in-house counsel, independent legal adviser, or both? From this study and others, the conclusion emerges that the role, responsibilities, loyalty, and even independence of the legal adviser shifts as the foreign policy decision-making process progresses. First, when a certain course of action or policy decision is being contemplated within the government, the legal adviser may be called on to provide the most independent advice as to the current state of international law and the parameters that it provides for the decision in question. Subsequently, the legal adviser may be confronted with different policy choices as the final decision is starting to take shape, while these choices may or may not remain within the boundaries of legal parameters. If not, all that remains for the legal adviser is to offer certain phrasing that should be included in the decision in order for it to be legally palatable, and/or to set out the various consequences and liabilities that arise from the different policy options.[119] Finally, the Legal Adviser may be called on to articulate and defend the legal side of the final policy.

To answer the question from the Davids Report, the legal adviser displays both the role of independent legal adviser or judge,[120] and in-house counsel in the first two phases respectively, but also that of attorney in the final phase.[121] Indeed, legal advisers sometimes speak in terms of their 'client', although it may be difficult to determine who or what should be considered the client; the Minister or Secretary of State, Prime Minister or President, the Government at large, the national interest, or ultimately the 'People'?[122] Moreover, the principle of attorney–client privileges extends to in-house counsel, including government legal advisers, in the UK.[123] The legal advice given is, therefore, confidential, and even when the advice is not privileged information, governments will still be highly reluctant to make the advice public. This is so not only because the government may wish to hide the fact that action may have been taken contrary to legal advice, but also

---

118 Answers from the Minister of Foreign Affairs to the questions of MP Timmermans, 3 March 2011, *Handelingen II (Aanhangsel)*, 2010/11, nr. 1635.

119 Berman 1994, p. 86.

120 In both capacities, the independent legal adviser and judge interpret 'international law as applied to a particular set of circumstances and advising on whether proposed actions would be consistent with the law.' Scharf and Williams 2010, p. 17.

121 Cf. Scharf and Williams 2009, p. 67.

122 See e.g. the discussion among former US Legal Advisers, as recorded by Scharf and Williams 2010, pp. 151–154. Also largely reproduced in Scharf and Williams 2009.

123 See e.g. Butler Report 2004, para 372.

because government lawyers must be free to advise the government as they see fit, without having to take into account future publication of that advice.

The manner in which the issues raised above are often characterized, namely as 'obstacles' and 'problems', betrays a bias that is inherent in most international lawyers. It is a bias in favor of a substantial, equal, or even defining role for international law in politics. Many, if not most international lawyers inherently and intuitively perceive their professional field to circumscribe and even trump political considerations. In their view, the Law defines the political playing field and supplies a set of rules to which policy-makers must adhere, and must therefore occupy a prominent place in the foreign policy decision-making structure.[124] However, as this and other studies show, the so-called 'vagueness' of international law is often invoked to either challenge that desired prominence or to claim elaborated room for political maneuvering.[125] In the extreme, international law is perceived by policy makers as only one factor in determining policy. At the same time, however, the indeterminacy of international law may only strengthen the legal adviser's commitment to upholding the rule of law in the face of political pressure.[126] Indeed, because of this indeterminacy the international lawyer may 'claim an allegiance to the law over and above a simple loyalty to the client.'[127] Consequently, the legal adviser in particular is caught in dialectic between his or her own commitment to international law and cynicism about its practical impact on policy making in a highly political environment.[128] A legal adviser may feel, simultaneously, 'a sentimental attachment to the field's constitutive rhetoric and traditions (...) and a pervasive and professionally engrained doubt about the profession's marginality, or even the identity of one's profession, the suspicion of its being 'just politics' after all (...).'[129] As noted earlier, however, that dual feeling of commitment and cynicism and the position between law and politics, between a rock and a hard place, is precisely what makes the legal adviser feel privileged to be in that line of work, even though it may conflict with one's conscience in extreme cases.

Thus, in the words of former Dutch Legal Adviser Riphagen:

> [i]n the final analysis, the role of the lawyer in the decision-making process in international relations depends on the approach of policy makers to 'foreign policy' and on the

---

124 See e.g. AJIL 1991, pp. 366–367.

125 See e.g. Note from Foreign Secretary Jack Straw to Michael Wood (FCO Legal Adviser) re Iraq: legal basis for use of force, 29 January 2003; Scharf and Williams 2010, pp. 204–205.

126 Sir Michael Wood stated to the Chilcot Inquiry: '[t]he events leading up to the use of force against Iraq in 2003 also raise the question of the role of government lawyers advising on public international law, in circumstances as acute as this, where the likelihood of the matter coming before an international or national court is remote. In my view, the seriousness of the matter and the absence of a court places a special responsibility on the lawyer to do his or her best that the law is upheld.' Statement by Sir Michael Wood, 15 January 2010, para 37.

127 Berman 1994, p. 86. Cf. Macdonald who also noted from legal adviser other descriptions of the role of legal advisers. Macdonald 1977, pp. 389–390.

128 Koskenniemi 1999, p. 511.

129 Koskenniemi 1999, p. 496.

approach of lawyers to 'law.' If the lawyer does not regard 'law' as a continuous process of creative imagination, and if the policy maker regards 'policy' as dictated *ad hoc* by the circumstances of the situation and the immediate interests involved, there is not much place for fruitful collaboration between them. Where, however, the policy maker has an eye for the general (not necessarily strictly 'legal') aspects of a case, he will be willing to listen to the advice of a lawyer who, on his part, is inclined (to borrow a phrase) 'to find a solution for every difficulty rather than to find a difficulty for every solution.'[130]

References

AJIL (1991) Current developments: the role of the legal adviser of the Department of State—a report of the Joint Committee established by the American Society of International Law and the American Branch of the International Law Association. Am J Int L 85:366–367

Attorney General Lord Goldsmith's legal advice, 'Iraq: Resolution 1441', 7 Mar 2003, http://news.bbc.co.uk/2/shared/bsp/hi/pdfs/28_04_05_attorney_general.pdf

Berman FD (1994) The international lawyer, inside and outside Foreign Ministries. In: Hill C, Beshoff P (eds) Two worlds of international relations. Routledge, London, pp 79–92

Bilder RB (1962) The Office of the Legal Adviser: the State Department Lawyer and Foreign Affairs. Am J Int L 56:633–684

Butler Report (2004) Review of intelligence on weapons of mass destruction report of a committee of Privy Counsellors, Chairman: The Rt Hon The Lord Butler of Brockwell KG GCB CVO (hereafter 'Butler Report'). http://www.butlerreview.org/

Carty A, Smith R (2000) Sir Gerald Fitzmaurice and the world crisis: a legal adviser in the Foreign Office, 1932–1945. Kluwer Law International, The Hague

Corell H (1991) Current development: legal advisers meet at UN headquarters in New York. Am J Int L 85:371–373

Corell H (1992) Second legal advisers' meeting at UN headquarters in New York. Nordic J Int L 61/62:3–6

Corell H (1999) Cooperation among legal advisers on public international law. In: Collection of essays by legal advisers of states, legal advisers of international organizations and practitioners in the field of international law. United Nations, New York, pp 97–119

Crawford J et al (2003) Letters: war would be illegal. In: The Guardian, 7 March 2003, http://www.guardian.co.uk/politics/2003/mar/07/highereducation.iraq. Accessed 18 Sept 2011

Davids Committee (2010) Rapport: Commissie van onderzoek besluitvorming Irak. Boom, Amsterdam

Gray C (2004) International law and the use of force, 2nd edn. Oxford University Press, Oxford

Koskenniemi M (1999) Between commitment and cynicism: outline for a theory of international law as practice. In: Collection of essays by legal advisers of states, legal advisers of international organizations and practitioners in the field of international law. United Nations, New York, pp 495–523

Lammers JG (2009) The role of the legal adviser of the Ministry of Foreign Affairs: the Dutch approach and experience. Tulane J Int Comp L 18:177–205

Macdonald RStJ (1977) The role of the legal adviser in Ministries of Foreign Affairs in 156 Recueil des Cours. In: Collected courses of the Hague Academy of International Law, 1977-III. Martinus Nijhoff Publishers, The Hague, pp 377–482

Manusama K (2006) The United Nations Security Council in the post-cold war era: applying the principle of legality. Brill, Leiden

[130] Riphagen 1964, p. 83.

Merillat HCL (1964) The legal adviser's place in government. In: Merillat HCL (ed) Legal advisers and Foreign Affairs. Oceana Publications, Dobbs Ferry, New York, pp 1–14
Murphy SD (2004) Assessing the legality of invading Iraq. Georgetown L J 92:173–257
NILR (2010) Report of the Dutch committee of inquiry on the war in Iraq—Chapter 8: The basis in international law for the military intervention in Iraq. Netherlands Int L Rev 57:81–137
Parry C (1964) United Kingdom—background paper. In: Merillat HCL (ed) Legal advisers and Foreign Affairs. Oceana Publications, Dobbs Ferry, New York, pp 101–152
Riphagen W (1964) The Netherlands—background paper. In: Merillat HCL (ed) Legal advisers and Foreign Affairs. Oceana Publications, Dobbs Ferry, New York, pp 79–83
Scharf MP, Williams PR (2009) International law in crisis: a qualitative empirical contribution to the compliance debate. Cardozo L Rev 31:45–97
Scharf MP, Williams PR (2010) Shaping foreign policy in times of crisis—the role of international law and the State Department legal adviser. Cambridge University Press, New York
Warbrick C, McGoldrick D (2003) The use of force against Iraq. ICLQ 52:811–814
Watson G (1988) Armed intervention in the 1956 Suez Canal Crisis: the legal advice tendered to the British Government. Int Comp L Q 37:773–817
Weller M (2010) Iraq and the use of force in international law. Oxford University Press, Oxford

Chapter 5
Whose International Order? Which Law?

Thomas Mertens and Janine van Dinther

Abstract The legality and legitimacy of the Iraq war in 2003 has been widely discussed before, during and after the hostilities. Though hardly anyone questions the lack of a legal basis for the military operation in Iraq, it has been argued that other grounds could have justified the undertaking of military action. The political support of the Dutch government for the American-led invasion in Iraq needs to be understood along these lines. This contribution focuses on the legal and intellectual trends that can be observed preceding the support given to the 2003 war. These trends could be summarised as a move from legality towards legitimacy, from positive law to morality, broadly understood. The support of the Dutch government for the war can be interpreted as a reflection of a certain discontent with existing international law and of changing attitudes vis-à-vis the international order. The following questions will be raised in this contribution: What was really relevant in this context: the international legal order of the Charter of the United Nations or some other international order dominated by certain values other than the ones embedded in the Charter? Moreover, what kind of a war was the invasion of Iraq: a legal war on the basis of international law broadly understood or an ethical war in accordance with the criteria of the just war tradition? These questions will be dealt with from the Dutch constitutional perspective and from the perspective of ethics.

The title is a paraphrase, as many will recall, of A. MacIntyre's *Whose Justice*? *Which Rationality*?, University of Notre Dame Press, Notre Dame, 1988.

T. Mertens (✉) · J. van Dinther
Faculty of Law, Radboud University Nijmegen, Nijmegen, The Netherlands
e-mail: t.mertens@jur.ru.nl

J. van Dinther
e-mail: j.vandinther@jur.ru.nl

I. F. Dekker and E. Hey (eds.), *Netherlands Yearbook of International Law 2011*,
Netherlands Yearbook of International Law 42, DOI: 10.1007/978-90-6704-849-1_5,

Keywords 2003 Iraq war · Davids Committee · Dutch constitution · International legal order · International ethics · Kant · Legality Legitimacy

Contents

5.1 Introduction

In his famous essay 'Towards Perpetual Peace', Kant wrote the following about the relationship between politics and right: '[f]or all politics must bend the knee before right, although politics may hope in return to arrive, however slowly, at the stage of lasting brilliance.'[1] Herewith, Kant rejects the position of Machiavellian politicians who subordinate the requirements of law and morality to power politics. He pleads instead for moral politicians who work towards the establishment of the legal conditions under which world peace can be obtained. These conditions include republican government on the domestic level, federalism on the international level and cosmopolitanism on the global level.

It might have been relatively clear what these three conditions entailed in Kant's world at the end of the eighteenth century, where hardly any republican governments were in place, where there was not even a glimpse of a true federal global structure in sight, and where an understanding of cosmopolitanism was nothing more than the vague hope that a violation of rights in one part of the world would be felt everywhere.[2] Kant calls for the replacement of the monarchical principle by the republican principle, in line with the French revolution, because of the republican attribution of the decision to go to war to its citizens; for the establishment of a permanent congress of states in which matters of controversy between states can be solved in a peaceful manner; and finally for foreigners and foreign communities to be respected and for the abolishment of colonialism.

Our world, at the beginning of the twenty-first century, looks very different. The principle of republicanism is widely enacted, at least on paper, with lip service to the principle of popular sovereignty everywhere. The world has witnessed the

[1] Kant 1970, p. 125.

[2] Ibid., p. 108.

establishment of at least two universal international organisations, the League of Nations and its successor, the United Nations. The idea of humanity as a community as such with shared values has been realised, at least in theory, since the almost universal recognition of human rights. Yet, the world has not yet witnessed the 'outbreak' of the peace Kant hoped for. Even after the end of the cold war, a moment some saw as the occasion for the realisation of Kantian ideals, conflicts occur on a regular basis. The question must be raised whether the way in which the international order is presently institutionalised is the kind of order that Kant had in mind as an essential requirement for the establishment of peace. Obviously, this is too large a topic for the modest contribution that we present here. But it is this larger question that motivates our reflection upon the decision of the Dutch government to lend political support to the American-led invasion of Iraq in 2003, prompted by the evaluation of that decision by the Davids Committee in its important 2010 report.[3] The conclusions of this Committee—that the Dutch government had lent its support to a war without a proper international legal mandate—led to fierce political discussions in The Netherlands. In this contribution we do not wish to discuss the well-established fact of the lack of a second Security Council resolution. This has been duly noted in a variety of comments, both at home and abroad;[4] nor will we discuss the so-called corpus-theory, endorsed by the Dutch government in the period leading up to the invasion, according to which the existing Security Council resolutions sufficed as authorisation of the use of force against Iraq. It is now widely agreed that the Iraq war could not be legally justified on the basis of this theory, a conclusion subscribed to by the Davids Committee.

What interests us here are the legal and intellectual trends that we think can be observed preceding the political support given to the 2003 war. These trends could be summarised most briefly as a move from legality towards legitimacy, from positive law to morality, broadly understood. The support of the Dutch government for the war can thus be understood as a reflection of a certain discontent with existing international law and of changing attitudes vis-à-vis the international order. Hence the question: whose international legal order and what kind of war? Formulated differently: What is really relevant, the international legal order of the Charter of the United Nations or some other international order dominated by certain values other than the ones embedded on the Charter? And, what kind of a war: a legal war on the basis of positive international law or an ethical war in accordance with the criteria of the just war tradition? These questions will be dealt with in two sections, the first dealing with the internal Dutch constitutional perspective. Here, we focus on the incongruity between the provisions of the Dutch constitution with regard to the international order and positive international law. The second section focuses on the transition from understanding the international

[3] Commissie van onderzoek besluitvorming Irak, Rapport commissie van onderzoek besluitvorming Irak [Committee Report on Investigation of Decision-Making on Iraq] 2010.

[4] See e.g. Sands 2005.

realm through positive law towards an understanding of this order from the perspective of ethics. Such a transition, at least according to Koskenniemi,[5] is taking place. It is our conjecture that these two movements complement each other: the Dutch constitution's emphasis on 'promoting' the international legal order (rather than on the legality thereof, i.e. the strict compliance with its positive law) seems now to be supported by the emphasis on the ethical, as opposed to strictly legal, dimension of international relations. Yet, the following caveat should be stressed: the fact that we try to put the intellectual underpinning of the Dutch support for the Iraq war in a broader context does not mean that we endorse its wisdom. Rather the contrary; with Kant, we defend the need for positive international law and, contrary to the proponents of the ethical just war tradition (Kant call them 'sorry comforters'), we are not in favour of a 'turn to ethics' in international relations. But it needs to be admitted that this turn to ethics has also affected the understanding of Kant's philosophy of law and led some commentators to present Kantian thinking as supporting the Iraq war.[6] We hold that this is incorrect.

5.2 Provisions in the Dutch Constitution

It is not a new observation, but nonetheless worth noting again that the provisions in the Dutch constitution do not unequivocally endorse the importance of positive international law. 'Promoting the international legal order', as the Dutch constitution requires,[7] need not be the same as respecting existing international law. This becomes evident from several military missions which have been decided in accordance with the Dutch constitution, but which were, it could be argued, not necessarily in accordance with positive international law. By means of a small historical survey, this paragraph will elaborate on this particular observation a little further.

Since the end of the Cold War, the Dutch government has increasingly deployed its military forces all over the world. Military troops have been dispatched to Cambodia, Iraq, Bosnia, Kosovo, Afghanistan and Somalia, to name but a few countries. Before the 1990s, however, the dispatch of Dutch soldiers abroad was rare, with Dutch participation in the Korean war in the 1950s and the military contribution to UNIFIL in Lebanon from 1979 to 1983 as the only examples of any significance.[8] Since 1989, that situation has changed drastically: the deployment of the Dutch army has increased in number, frequency and goals, and now encompasses peace keeping, peace enforcement and humanitarian aid. The legality of these missions has been based on Articles 90 and 97(1) of the Dutch constitution. The former stipulates that the Dutch government has the duty to promote the development of the international

[5] Koskenniemi 2002.

[6] Gerhardt 2003, pp. 557–569; Scruton 2003.

[7] Articles 90 and 97 para 1.

[8] van Genugten et al. 2007, p. 404.

legal order, whereas the latter describes the tasks of the military as follows: 'There shall be armed forces for the defence and protection of the interests of the Kingdom, and in order to maintain and promote the international legal order'.

It is obviously the definition of the concept of 'international legal order' that is important here. How does the Dutch constitution define 'international legal order'? To what extent and in what manner are Articles 90 and 97 applied as justification for deploying the military?[9] As Article 97(1) is relatively new, having obtained its current form in 2000, and since its meaning is mostly derived from Article 90, the emphasis in defining this concept is on the latter provision. It is clear that 'international legal order' is a rather vague notion. This has not gone unnoticed. During the early 1950s, Members of Parliament were concerned about the supposed obscurity of the provision and pointed out that its vagueness could be used to endorse any governmental policy. The then Minister of Internal Affairs, L.J.M. Beel, after some debate, acknowledged the difficulty of defining the term 'international legal order' clearly. Mr. Beel stated that the international legal order changed with the structure of society and was under the constant influence of the prevailing *Zeitgeist*.[10]

These remarks are in line with the constitutional history of Article 90, which starts in 1922. At that time, the predecessor of Article 90 (Article 58) was included in the Dutch constitution. It read as follows: '[t]he King shall attempt to resolve conflicts with foreign powers through judicial and other peaceful means. He shall not declare war unless the States General gives their prior assent'. A first draft of the provision only contained the second sentence.[11] The first sentence was added only to make clear that declaring war was not a normal 'aspect' of Dutch foreign policy as long as the States General were to give 'their prior assent'.[12] The reference to 'judicial and other peaceful means' gives the predecessor of Article 90 a somewhat idealistic ring.[13] This is understandable in the context of the early 1920s, where the end of the First World War occasioned the founding of the League of Nations and the will, of not only the Dutch parliament, to prevent another war. The idea was to pursue peace through (international) law.[14]

---

[9] Noteworthy to mention is that the Articles 90 and 97 para 1 are to be understood, in a constitutional sense, as tasks. Generally, this means that the 'attributive' and 'regulative' aspects of the Articles are debatable. Here, we rely on Besselink 2003, pp. 118–135.

[10] *Aanhangsel Handelingen I* [Proceedings of the First Chamber of Parliament] 1951/1952, 2374, pp. 854–855.

[11] Verslag van de Staatscommissie ingesteld bij Koninklijk Besluit van 20 December 1918 [Report of the State Commission established by Royal Decree of 20 December 1918, No. 78, which has been commissioned to prepare a revision of the Constitution] 1920, p. 4.

[12] Attached note of J.H.A. Schaper in: Verslag van de Staatscommissie ingesteld bij Koninklijk Besluit van 20 December 1918, pp. 3–4.

[13] Besselink 2003, p. 99.

[14] *Handelingen II* [Proceedings of the Second Chamber of Parliament] 1921/1922, nr. 90, pp. 406–407. The writings of Cornelis van Vollenhoven, a Dutch scholar in public international law, on war, peace and law were highly influential at that time, see Boogman 1984, p. 166.

In 1953, the constitutional provisions concerning foreign affairs were thoroughly revised in the light of the acknowledgment that the Netherlands could no longer hold on to its policy of neutrality.[15] The new objectives were focused on international cooperation and (European) integration. The Netherlands joined several international organisations (e.g. the United Nations, North Atlantic Treaty Organisation and European Coal and Steel Community). The constitution needed to reflect the development of these intergovernmental and supranational organisations and the subsequent limitation of state sovereignty. The predecessor of Article 90 was amended to read as follows: '[t]he King shall have supreme authority over foreign affairs. He shall promote the development of the international legal order'.[16] The new second sentence was intended to broaden the original meaning of the provision. It was no longer solely the government's task to resolve peacefully disputes with foreign powers but it was also entrusted with the development of international cooperation and integration.[17] At the time, a Member of Parliament stated that one could object to 'promoting the development of the "international legal order" as *Leitmotiv'*, because it is insubstantial, difficult to determine and therefore holds the danger of being too broad'.[18] Another Member argued that the obscurity of the provision could be taken to support a broad array of policies.[19] The Minister acknowledged this but argued that it would be impossible to give a clear-cut definition, as the 'international legal order' changed with the structure of society.[20]

Article 90 acquired its present text in 1983: '[t]he Government shall promote the development of the international legal order'. Contrary to the debates in the 1920s and 1950s, the government now provided extensive elaboration on the meaning of 'the development of the international legal order'. It described the international legal order as based on legal norms of universal validity; it linked the content of the provision to a number of policy objectives, i.e. the promotion of universal human rights in the broadest sense possible (not only civil and political rights, but also economic, social and cultural rights), the promoting of the well-being of the world population,[21] the strengthening of relations with other nations by means of the conclusion of treaties, compliance with written legal standards,[22] the promotion of a new international economic order and, finally, the pursuit of

15 Voorhoeve 1979, p. 47; Bovend'Eert and Kummeling 2010, p. 354.

16 Eindrapport van de Staatscommissie tot herziening van de Grondwet ingesteld bij Koninklijk Besluit van 17 April 1950, No. 25 [Final Report of the State Commission to amend the Constitution, established by Royal Decree of 17 April 1950, No. 25], 1954, p. 8.

17 Ibid., p. 152.

18 *Handelingen I* 1952/1953, p. 469.

19 *Handelingen II* 1951/1952, 2374, 1933.

20 *Aanhangsel Handelingen I* 1951/1952, 2374, pp. 854–855.

21 *Kamerstukken II* [Parliamentary Documents of the Second Chamber] 1979/1980, 15049 (R 1100), nr. 7, p. 5.

22 *Kamerstukken I* [Parliamentary Documents of the First Chamber] 1980/1981, 15049 (R 1100), nr. 19, p. 2.

lasting international peace and security.[23] All in all, the provision was seen as the embodiment of various policies of that time.[24] Interestingly, however, the government noted that the objectives of peace and of promoting the development of the international legal order, though connected, need not necessarily be in accordance with each other. It was suggested that the objective of peace could be overruled by the objective of promoting the development of the international legal order,[25] implying that respect for the existing international legal order is not an absolute requirement or, perhaps better, that the 'international legal order' in the Constitution need not necessarily coincide with positive international law. On this point, at least, the lack of clarity was not removed. The constitutional history of Article 90 reveals an idealistic spirit coupled with a certain, though not unrestricted, commitment to international law. Article 90 is therefore best described as an open norm.

Given this lack of clarity, it does not come as a surprise that the government has been able to justify and support a variety of military operations on the basis of Article 90 and, since 2000, Article 97—ranging from a military contribution to the UN-mission UNMEE in Ethiopia and Eritrea to the dispatch of military engineers to Poland to help cope with flooding.[26] There is little doubt that these military operations were in accordance with positive international law. However, this does not apply to the Kosovo intervention and to political support for the Iraq war. Despite the questionable legality of these latter cases under international law, the Dutch government nonetheless gave its military support to NATO's Operation Allied Force in Kosovo in 1999 and its political support for the Iraq war in 2003. Could these decisions be justified by reference to the constitutional objective of promoting the international legal order? Is promoting the development of the international legal order compatible with a breach of positive international law?

As the literature on Articles 90 and 97 suggests, these provisions indeed have a broader meaning than merely the observation of and compliance with existing international law, due to the use of the dynamic words 'promoting' and 'development'.[27] The main focus in these provisions is not merely existing law but the promotion of *new* desired law as well.[28] Over the last 20 years, statements and actions of the government confirm this. In 1993, the government explicitly endorsed this position when the then Minister of Foreign Affairs, P.H. Kooijmans, stated that 'at times international law can hamper the promotion of the international legal order'. When different views on the content of international law, including as to what it prohibits, obstruct decision-making, he further stated, 'it may be necessary to conclude—preferably with other states—that the use of

---

[23] *Handelingen II* 1979/1980, 4086.

[24] Besselink 2003, p. 105.

[25] *Kamerstukken II* 1979/1980, 15049 (R 1100), nr. 7, p. 5.

[26] *Kamerstukken II* 2001/2002, 22 831, nr. 37, p. 10; *Handelingen I* 1997/1998, nr. 22, p. 1080.

[27] Besselink 2003, pp. 105–110.

[28] Besselink 2008, p. 91.

military means is necessary to promote the objective of the international legal order. In these particular circumstances, military action can influence the development of law'.[29] This statement did not go unnoticed. One Member of Parliament, M. van Traa, responded that military action should never be in violation of international law. He stated that it should never be the case that 'we would encourage everyone to determine on its own what international law is'.[30] The Minister clarified his remarks, noting that they referred to situations in which international law was not clear or sufficiently responsive: 'the development of principles of international law should not be determined by the one with the slowest pace, which is why in such diffuse situations it can be important to take cooperative action with other countries (…).'[31]

The importance of this discussion between the Minister and Parliament can hardly be overstated. It suggests that the constitutional duty of the government is not always towards the strict observance of positive international law. Moreover, it is remarkable that the Dutch government has refused explicitly to rule out the use of force where the Security Council is incapable or unwilling to respond to what is widely viewed as a (humanitarian) crisis. A number of government statements and decisions make clear that its policy is not to be exclusively centred on (conformity with) the United Nations Charter, as illustrated most explicitly by the military support for the Kosovo intervention in 1999. Since 1999, the government has argued on several occasions that a resolution of the Security Council is not a *conditio sine qua non* for the legitimacy of military action.[32] When fundamental human rights are violated on a large scale, the use of force is by and large considered to be justified on moral and political grounds, even if a legal basis is lacking.[33] The government has justified this line of argument by referring to, unsurprisingly, the objective of the international legal order.[34]

It is worth considering the government's statement 'that in case of a humanitarian emergency, the use of force can be justified on moral and political grounds, even when a clear legal basis is lacking',[35] from the perspective of the important debate between Simma and Cassese on the legitimacy of the Kosovo intervention.[36] The government has explicitly referred to Cassese's arguments as justification for intervention. Cassese famously held in his exchange with Simma that we might be witnessing the emergence of a new doctrine in international law

---

29 *Handelingen II* 1992/1993, nr. 70, p. 5005.

30 Ibid.

31 Ibid.

32 *Handelingen II* 1998/1999, nr. 61, p. 3793; *Handelingen II* 2002/2003, nr. 95, p. 5665; Hellema and Reiding 2004, p. 8.

33 *Kamerstukken II* 2006/2007, 29521, nr. 41, pp. 7–8.

34 *Handelingen II* 1998/1999, nr. 61, pp. 3784–3799; without mentioning the concept of 'promoting'.

35 *Kamerstukken II* 2006/2007, 29521, nr. 41, p. 8.

36 Cassese 1999, pp. 23–30; Simma 1999, pp. 1–22.

according to which the use of force is allowed 'to impede a state from committing large scale atrocities on its own territory, in circumstances in which the Security Council is incapable of responding adequately to the crisis'. Indeed, governmental advisory committees have described this idea of an emerging doctrine of humanitarian intervention as 'customary international law'.[37]

To sum up this section, then, the Dutch government has quite consistently stressed the importance of existing international law,[38] but it has also argued that international political and legal developments evolve and influence each other.[39] Political considerations thus have an independent importance. Articles 90 and 97(1) of the Dutch constitution do not therefore command 'politics' to bend the knee always before positive 'right'. In the light of this and from a strictly constitutional perspective, the critical findings of the Davids Committee and its emphasis on positive international law could thus have come as a surprise. The reasons for its establishment are clear. Both the legality and legitimacy of the Iraq war in 2003 had been challenged widely and fiercely before, during and after the hostilities.[40] In the wake of these exchanges, the Davids Committee was therefore given the task 'to investigate preparations and decision-making in the period from summer 2002 to summer 2003 regarding The Netherlands' political support for the invasion of Iraq in general, and with regard to matters pertinent to international law, to intelligence and information provision and to alleged military involvement in particular'.[41] Unsurprisingly, the Committee concluded that the decision to support the invasion of Iraq was based not on positive international law but 'mainly on international political considerations', such as Trans-Atlantic solidarity and the desire for continuity in Dutch policy with regard to Iraq.[42] Unsurprisingly again, the Committee argued that this continuity was dubious since, by 2003, the US and Britain were pursuing a radically different objective (regime change) than during the 1990s (penalising aggression).[43] As regards the law, the Committee concluded that the military intervention in 2003 had no sound mandate under existing positive international law. The Committee rejected the government's view that a new Security Council mandate for the use of force was politically desirable but not legally indispensable. Further, it rejected the so-called 'corpus-theory', according to which various earlier Security Council resolutions on Iraq passed since 1990 constituted, taken together, a mandate for the use of force that was still valid in March 2003.[44] All this suggests that the Davids Committee's findings are in line with positive international law and with most international legal

---

37 *Kamerstukken II* 2006/2007, 29521, nr. 41, pp. 7–8.

38 Ibid., p. 3.

39 Ibid., p. 9.

40 Walzer 2004; Nollkaemper 2007.

41 Commissie van onderzoek besluitvorming Irak 2010, p. 521.

42 Ibid., pp. 426, 530.

43 Ibid.

44 Ibid., p. 524.

commentaries, which state that the use of force is only legitimate when it is based on a Security Council Resolution.[45]

Yet, and this is where the surprise comes in, we have seen that this is not necessarily a position supported by the Dutch constitution. The requirement in Article 90 to promote international legal order is not equivalent to the requirement to respect positive international law. As a result, the Committee's findings have been criticised. While no-one questions the lack of a formal international legal basis for the war against Iraq, some have argued, most prominently A.P. van Walsum (one of the members of the Committee, in a separate comment), that other grounds should be considered sufficient to justify the policy of support adopted by the government. Van Walsum pointed out that the prevention of the proliferation of weapons of mass destruction-programs sufficed as a political ground for the use of force.[46] The Davids Committee's report hardly discusses this different opinion, and that is unfortunate, as the government, in response to the Committee's finding, maintained the legitimacy of military action even in the absence of a Security Council mandate. Such a situation, the government holds, occurs in cases of a (threatened) humanitarian catastrophe, most notably genocide, where there is broad international support for military action although not broad enough to make a Security Council mandate possible.[47] Thus, the Dutch government is insistent on keeping the option of humanitarian intervention open, even if such a military action is not mandated by the Security Council. This development is especially interesting as academic discourse involving both legal scholars and philosophers contains this line of argumentation too.[48] Arguing away from strict compliance with positive international law could be understood, with Koskenniemi,[49] as the turn to ethics in international law, or with Walzer, as 'the triumph of just war theory'[50] over international law. It is to these theoretical developments we now turn.

5.3 From International Law to International Ethics

It is of course impossible to give a full account of the move to ethics in the context of this comment on the findings of the Davids Committee. Yet, a good starting position for some tentative remarks is indeed the discussion between Simma and Cassese in the *European Journal of International Law*,[51] published at the very

---

45 Nollkaemper 2010, p. 144.

46 Commissie van onderzoek besluitvorming Irak, p. 270.

47 *Kamerstukken II* 2009/2010, 31847, nr. 18, pp. 4–5.

48 Especially among liberal philosophers, there seems to exist a consensus about the desirability of humanitarian intervention, See e.g. Tesón 2003.

49 Koskenniemi 2002.

50 Walzer 2004, pp. 3–22.

51 Simma 1999, pp. 1–23; Cassese 1999, pp. 23–30.

moment of the Kosovo intervention, not only because the Dutch government endorsed Cassese's position but also because many see this discussion as a pivotal moment in the development of our thinking about the ethics of international law.

Cassese, a distinguished international law professor and judge, argued that 'ex iniuria ius oritur'[52] and that we are indeed, under very strict conditions, moving towards a scheme under which intervention for humanitarian purposes is legitimate even if there is no proper international legal justification. This conclusion results from his reflection on the Kosovo intervention, which, he says, is a clear and blunt violation of international legality. Yet, from an ethical standpoint the resort to armed forces was justified and can be seen as rooted in 'contemporary trends of the international community', such as the *erga omnes* character of human rights that gives rise to a responsibility for states to protect citizens of other states, particularly in circumstances that shock the conscience of mankind. If a decision by the Security Council is impossible, a group of states has, in other words, sufficient authority to take the decision to intervene. The argument continues: this could then develop into a new, independent exception to the UN Charter's system of collective enforcement, in addition to the exception recognised in the UN Charter, namely self-defence. The resort to armed force is thereby justified not only in the case of self-defence but also in the case of the defence of others. If one can defend oneself, why would one not be justified in defending others, a reasoning which dates back to Augustine? Cassese admits that the addition of such an exception to the prohibition to use military force internationally, even if it is tied to the most stringent conditions, can never be tight enough so as to preclude possible abuse, but it is a price worth paying.

Simma, in the article to which Cassese replies, is clearly more worried about opening Pandora's Box, to which unauthorised humanitarian intervention might lead, and stressed that the Kosovo intervention cannot be seen as setting a precedent. But Simma's piece is not only interesting because of its warning regarding the potential abuse of a non-Security Council authorised threat or use of force. It is also interesting when considered in connection with our reading of the Dutch constitution, according to which a distinction can be made between existing positive international law with the UN Charter as its 'constitution' and the possibility of a future 'international legal order' that needs to be promoted. Why would it not be possible for organisations other than the UN to present themselves as the defenders or promoters of this order?

Simma carefully analyses, in the context of the Kosovo crisis, the evolving relationship between the UN and NATO, in which the latter is moving beyond its original mission of collective self-defence towards 'venturing into the field of "enforcement action" against third states'. In the statements made by leading NATO politicians in the context of 'Kosovo', Simma notes a blurring of the strict legal relationship between UN and NATO, when it is defined in terms of synergy and cooperation rather than as one of hierarchy. In particular, a careful analysis of

---

[52] Cassese 1999, pp. 23–30.

the statement by US Deputy Secretary of State Talbott warrants, according to Simma, the conclusion that NATO, at least according to this powerful voice, should be entitled to take action with regard to the defence of 'its common interests and values, including when the latter are threatened by humanitarian catastrophes, crimes against humanity, and war crimes', even if a Security Council mandate or authorisation of such NATO missions (i.e. beyond collective self-defence) cannot be obtained. According to Simma, this argument entails that self-defence, enshrined in Article 51 of the UN Charter, would include the defence of what NATO considers 'common interest and values', suggesting a broader scope of self-defence than foreseen in positive international law.

Simma's article is often read as a warning against the use of the Kosovo intervention as legal precedent. True as that is, his concerns run deeper. Simma was particularly worried by the blurring of the hierarchical relation between the UN and 'regional organisations' such as NATO and the fundamental challenge to the legal primacy of the Charter. Discussing the legitimacy of the prevailing system of positive international law led NATO to the conclusion, according to Simma, that the legal primacy of the obligations flowing from the UN Charter should be relativised. His worry is thus not merely that Kosovo will function as a precedent, but specifically that 'other states or new alliances in Europe or in other parts of the world might [also] proclaim to 'stand ready to act' without the Security Council, or decide to defend 'certain interests and values' by armed force'. What concerns Simma most, therefore, is the erosion of respect for positive international law based on the Charter by the desire for a (new) international legal order, in which NATO or any other coalition (a coalition of the willing?) claims for itself the right to act in defence of 'common interests and values', such as protection against weapons of mass destruction, in place of the UN Security Council.[53]

The implications of NATO's intervention in Kosovo for the relationship between legality and legitimacy were publicly discussed not only by leading European legal scholars but also by philosophers, such as Jürgen Habermas. Habermas's comment on the Kosovo intervention is cautiously entitled: 'Bestiality and Humanity: a War on the Border between Legality and Morality'. This carefully drafted text, the Kosovo intervention was a particularly sensitive issue in Germany, makes clear that Habermas sympathises with the pacifist's rejection of every war and with the international lawyer's rejection of the Kosovo intervention as illegal, at the same time, however, he welcomes the intervention as protecting human rights. Therefore it can be seen, he argues, as a step within the transition from an international legal community of states towards a cosmopolitan world community. Habermas distinguishes between positive international law as the law between states with the United Nations at its centre and a future world community, in which human rights carry more moral weight than state sovereignty. Therefore, an illegal war should not necessarily be identified as an unjust war. Legitimacy may trump legality. Hesitantly, Habermas agrees with the Kosovo intervention

[53] Simma 1999, pp. 1–23, especially pp. 10, 16, 18 and 20.

despite its lack of legality and the risk of unilateralism, acknowledging that the acceptance of humanitarian intervention could pave the way for expansionism and for the blurring of the distinction between intervention and aggression. He therefore pleads for the establishment of an independent judicial body that would determine when humanitarian intervention is justified.[54]

Whereas Habermas seems to side, in the end, with Cassese, Simma's position seems to be supported by Koskenniemi. His well-known article 'The Lady Doth Protest too Much'[55] is primarily an effort to understand what he calls the turn to ethics in international law. There is little doubt that he regrets the preference given by most international scholars in the discussion on the Kosovo intervention to its moral desirability rather than to its illegality. The main reason for rejecting such a moralisation of international relations at the cost of formal (international) legality is that it 'transforms international law into an uncritical instrument for the foreign policy choices of those whom power and privilege has put into decision-making positions'. Formal law is thus seen as a bulwark against power politics dressed up in morality's clothing.

In his article, Koskenniemi describes the process that enables international lawyers to transform themselves into moralists. For us, in the context of this paper, it is telling that the teleological element in the Dutch constitutional provision of 'promoting' the international legal order is prominent in this process. In what Koskenniemi calls 'instrumentalism', the aim of positive international law is sought and then the (black) letter of the Charter is subordinated to this aim, namely its 'substantive morality' of, among other things, human rights. This moving away from the letter of the law is further confirmed by what Koskenniemi properly calls the 'turn to ethics'. Here the argument is typically that the formality of the law should be 'complemented' by a careful consideration of the particularity of situations and that the responsibility of decision-makers cannot be reduced to the mere application of formal rules. In exceptional situations, so the argument continues, decisions need to be taken on the basis not of strict rules but of the moral responsibility of the decision-makers. In those circumstances, a decision is 'born out of the legal nothingness' as a response to what a situation demands. In other words, one should not evade moral responsibility through reference to inapplicable rules. Here, Koskenniemi argues, the true nature of the international order reveals itself and it does not lie 'in the Charter of the United Nations nor in the principles of humanitarianism but in the will and the power of a handful Western civilian and military leaders'. The main fear that drives Koskenniemi's rejection of the turn to ethics is, to paraphrase Kelsen, that behind the mask of ethics one finds 'staring at him the Gorgon head of power'[56] or, to use his own words, that what counts as law 'is decided with conclusive authority by the sensibilities of the Western Prince'.[57]

---

54 Habermas 1999, pp. 263–272. Many cosmopolitans are in favour of international 'independent' bodies. Sceptics would of course ask how these bodies could be established and composed.

55 Koskenniemi 2002.

56 Veröffentlichungen der Vereinigung der Deutschen Staatsrechtslehrer 1927, pp. 54–55.

57 Koskenniemi 2002, pp. 159–175, especially pp. 159, 165 and 170-1.

5.4 Concluding Remarks

The turn to ethics thus reveals the political element in the decision to intervene, on humanitarian grounds of course, in Kosovo. According to Koskenniemi, this turn to ethics forms part of the general movement of international law between apology and utopia, between formalism and anti-formalism, between reason and emotion. In 'The Lady Doth Protest Too Much' he regrets the departure from positive international law, precisely because 'the culture of formalism' is able to set 'limits to the impulses—moral or not—' and to constitute 'a horizon of universality, embedded in a culture of restraint'.[58]

With this in mind, it is remarkable that the Davids Report does not contain a constitutional analysis of Article 90 and the possible distinction between obligations following from positive international law and obligations resulting from the duty to promote the international legal order; nor does it contain a thorough discussion on the legal versus the moral aspects of the Kosovo intervention. This is not only remarkable because a gap of merely 4 years separates the bombing of Belgrade from that of Baghdad, but also because one member of the Committee, van Walsum, in August 2002, published an op-ed in the Financial Times in which he presented precisely this argument in favour of invading Iraq and explicitly referred to the Kosovo precedent. In this piece, worth quoting at length, van Walsum comments on the statement made by the French President and the German Chancellor that military intervention could only be justified on the basis of a specific resolution of the Security Council. Van Walsum did not then agree with such a 'narrow interpretation of international law'. He endorsed the position taken by the then UK Prime Minister, Tony Blair, according to which 'any action should be taken in accordance with international law'. On the basis of the 'historic precedent' during the Kosovo crisis in which 'a military intervention [was] undertaken neither in the exercise of self-defence nor on the basis of a Security Council mandate', the rule that 'military intervention is only justified if it is based on a specific Security Council resolution has been superseded by two principles: first, a threat can be so exceptional that it justifies military intervention with a Security Council mandate; second that military intervention can be legally based on a country's consistent non-compliance with a binding Security Council resolution.'[59] It is easy to recognise in van Walsum's second principle the corpus-theory, later explicitly rejected by the Committee of which he was a member; but it is remarkable that the first principle, and its connected idea that only a 'narrow interpretation' requires a specific resolution on the use of force, was not discussed by the Committee at all.

The preference for a much broader interpretation has even made its way, as mentioned before, into Kant scholarship. Despite Kant's explicit rejection of humanitarian intervention, Habermas endorsed the Kosovo war, and, in the run up

[58] Ibid., p. 174 (emphasis left out from the original).

[59] van Walsum 2002.

to the Iraq war other Kant scholars defended that invasion on 'Kantian' grounds.[60] Most Kant scholars, Habermas included, did not agree but it is apparently less easy to know how politics is to bend its knee before 'right' now than in the context of the eighteenth century. Is it the 'right' of 'the constitutionalization of international law'[61] or that of the law of the Charter?

In Koskenniemi's terminology, the Committee's standpoint is a return to formalism and many have applauded the Committee for that; but, unfortunately, the really interesting issue is not this return to positive international law, nor is it the question asked by Nollkaemper of whether the decision to support the Iraq war was based on the wrong legal argument or on a political argument instead of a legal one.[62] The important question is: 'whose international order and which law'? Is there an independent 'international legal order' or does the ultimate decision on what it is lay with the global hegemon?[63] Is there a gap between the duty to respect positive international law and the duty to promote the international legal order? This really important issue needs discussing.[64]

References

Besselink LFM (2003) The constitutional duty to promote the development of the international legal order: the significance and meaning of article 90 of the Netherlands Constitution. Neth Yearb Int Law 34:89–136

Besselink LFM (2008) Geweldsmonopolie, Grondwet en krijgsmacht. In: Bovend'Eert PPT, Besselink LFM, van Schooten-van der Meer J, De Lange R (eds) Grondwet, krijgsmacht en oorlog. Wolf Legal Publishers, Nijmegen, pp 67–125

Boogman JC (1984) De Nederland-Gidsland-conceptie in historisch perspectief. Ons erfdeel: kultureel tijdschrift voor Zuidvlaamse werking in Vlaams-Nederlands-Suidafrikaanse samenwerking 27:161–170

Bovend'Eert PPT, Kummeling HRBM (2010) Van Raalte's Het Nederlands parlement. Kluwer, Deventer

Cassesse A (1999) Ex iniuria ius oritur: are we moving towards international legitimation of forcible humanitarian coutermeasures in the world community? Eur J Int Law 10:23–30

Commissie van onderzoek besluitvorming (2010) Rapport commissie van onderzoek besluitvorming Irak. Boom, Amsterdam

Eindrapport van de Staatscommissie tot herziening van de Grondwet ingesteld bij Koninklijk Besluit van 17 April 1950, No. 25 (1954). Staatsdrukkerij en Uitgeverijbedrijf, The Hague

Fasseur C (2010) Doorbreek stilzwijgen over aanbevelingen Davids, De Volkskrant, November 17, pp 20–21

Gerhardt V (2003) Die Macht im Recht. Ideologie und Politik nach dem 11 September 2001. Merkur 57:557–569

---

[60] Gerhardt 2003, pp. 557–569; Scruton 2003.

[61] Habermas 2006, pp. 115–193. On why it is wrong to understand Kant's philosophy as representing the just war tradition, see Mertens 2012.

[62] Nollkaemper 2010.

[63] http://georgewbush-whitehouse.archives.gov/nsc/nss/2002/.

[64] Fasseur 2010.

Habermas J (1999) Bestialität und humanität, Die Zeit, April 29, pp 1–8 (trans: 6 Constellations (1999), pp 263–272)
Habermas J (2006) Does the constitutionalization of international law still have a chance? In: Habermas J (ed) The divided west. Polity Press, Cambridge, pp 115–193
Hellema DA, Reiding H (2004) Humanitaire interventie en soevereiniteit: de geschiedenis van een tegenstelling. Boom, Amsterdam
Kant I (1970) Zum ewigen frieden. In: Reiss H (ed) Kant's political writings. Cambridge University Press, Cambridge
Koskenniemi M (2002) 'The Lady Doth protest too much' Kosovo, and the turn to ethics in international law. Mod Law Rev 65:159–175
Nollkaemper A (2007) Nederland dient koers in international rechtsorde te herzien. Zomer Christen Democratische Verkenningen 3:185–193
Nollkaemper A (2010) Na de Commissie Davids, Nederland, Irak en het volkenrecht. Nederlands Juristenblad 85:144–150
Mertens TH (2012) Kant and the just war tradition. In: Justenhoven HG, Barbieri W (eds), From just war to modern peace ethics, De Gruyter, Berlin-Boston (forthcoming)
Sands P (2005) Lawless world making and breaking global rules. Penguin Books, London
Simma B (1999) NATO, the UN and the use of force: legal aspects. Eur J Int Law 10:1–22
Scruton R (2003) Immanuel Kant and the Iraq war. Open Democracy. Available at www.opendemocracy.net/faith-iraqwarphiloshophy_1749.jsp
Tesón FR (2003) The liberal case for humanitarian intervention. In: Holzegrefe JL, Keohane RO (eds) Humanitarian intervention. Cambridge University Press, Cambridge, pp 93–129
van Genugten W, Grünfeld F, Leurdijk D (2007) Internationale rechtshandhaving. In: Norbach N, Lefeber R, Ribbelink O (eds) Handboek internationaal recht. TMC Asser Press, The Hague, pp 385–436
Veröffentlichungen der Vereinigung der Deutschen Staatsrechtslehrer (1927), vol 3. De Gruyter, Berlin
Verslag van de Staatscommissie ingesteld bij Koninklijk Besluit van 20 December 1918, No. 78, aan welke is opgedragen de voorbereiding van eene herziening van de Grondwet (1920). Algemeene Landsdrukkerij, The Hague
Voorhoeve JJC (1979) Peace, profits and principles: a study of Dutch foreign policy. Nijhoff, The Hague
van Walsum P (2002) Iraq and International Law, Financial Times, August 19, 10
Walzer M (2004) Arguing about war. Yale University Press, New Haven, pp 3–22

Chapter 6
Forging International Order: Inquiring the Dutch Support of the Iraq Invasion

Tanja E. Aalberts

Abstract This article analyzes the Iraq inquiry in The Netherlands as presented by the Davids Committee (Rapport Commissie van onderzoek besluitvorming Irak. Boom, Amsterdam, 2010). It discusses the so-called corpus theory that informed the Dutch position that the invasion in Iraq was in accordance with international law, and its deconstruction by the Davids Committee. However, this article also argues that the corpus theory was only part of the story. In the search for justifying its political support of the war, the corpus theory interacted with two other claims for legitimacy put forward by the Dutch government. These alternative strands of legitimacy moved beyond positive law to include extra-Charter values (notably with regard to state roguery in the New World Order) on the one hand, and to circumvent the politics within the Security Council (legitimacy through defiance), on the other hand. The analysis discloses how any legal argumentation and bids for legitimacy are based on a particular vision of the international society and how to safeguard law, peace, and freedom in the contemporary international order. Together this leads to a more nuanced view, which does not alter the conclusion that the Iraq war was illegal, but which does show that it can be deceptive to reduce international policy-making to a zero-sum choice between law and politics narrowly defined.

Keywords Davids Committee · Iraq inquiry · The Netherlands · Use of force · Resolution 1441 · Corpus theory · Justifications · Liberal antipluralism · Rogue states · Security Council · International responsibility · International community

---

The author would like to thank Jean d'Aspremont and the editors for their comments.

T. E. Aalberts (✉)
Leiden University, Leiden, The Netherlands
e-mail: taalberts@fsw.leidenuniv.nl

I. F. Dekker and E. Hey (eds.), *Netherlands Yearbook of International Law 2011*,
Netherlands Yearbook of International Law 42, DOI: 10.1007/978-90-6704-849-1_6,

Contents

6.1 Introduction

The 2003 invasion in Iraq has aroused a heated debate on its legality and/or legitimacy within the international community and national parliaments alike, both prior to the deployment of armed forces on 20 March 2003 but no less in the years afterwards. After continuous requests by the parliament, in 2009 the Dutch government at last decided to launch an official independent investigation[1] into the decision-making process leading up to the support of and participation in the invasion.[2] The immediate instigator was a publication in a renowned newspaper that critical advice regarding the legal justification for political support of the war in Iraq had been withheld from the Minister of Foreign Affairs, Jaap de Hoop Scheffer.[3] In March 2009 the Davids Committee—named after its chair and former President of the Supreme Court in The Netherlands, Mr. Willibrord Davids—was formally installed with the assignment to investigate the preparation and decision making in the period summer 2002–summer 2003 regarding the political support

[1] However, it decided against an official investigation by the Parliament itself or the even heavier parliamentary 'enquête', in which case all hearings are public and under oath, and continuous refusal to testify can lead to prosecution.

[2] Officially, the government provided political but not military support. The distinction is not always clear and not maintained by the US government, Davids Committee 2010, pp. 106–110, 426, conclusion no. 11. Moreover, political support can have legal consequences too, as international law obligates all states to end violations of fundamental norms, such as the nonuse of force, Nollkaemper 2010, p. 149.

[3] Joost Oranje, 'Buitenlandse Zaken hield kritisch Irak-advies achter', *NRC Handelsblad*, 17 January 2009; 'Memorandum DJZ/IR/2003/158', *NRC Handelsblad*, 26 January 2009. In his letter the Minister President more generally refers to the lists of questions raised in Parliament in the preceding weeks, Letter, 2 February 2009, *Kamerstukken II*, 31847/1; Davids Committee 2010, pp. 17–18.

of The Netherlands to the invasion in Iraq in general, and with special attention for aspects of international law, intelligence and information services, and the alleged military support.[4] On 12 January 2010 the Committee published its report.[5]

Apart from the question about the (il)legality of the invasion which occupied the parliamentary debate ever since the 2002 preamble to the war in Iraq, from an academic perspective it is even more interesting to analyze how the justification for the use of force is (de)constructed within political and legal discourse. The question on (il)legality is rather straightforward, but somewhat misleadingly so. Rather than a mathematical formula with one correct answer, law is better understood as a scheme of interpretation. It is the outcome of legal practice, which not only means law is always in process but it is also interacting with other forms of legitimacy in the search for justification of international policy-making. As famously postulated by Koskenniemi: 'legal arguments do not produce substantive outcomes but seek to justify them'.[6] As international law, like any other law, is not a formula where legal questions lead to readymade answers, it is interesting to look into the deliberations that led different parties to different answers to the question whether its conduct falls within the confines of international law. In this light it is unfortunate, as Nollkaemper in his commentary on the Davids Report notes,[7] that the analysis of the legal mandate in Chap. 8 of the report discusses and dismisses the justification put forward by the Dutch government in less than two pages. The Committee predominantly focuses on the so-called 'corpus theory', which distils the authorization of a forceful intervention from the body of resolutions issued by the Security Council against Iraq since the early 1990s.[8] This is indeed the legality argument put forward most explicitly by the Dutch government. However, this article will argue that the corpus theory interacted with other justificatory schemes that emerged in the deliberation of the Dutch government with the parliament. Using Berman's classification of international legitimacy, this analysis will identify three justification strands: (i) the legal justification informed by the corpus theory (Sect. 6.2); and then two alternative strands of justification: (ii) synergy between Charter and extra-Charter values (Sect. 6.3); and (iii) bidding for legitimacy through defiance (Sect. 6.4).[9]

---

[4] *Instellingsbesluit*, 6 March 2009, nr. 3075101, Davids Committee 2010, Appendix A.

[5] Davids Committee 2010. See http://www.rijksoverheid.nl/onderwerpen/irak/commissie-davids. The 551 page report is published in Dutch, but the conclusions and summary are available in English on the official website. Chap. 8, on the legal foundation, was translated and published ad verbatim in the *Netherlands International Law Review* (NILR 2010, pp. 81–137). All translations are by this author; quotes from Chap. 8 are taken from the translation by the *NILR*.

[6] Koskenniemi 2006 [1989], p. 570.

[7] Nollkaemper 2010.

[8] Davids Committee 2010, pp. 22, 263, 271–272.

[9] Berman 2005. He distinguishes three justification strands: (i) innovation through violation; (ii) legitimacy through competing coherence, which can entail either teleological interpretation or synergy; and (iii) legitimacy through defiance.

It should be made clear from the outset that such a more extensive analysis does *not* change the overall conclusion about the illegality of the military intervention under the UN Charter framework. However, it does lay bare how legal analysis is never a simple mathematical equation, but a structure of argumentation which always involves a process of interpretation which is inherently political.[10] Like any law, international law is not a manual that dictates the legal outcome of any particular situation to which it is applied. Several points follow from this. It means, first of all, that any reading of positive international law is (often implicitly) informed by a broader vision on international society and its relation to the international legal order. It also means that in addressing questions of legality different parties can reach opposite conclusions, either because they rely on different legal regimes to frame the issue at hand,[11] or because they interpret the same articles (of, for instance, the UN Charter) differently in light of their vision of the international legal order. Moreover, international justification need not confine itself to positive international law, but can explore and seek to expand the boundaries of legality and legitimacy based on a particular vision of what the international society is or should be. This article illustrates these points by deconstructing the different justification strands put forward by the Dutch government for its political support of the Iraq invasion, along the aforementioned lines of Berman's distinction—thus including but not limited to the legal argumentation analyzed by the Davids Committee.[12]

6.2 (De)constructing Legality

Both the Dutch government and the Davids Committee identified the United Nations (UN) Charter as the relevant legal paradigm for questions of war and the international use of force.[13] Launched right after the Second World War, the United Nations aimed to provide a framework for the peaceful settlement of international disputes and managing the use of force by distinguishing (i) unlawful acts of aggression (Article 2(4) UN Charter); (ii) the inherent right to individual or collective self-defence (Article 51 UN Charter); and (iii) collective enforcement authorized by the Security Council (Article 39 and 42 UN Charter). The latter refers to the so-called Chapter VII procedure, which holds that the Security Council can declare a situation to be a threat to international peace and security

---

[10] Nollkaemper 2010, p. 145.

[11] Koskenniemi 2007.

[12] Unlike the Chilcot inquiry in the United Kingdom, the hearings of the Davids Committee have not been made public. Hence apart from the Davids Report itself, this analysis relies on letters and transcripts of parliamentary debates, and other documents, all of which are available at https://zoek.officielebekendmakingen.nl/. All translations are by the author.

[13] *Cf. Handelingen II*, 30 January 2003 (38/2821–2849), p. 2839; Davids Committee 2010, section 8.2.

and 'make recommendations, or decide what measures shall be taken ... to maintain or restore international peace and security' (Article 39 UN Charter). These measures can—subsequently—entail both economic and diplomatic sanctions (Article 41 UN Charter) or ultimately the use of military force (Article 42 UN Charter).[14] The latter is implied when a Security Council resolution uses the diplomatic language of 'all necessary means' (also: measures). All Security Council Resolutions have to be supported by 9 out of the 15 members, including the 5 permanent members,[15] and are legally binding.

Since the end of the Cold War the Security Council has used its discretion to interpret Article 39 UN Charter in a broader sense, by increasingly identifying humanitarian crises as threats to international peace and security, and mandating forceful humanitarian interventions. This development has given rise to the so-called Responsibility to Protect paradigm, a concise version of which was adopted at the World summit in 2005. The paradigm appears to reconceptualize the relationship between sovereignty and human rights and can be summarized in two steps: first, by identifying sovereignty not as a state's privilege (with accompanying rights of non-intervention), but as a responsibility to protect the rights of its citizens; and secondly, by transferring this responsibility to the international community in case a state does not fulfill its sovereignty obligations. The new paradigm also implies that a state that does not fulfill its obligations forfeits its rights as a sovereign member of the international society. As such the paradigm at once allegedly provides a basis for humanitarian intervention as a right—or even duty—on the part of other member states in case of gross violations of human rights of the population of any state. To be clear, while the Responsibility to Protect paradigm has been adopted by the General Assembly, and indeed has been referred to in Security Council resolutions, it is a diplomatic formula the legal status of which remains dubious.[16] Moreover, the humanitarian card has not been pushed by the Dutch government (or any other state for that matter) in the case of Iraq. Nevertheless, a similar logic of shifting responsibilities did transpire in the Dutch justification for its political support of the intervention in Iraq.

---

[14] Article 42 reads: '[s]hould the Security Council consider that measures provided for in Article 41 would be inadequate or have proved to be inadequate, it may take such action by air, sea, or land forces as may be necessary to maintain or restore international peace and security. Such action may include demonstrations, blockade, and other operations by air, sea, or land forces of Members of the United Nations.'.

[15] The P5 are United States, United Kingdom, France, Russia, and China. Whereas art 27(3) UN Charter demands a positive vote of the P5, in practice it is interpreted in a broader sense (i.e., no negative vote from the P5) so that they have the option of abstaining without blocking the decision-making procedure all together.

[16] This paradigm was referred to by the Security Council for the first time in its Resolutions 1674 (2006), and 1894 (2009) on the Protection of Civilians in Armed Conflicts, and explicitly invoked in the context of the situation in a particular country in Resolution 1706 (2006) on the conflict in Darfur, and Resolutions 1970 (2011) and 1973 (2011) regarding the crisis in Libya, and Resolution 1975 (2011) on the situation on Côte d'Ivoire. On its legal status, see inter alia Stahn 2007.

However, in order to make this justificatory claim, the Dutch government had to move beyond the confines of the Charter and bid for 'legitimacy through defiance', as will be discussed in the last section.

6.2.1 Dutch Government: Corpus Theory of Security Council Authorization

In its justification for the political support to the invasion in Iraq under the Charter framework, the Dutch government argued that the issue should to be considered in the broader and historical context of the relationship between Iraq and the United Nations, with a particular focus on the developments since the early 1990s.[17] This relationship started with the Security Council condemnation of the invasion and annexation of Kuwait by Iraq and its call for the immediate withdrawal of Iraqi troops and restoration of Kuwait's territorial integrity in Security Council Resolution (UNSC) 660. To summarize the long history that evolved, three resolutions play a particularly crucial role: UNSC 678, UNSC 687, and UNSC 1441.[18] When subsequent resolutions to further enforce the withdrawal proved ineffective, the Security Council issued Resolution 678 on 29 November 1990 in which it authorized the use of 'all necessary means' to enforce compliance with Resolution 660 and 'all subsequent relevant resolutions'[19] in order to 'restore international peace and security in the area'. The mandate for the use of force thus was included in this Resolution 678 and no further consultation or decision by the Security Council was required. After the Iraqi withdrawal, the Security Council in a subsequent Resolution (UNSC Resolution 687, 3 April 1990) formulated a seize fire conditional upon formal acceptance by the Iraqi government of the peace package contained in the resolution. '[R]eaffirming the need to be assured of Iraq's peaceful intentions' and referring to previous Iraqi threats and actual use of biological and chemical weapons, one of the conditions was that Iraq would destroy, remove, or dismantle under international supervision all its chemical, biological, and nuclear weapons facilities in order to restore international peace and security in the area.[20] As such, this resolution broadened the issue from the conflict between Iraq and Kuwait, to the possession of weapons of mass destruction as a threat to

---

[17] See also Davids Committee 2010, para 8.3.

[18] See also Davids Committee 2010, pp. 43–44, 225–229. In total there were 59 UNSC resolutions regarding Iraq in 1990 (S/RES/660) until 2002 (S/RES/1409), the majority of which was issued under Chapter VII and hence had a binding character. See Letter of the MoFA, 25 September 2002, *Kamerstukken II*, 28618/5.

[19] In the resolution itself reference is made to the preceding UNSC Resolutions 661(1990), 662(1990), 664(1990), 665(1990), 666(1990), 667(1990), 669(1990) 670(1990), 674(1990), 677(1990).

[20] Being a signatory of the Nuclear Non-Proliferation Treaty (1970) and Biological Weapons Convention (1972), Iraq was already forbidden to possess nuclear and biological weapons, as the

international peace and security at large.[21] In the following years, the Iraqi government proved to be very reluctant to comply with the inspection regime, and ultimately unilaterally declared the end of the UNSCOM mission in 1998, after which the UN inspectors were withdrawn.

After 9/11 there was an important shift in the international political climate and in particular the US position toward so-called rogue regimes, among which Iraq.[22] Identifying the latter as a prominent entity within the 'axis of evil', these states were categorized as irresponsible regimes who would not hesitate to provide weapons of mass destruction to international terrorists.[23] Given the ineffectiveness of the inspection regime from its very beginning, more severe (i.e., military) measures were called for. From September 2002 it became clear that the US was planning to pursue these measures via a multilateral pathway, developing not only a 'coalition of the willing' to cooperate in the fight against the Iraqi regime, but also by seeking legitimation via the legal framework provided by the UN Charter.[24] However, in light of the latter, it soon became clear that there were different standpoints on what the aim of such measures should be (regime change or disarmament) and what such a legal justification would require, in particular whether a new resolution with an explicit authorization under Chapter VII would be necessary to mandate a forceful intervention in Iraq. While the Security Council agreed with the necessity to reinstall and sharpen the inspection regime, several of its members, and in particular permanent member France, were reluctant to automatically mandate the use of force in case of continued non-compliance. Instead, France proposed a two-step approach, with a first resolution to give Iraq a final opportunity to cooperate with the UN and terminate the situation of material breach; and a second resolution to decide upon the measures to be taken in case of further non-compliance. Resultant UNSC Resolution 1441 (8 November, 2002) was a compromise to accommodate the different perspectives. It recalls all the relevant resolutions since 1990, including the authorization of force under UNSC resolution 678 ('all necessary means') to implement UNSC resolution 660 as well

(Footnote 20 continued)
Resolution also states. The Chemical Weapons Convention only came into force in 1997, and was entered by Iraq in 2009.

[21] In a subsequent resolution (UNSC 688), the Security Council condemned the oppression of Iraqi civilians as a threat to international peace and security. However, it did not invoke the Chapter VII procedure and authorizing the use of force to restore the peace. Nevertheless, the Security Council also refrained from condemning the following forceful humanitarian intervention (operation *Provide comfort*) led by the US. This was one of the first operations of a series of unilateral and multilateral humanitarian interventions in the 1990s.

[22] Davids Committee 2010, pp. 57–58, 155.

[23] State of the Union address by President George W. Bush, 29 January 2002 (available at http://www.washingtonpost.com/wp-srv/onpolitics/transcripts/sou012902.htm). In reaction to this speech Iraq stated to be willing to discuss the return of the UN weapon inspectors. See Verslag van een Algemeen Overleg d.d. 7 Februari 2002, *Kamerstukken II,* 21501/02.

[24] See the speech delivered by President George W. Bush to the UN General Assembly, 12 September 2002, Meeting Records A/57/PV.2.

as the obligations imposed on Iraq under UNSC resolution 687, both aimed to restore international peace and security in the area (according to the Dutch, US, and UK readings of these texts). 'Deploring' inter alia the lack of 'accurate, full, final and complete disclosure' of its weapons of mass destruction and its repeated obstruction of the inspection regime, in Resolution 1441 the Security Council decided that Iraq 'has been and remains in material breach of its obligations under relevant resolutions' (§ 1) and would be given a final opportunity to comply with the disarmament obligations (§ 2). Apart from a number of specific conditions, the Security Council generally demands 'that Iraq cooperate immediately, unconditionally, and actively' with the inspectors (§ 9). In case of further material breach the Council would 'convene... in order to consider the situation' (§ 4 and 12). In the penultimate paragraph of the resolution, it recalls that 'the Council has repeatedly warned Iraq that it will face serious consequences as a result of its continued violations of its obligations' (§ 13).[25]

From September 2002 onwards, the issue of Iraq was high on the political agenda in The Netherlands and subject to continuous deliberation between the Minister of Foreign Affairs (MoFA), Mr. Jaap de Hoop Scheffer, and parliament. Drawing on the UN framework, the Dutch government position from the very beginning was based on four related points[26]:

i. the real and serious threat to international peace and security posed by the possession of weapons of mass destruction by Iraq;
ii. the continuous non-compliance by Iraq with binding resolutions of the Security Council since the 1990s;
iii. the corpus theory of authorization; and
iv. the politics and credibility of the Security Council.

In line with the overall stance in the international community, the government made an issue of dealing with the situation on a step-by-step basis. In order to deal with the first two points, the international community would initially have to organize an unconditional and immediate return of the weapon inspectors to reestablish the inspection regime with the ultimate goal of disarming Iraq of its weapons of mass destruction.[27] While not wanting to anticipate what would happen next in case of continued rejection to admit the inspectors, and refusing to 'defin[e] the endgame', the MoFA did identify the use of force as '*ultissimum remedium*', indicating both that it would be only the last in a line of other

---

[25] This was also the language used in inter alia Resolutions 688 (1991) and 1194 (1998). See Davids Committee 2010, p. 238. The Davids Committee discusses Resolution 1441 in paragraph 8.6 of the report.

[26] *Cf. Handelingen II*, 5 September 2002, 95/5648–5671. See also Letter of the MoFA, 4 September 2002, *Kamerstukken II*, 23432/56; Letter of the MoFA, 18 March 2003, *Kamerstukken II*, 23432/94.

[27] This had been the repeated demand of several resolutions since 1998, most recently UNSC Resolution 1284 of 17 December 1999. For a comparison of Resolutions 1284 and 1441, see Davids Committee 2010, p. 236.

diplomatic and political steps, but explicitly not ruling the option out either:[28] '[t]he UN trajectory is aimed at the return of the weapon inspectors and the prevention of military intervention [....] Use of force was and is the ultimum remedium. "Was the ultimum remedium" because resolutions 687 and 1284 legitimize the use of force under circumstances'.[29] This reasoning was based on the argument that excluding the possibility of military intervention at this early stage would leave the Security Council toothless in its attempt to force the Iraqi regime to comply with its demands. Pushed by Members of Parliament to elaborate on how such enforcement could be legitimated if push would come to shove, Minister de Hoop Scheffer pointed to the body of resolutions that had already been issued against Iraq. They could provide a legal ground for the use of force against Iraq in case of (continued) material breach of the conditions put forward by the international community, in casu the disarmament of its weapons of mass destruction. Against the background of the immense threat to international peace and security posed by Iraq (as a rogue state in possession of weapons of mass destruction), so de Hoop Scheffer argued, it would render a new resolution with an explicit authorization 'politically desirable' but not a legal '*conditio sine qua non*' given the 'corpus of resolutions of the Security Council' (without further specification).[30] This corpus of resolutions hence by itself would suffice as legal basis, and in addition would circumvent the possibility of international action being blocked by a veto of one of the P5.[31]

Over the course of the months in which the possibility of a new resolution, and an additional second one, was discussed by the Security Council, the Dutch government continued this line of argumentation.[32] And when the new resolution, UNSC 1441, was finally issued, the government conceived it as a confirmation of the corpus theory. As the Dutch government noted in an appendix to its letter to the Parliament of 18 March 2003, the term 'serious consequences' in the penultimate paragraph of the resolution clearly differed from the diplomatic jargon normally used to explicitly authorize military measures. Nevertheless, the government maintained that such authorization follows from the direct link between Resolution

[28] *Handelingen II*, 5 September 2002, 95/5648–5671, p. 5665.

[29] Verslag van een Algemeen Overleg d.d. 1 October 2002, *Kamerstukken II*, 23432/61; Letter of the MoFA, 31 October 2002, *Kamerstukken II*, 23432/62.

[30] *Handelingen II*, 5 September 2002, 95/5648–5671; *Handelingen II*, 30 January 2003, 38/2821–2849; *Handelingen II*, 12 February 2003, 43/2992–3038; Letter of the MoFA, 18 March 2003, *Kamerstukken II*, 23432/94. See also Davids Committee 2010, pp. 116, 246, 263. The full explanation of the alleged relationship between the different resolutions, was provided by the government at the Parliamentary debate of 18 March 2003, see *Handelingen II*, 18 March 2003, 50/3275–3327.

[31] *Handelingen II*, 5 September 2002, 95/5648–5671, pp. 5665, 5666 and 5668. Further legal advice by the Commissie van Advies inzake Volkenrechtelijke Vraagstukken (Advisory Commission on Public International law) was deemed unnecessary, as the MoFA replied to a question of MoP Koenders, 26 September 2002. See also Davids Committee 2010, p. 247. On the role of legal advisors in the decision-making leading to the invasion in Iraq, see Manusama 2011.

[32] See also *Handelingen II*, 18 March 2003, 50/3275–3327.

1441 and the body of resolutions issued since 1990: '[t]hrough the recapitulation in 1441 of all previous resolutions—in particular 678 (force mandate) and 687 (weapons of mass destruction)—the authorization of the use of force [of 678] was reinvoked'.[33] Hence, from the perspective of the Dutch government, Resolution 1441 added to and confirmed the body of resolutions that had been issued since the 1990s:

> Resolution 1441 ... must indeed be read as part of and is the consequence of the developments of the last eleven years, in which no action [against the total and permanent material breach of previous resolutions by Iraq] was undertaken because the international community and the United Nations for all kinds of political reasons lacked the bones to do so, causing a threat to the Security Council's credibility[34]

According to the Dutch government, the continuity narrative was hence still applicable, and the corpus theory was reinforced with the adoption of Resolution 1441. The Resolution itself confirmed this by referring to the material breach as formulated in UNSC Resolution 678.[35] Consequently, while explicit information on further measures and their authorization was lacking, the 'serious consequences' referred to in the penultimate paragraph of Resolution 1441 'means that the Security Council [in case of non-compliance by Iraq] will not start a whole new debate: "serious consequences" can according to the minister [of Foreign Affairs] only be read as "the use of force"'.[36] Moreover, no explicit decision by the Security Council would be necessary to determine the 'further material breach', as the Resolution confirmed the material breach that had been ongoing for over a decade, and in terms of procedural matters it merely stated that the Council will convene to 'consider' the situation, not that it 'would decide what needed to

---

[33] Letter of the MoFA, 18 March 2003, *Kamerstukken II,* 23432/94. In this letter the MoFA gives an update on the international situation and the position of the Dutch government once it became clear that Iraq would not comply with Resolution 1441 and the Security Council was divided on the interpretation of the expression 'serious consequences' in the resolution text.

[34] Verslag van Algemeen Overleg d.d. 19 November 2002, *Kamerstukken II,* 23432/66; see also Davids Committee 2010, pp. 259–260.

[35] *Handelingen II,* 18 March 2003, 50/3275–3327; Verslag van Algemeen Overleg d.d. 19 November 2002, *Kamerstukken II,* 23432/66; Appendix to the letter of the MoFA, 18 March 2003, *Kamerstukken II,* 23432/94; see also Davids Committee 2010, p. 262.

[36] Letter of the MoFA, 11 November 2002, *Kamerstukken II,* 23432/63; Verslag van Algemeen Overleg d.d. 19 November 2002, *Kamerstukken II,* 23432/66. In a later debate in parliament the MoFA identified this as a 'very clear passage', *Handelingen II,* 30 January 2003, 38/2821–2849, pp. 2834, 2839. See also Letter of the MoFA, 18 March 2003, *Kamerstukken II,* 23432/94. In the US line of argumentation, that Berman analyses, the term 'serious consequences' amounts to another strand of justification as the US administration linked it to extra-Charter values (which are not further specified in the analysis). As such it illustrates a synergy argument. The Dutch interpretation of 'serious consequences', however, remains within the parameters of the Charter framework and hence falls under the justification through legality, even though this legal argumentation ultimately was not valid.

be done to restore international peace and security'.[37] This literal reading of the resolution was supplemented by another key rule of interpretation, taking into account the discussion leading up to the adoption of the text.[38] In this context, the MoFA applied an *a contrario* construction to the compromise formulation, drawing on the inconclusive phrasing with regard to the necessity of a second resolution to authorize the use of force in case of 'further material breach'. It argued that as France, despite its persistent efforts, did not succeed to have this reference to a follow-up resolution incorporated as an explicit *conditio sine qua non* in Resolution 1441, it follows that it is not required that the Security Council has to decide upon the compliance with the Resolution.[39]

At the eve of the invasion, the corpus theory was again put forward as sufficient legal basis for military action. Moreover, the government in the debate with Parliament cunningly remarked that it was not a new legal argumentation that was being presented: it had been around since the 1990s, with the Parliament's approval at the time.[40] It further justified this 'legal construction'[41] by referring to the parallel 'revival theory' that the then Attorney General of the UK, Lord Goldsmith had formulated the previous day in a memo to the Parliament (17 March 2003) as the legal ground for military action against Iraq.[42] This hence was

[37] 'Nowhere in 1441 it says ... that the Security Council has to take a decision about what should follow after that resolution. If that would have been the case, the resolution would have stated that the Security Council "would decide what needed to be done to restore international peace and security". It does not say so, but it does say that the Security Council "will consider the matter". From this it can be derived that no further decision is necessary.' *Handelingen II*, 18 March 2003, 50/3275–3327, pp. 3309–3310. See also *Handelingen II*, 30 January 2003, 38/2821–2849. This differed from what was discussed in the Council of Ministers on the eve of the adoption of Resolution 1441, see Davids Committee 2010, pp. 256, 262. This issue of wording was also discussed the British Chilcot Inquiry on the invasion in Iraq. In his testimony before the Inquiry, Lord Goldsmith, Attorney General at the time, used the same line of argumentation as the Dutch MoFA: '[i]n one sense, the wording is crystal clear, because these members of the Security Council, who know the difference between the word "decide" and "consider the situation", chose, I believe quite deliberately to use the words "consider the situation", and they could have said "decide" if that's what they meant.' Rt Hon Lord Goldsmith QC, Oral Evidence for the Iraq Inquiry, 27 January 2010, p. 49, available at www.iraqinquiry.org.uk/media/45317/20100127goldsmith-final.pdf.

[38] Legal Consequences for States of the Continued Presence of South Africa in Namibia Notwithstanding SC Resolution 276, Advisory Opinion, ICJ Reports 16, 1971.

[39] *Handelingen II*, 18 March 2003, 50/3275–3327, p. 3310. See also the explanation by Lord Goldsmith, *infra*, note 52.

[40] *Handelingen II*, 18 March 2003, 50/3275–3327, pp. 3298, 3310. See also Handelingen II, 5 September 2002, 95/5648–5671, p. 5665; *Handelingen 2002–2003,* Aanhangsel nr. 910; Letter of the MoFA, 18 March 2003, *Kamerstukken II,* 23432/94; Davids Committee 2010, pp. 53–54, 228 and 261.

[41] *Handelingen II*, 18 March 2003, 50/3275–3327, p. 3298.

[42] *Handelingen II*, 18 March 2003, 50/3275–3327, p. 3299; *Kamerstukken II,* 23 432/171, appendix. See also Davids Committee 2010, pp. 263–265, 272. As turned out later, this was only a summary of a larger and more cautious memo sent by Lord Goldsmith to Tony Blair on 7 March 2003, in which the Attorney General concluded that a further decision by the Security

the central line of argumentation formulated by the Dutch government on the basis of the Charter framework, and the one that was scrutinized by the Davids Committee and rejected as sufficient legal basis for the invasion, as will be discussed in the next paragraph. However, the above quote also hints at two alternative strands of justification that were interacting with this particular legal argumentation. These alternative strands concern first the permanent non-compliance with international legal obligations, rendering Iraq not only a brutal regime but also a disobedient member of international society.[43] It is based on a particular vision of international society that moves beyond the template of the United Nations with its emphasis on the principle of sovereign equality. As will be discussed below, this translates into a legitimacy argument that can be conceptualized as justification by synergy, as a first alternative strand of justification. In this case extra-Charter values and processes are added to complete the partial legal argumentation on the basis of the Charter framework.[44] This 'paralegal' justification is supplemented by a third bid for legitimacy which explicitly defies the Charter framework. Such 'legitimacy by defiance' (the second alternative strand of justification) can be identified in the final point put forward by the MoFA de Hoop Scheffer in the above quote (footnote 33) i.e., the politics of the Security Council and its resultant lack of action and credibility. Before addressing these alternative strands of justification the next section will discuss how the Davids Committee criticized the legal justification based on the corpus theory.

6.2.2 Davids Committee: Inadequate Legal Mandate

The corpus theory, as the backbone of the legal strand of justification put forward by the Dutch government, was deconstructed by the Davids Committee. The Committee concludes—in line with the general consensus among international

(Footnote 42 continued)
Council was warranted as legal ground for the intervention. This secret memo (which only was made public by Tony Blair after its leaking in Spring 2005) was never sent to the Dutch Government, who only received the summary. As the Davids Committee also notes, the role of the Attorney General in the course of the events changed from an independent legal advisor to an advocate for the government. Davids Committee 2010, p. 264. See also Manusama 2012; and Ralph 2011. See also the records of Lord Goldsmith's testimony in front of the UK Iraq Inquiry, on 27 January 2010, available at www.iraqinquiry.org.uk/transcripts/oralevidence-bydate/100127.aspx. The memo of 7 March 2010 is available at www.ico.gov.uk/upload/documents/library/freedom_of_information/notices/annex_a_-_attorney_general's_advice_070303.pdf.

[43] In a later paragraph it is stated that 'the international community [should] take an extremely critical position towards a dictator who enslaves his population, possesses weapons of mass destruction and has shown to be prepared and use these weapons.' Verslag van Algemeen Overleg d.d. 19 November 2002, *Kamerstukken II,* 23432/66.

[44] Berman 2005, pp. 106, 109.

legal scholarship—that it could not pass the legality test.[45] This conclusion is based on two fundamentally different standpoints regarding the importance and meaning of Resolution 1441.

The first point considers the continuity narrative as the basis for the corpus theory. Rather than its confirmation, Resolution 1441 established a new phase in the relationship between Iraq and the United Nations, making it necessary to distinguish between the period 1991–2002 and the period after 8 November 2002.[46] In fact, the corpus theory had already lost its potential legal weight before the definite adoption of the resolution. The Dutch position, that a new resolution with an explicit authorization was the politically preferred course but not a legal necessity,[47] might have been a legitimate option in the early phases of the discussion when the debate in the Security Council had not crystallized yet, as Nico Schrijver (professor of International Law and member of the Davids Committee) explained in the roundtable discussion with Parliament upon the completion of the report. However, this changed when the objections of particularly France became clear.[48] In any case, the corpus theory definitely lost validity as a legal justification for the intervention in November 2002, when a new phase in the decision-making process started with the adoption of Resolution 1441. Like the Dutch government, the Davids Committee bases its argumentation on both the formulation of the Resolution text, and the context of its drafting, yet it draws completely opposite conclusions, as will be discussed next. Finally, the corpus—or revival—theory was further undermined by the 'frantic attempts in the Spring of 2003 to get a so-called "second resolution" adopted which would authorize *expressis verbis* the use of force'.[49]

One could argue that from the adoption of Resolution 1441 onwards the legality question became more like a mathematical exercise: no authorization, hence no legality.[50] However, the discussions following the adoption of UNSC 1441 again illustrate how law is a scheme of interpretation. The second critical point concerns the meaning and legal consequences of Resolution 1441. While relying on the same traditional rules of interpretation—literal reading combined with contextual

---

45 Davids Commitee 2010, pp. 271–272.

46 Davids Commitee 2010, p. 236; translation in NILR 2010, p. 135. With regard to the claim of its prior legitimacy in 1998, the Davids Committee refers to a similar practice of creative readings of Resolutions 678 and 687, neglecting the context of their drafting, as well as parallel attempts to obtain Security Council authorization via an additional resolution. Davids Committee 2010, pp. 228, 249.

47 This position was developed by the government in August 2002 and maintained over the course of the months leading to the invasion in March 2003.

48 Verslag van een Rondetafelgesprek d.d. 19 January 2010, *Kamerstukken II*, 31847/17, pp. 14, 16.

49 Davids Committee 2010, p. 272. Tellingly, the draft resolution submitted by the United States, the United Kingdom and Spain was modelled after Resolution 678 (1991).

50 The other exception to the prohibition of the use of force (self-defence) does not apply either, and indeed was not invoked.

understanding—the conclusion of the Davids Committee about its legal meaning is the complete reverse of the Dutch position in the run-up to the war in Iraq. For one thing, the Committee rejects the argument that 'serious consequences' could not mean anything but the use of force, as the MoFA de Hoop Scheffer maintained. The significance of the formulation of 'serious consequences' lies exactly in what it did *not* formulate, i.e., the authorization formula of 'all necessary means'. As such, the former is a less heavy, but still threatening formulation in UN practice, entailing a message of possible future authorization—i.e., supporting the two-stage approach preferred by the majority of the international community.[51] Note that this focus on what was *not* expressed is in fact the same logic that the Dutch government applied to the formulation of 'consider' as opposed to 'decide' (see footnote 36). However, in that latter case there is not a specific prescription in diplomatic practice with a similar heavy legal weight as the coded language of 'all necessary means'. Rather than taking this choice of words at their face value and apply an *a contrario* argumentation, the correct legal meaning of 'consider' follows from the broader, contextual reading of the Resolution, as the Davids Committee argues. In particular the voting statements of the Security Council members are unequivocal in this regard.[52] All members—including the United States and the United Kingdom—explicitly stated that the Resolution 'contains no "hidden triggers" and no "automaticity" with respect to the use of force'.[53] In other words, in case of further material breach of Iraqi's disarmament obligations as formulated in Resolution 1441 'the matter will return to the Council for discussion as required in para. 12'.[54] This was spelled out by the French

[51] Davids Committee 2010, pp. 238, 240–241.

[52] Meeting records S/PV.4644, 8 November 2002. (All records of Security Council meetings and decisions are available at www.un.org/Depts/dhl/resguide/scact.htm). See also Davids Committee 2010, pp. 241–242. MoFA in fact also refers to the context of the drafting to support his reading of Resolution 1441. However, he does not further specify this. See *Handelingen II*, 18 March 2003, 50/3275–3327, p. 3310. In his oral evidence to the Chilcot inquiry Lord Goldsmith also refers to the history of the drafting to substantiate his interpretation of the expressions 'consider' and 'serious consequences'. However, rather than focusing on France's objection and potential veto of any 'hidden triggers', he argues that from the context and history of the drafting it was clear that in fact the US would veto any reference to further decision-making for authorisation—that was a 'red line' for the US, and if it would be crossed they would have gone ahead without any Resolution whatsoever. Rt Hon Lord Goldsmith QC, Oral Evidence for the Iraq Inquiry, 27 January 2010, pp. 87, 111, 114 and 142, available at www.iraqinquiry.org.uk/media/45317/20100127goldsmith-final.pdf. In other words, 'serious consequences' was as much a compromise to satisfy France, as it was to keep the US on board. Seen in this light, all members knew what they would get by accepting serious consequences, or so Goldsmith argues.

[53] Statement by the US ambassador to the UN, Mr. Negroponte. He finishes the paragraph by stating that the resolution does not constrain the right to self-defense, and—more controversially—'constrain any Member State from acting … to enforce relevant United Nations resolutions and protect world peace and security.' S/PV.4644, p. 3. He also recalls the different opinions about the 'shape and language' of the resolution. Ibid., p. 4.

[54] Statement by the UK ambassador to the UN, Sir Jeremy Greenstock, S/PV.4644, p. 5. He too anticipates that the UK will take further action, with or without the other members of the Security

representative, who pointed to the unambiguous adoption of the two-stage approach: in the event of a non-compliance of Iraq 'the Council would meet immediately to evaluate the seriousness of the violations and draw the appropriate conclusions'.[55] Against the backdrop of these statements and the overall drafting history of Resolution 1441 it is clear that 'serious consequences' does not equal 'all necessary means', and hence does not contain an authorization of military intervention.

Apart from the fact that the corpus theory in and of itself is not legally waterproof—the Davids Committee regards the authorization of 'all necessary means' in UNSC resolution 687 as pertaining to the issue of Kuwait's territorial integrity rather than a broader focus on weapons of mass destruction as a threat to international peace and security at large[56]—the Committee concludes that the Dutch government incorrectly adds Resolution 1441 to the corpus of existing resolutions from the period since 1991. In fact it could be argued that the Dutch government, on the one hand, unduly reduces UNSC 1441's legal significance as an independent resolution and defining moment in the history of Iraq and the UN by seeing it merely as an extra confirmation of the corpus theory. On the other hand, the Dutch government was raising the stakes of the same resolution by implying it could by itself serve as a second resolution (in addition to the corpus of resolutions of the 1990s) through its reference to 'serious consequences', which would entail an implicit authorization of military measures. However, despite some ambiguous formulations, the Davids Committee concludes that there is no ground to interpret the resolution as a *carte blanche* for individual member states to unilaterally enforce Iraq's compliance with its obligations under Security Council resolutions. All together, this means that the military action against Iraq lacked an 'adequate legal mandate'.[57]

While both the Dutch government and the Davids Committee address the legality question in the context of positive law and the Charter framework in particular, they reach diametrically opposed conclusions. Their lines of argumentation run parallel to the discussions in the Security Council in March 2003, where both opponents and defenders of the Iraq intervention emphasized the importance of compliance with UN rules and resolutions, as well as respect for international law at large. For instance, as an opponent of the war France at that time emphasized respect for international law as the cornerstone of the international order; while Great Britain defended its support by stating just a couple of hours before the beginning of the intervention that 'any action which the United Kingdom has to take will be in accordance with international law and based on

(Footnote 54 continued)
Council, without relying on the current text as a legal ground or specifying the action for that matter ('the United Kingdom –together we trust, with other Members of the Security Council—will ensure that the task of disarmament required by the resolutions is completed').

55 Statement by the French Ambassador to the UN, Mr. Levitte, S/PV.4644, p. 5.

56 Davids Committee 2010, pp. 237–238.

57 Davids Committee 2010, pp. 241, 426, conclusions nos. 18 and 20.

relevant resolutions of the Security Council'.[58] In other words, both antagonists and advocates of the war use the 'grammar' of international law and draw on the same 'data' to produce legal arguments in support of their standpoint. This practice illustrates how (international) law is a 'language of justification', and an instrument for articulating particular standpoints in a formal way as input for seeking international legitimacy.[59] As such, international law does not dictate legal outcomes—or as the Davids Committee puts it: the UN Charter is not an instruction manual[60]—but only structures the justifications that can be put forward by key players within the international field. This indeterminacy does not equal a radical relativism, where any argument is as good as any other. Like any language system, legal grammar is defined by specific rules of argumentation. Moreover, obviously some justification schemes have more international leverage as the controversies on the Iraq war clearly show. It does mean, however, that like any other form of justification, legal argumentation is based on and reveals a broader vision on the international society and its relation to the international legal order. In other words, different interpretations of the (il)legality question ultimately stem from underlying differing views on the international community and how to safeguard law, peace, and freedom in the contemporary international order.

The remainder of this article will analyze how the legal justification put forward by the Dutch government interacted with a particular vision of international society and the international (legal) order, which informed two additional lines of argumentation to legitimize the political support of the Iraq war. The first of these alternative justifications concerns a qualification of the principle of sovereign equality as a defining principle of international society. In terms of Berman's scheme, this justification can be conceptualized as an argument for legitimacy by synergy. The second alternative line of argumentation concerns the assertion that legal procedures are sometimes blocked by politics within the Security Council, as the supreme authority of the international community. This results in an argument for legitimacy through defiance.

6.3 Claiming Legitimacy (1): The Dutch Vision on International Society

6.3.1 Of Good Sovereigns and Bad States

The outlawing of the use of force within the UN Charter is linked to one of the other fundamental principles of the United Nations, the principle of sovereign

58 Meeting records S/PV.4721, 19 March 2003; *cf.* US statement in the Security Council meeting of March 24 2003, S/PV.4726.

59 Koskenniemi 2006 [1989], p. 570.

60 Davids Committee 2010, p. 268; translation in NILR 2010, p. 132.

equality of the states (Article 2(1) UN Charter). As a radical break away from colonial history, when international society was exclusionary and the right to equality as a legal principle was based on a logic of difference and a standard of civilization,[61] the post-World War II UN Charter postulated an inclusive society, based on the principles of universality and equality. It was celebrated as a project of homogenization and equalization by which the pluralist premises of the Westphalian template (*cuius regio, eius religio*) in their secularized form were transposed into the new charter for the emerging global international society. In this society states would cohabit peacefully under a shared framework of norms and rules based on mutual recognition of their sovereignty and territorial integrity.[62] This was the liberal internationalism 1.0 as envisioned by Woodrow Wilson at the beginning of the twentieth century.[63] As a volte-face of the colonial logic of sovereignty, equality in this framework is a matter of principle, a legal status, and decoupled from substantial (political and/or material) equality, with membership available for peaceful states, regardless of their internal architecture and ideology.[64] As is stated in Article 4(1) UN Charter: '[m]embership in the United Nations is open to all other peace-loving States which accept the obligations contained in the present Charter and, in the judgment of the Organization, are able and willing to carry out these obligations'. This article consists of an exhaustive list of criteria, as the ICJ concluded in the *Admission* case.[65] At the same time, the decision as to whether the conditions are fulfilled remains with the other member states (Article 4(2) UN Charter), and 'peace-loving' is vague and broad enough a description to include other considerations in the decision (e.g., how peace-loving

---

[61] Gong 1984; Anghie 2005.

[62] In IR theory, the international society is distinguished from a mere international system of regular interaction between states, on the basis of a shared conception among its members 'to be bound by a common set of rules in their relations with one another, and share in the working of common institutions'. This means that '[m]ost states at most times pay some respect to the basic rules of coexistence in international society, such as mutual respect for sovereignty, the rule that agreements should be kept, and rules limiting resort to violence'. These include both formal principles having the status of international law, as well as rules of morality, custom, etiquette, or operational rules of the game. Bull 1995 [1977], pp. 13, 40 and 52.

[63] Ikenberry 2009.

[64] See the Declaration on the Granting of Independence to Colonial Countries and Peoples, GA Resolution 1514 (XV), December 14, 1960 in comparison to Lorimer's infamous quote about equal and unequal states: '[a]ll States are equally entitled to be recognized as States, on the simple ground that they are States; but all States are *not* entitled to be recognized as *equal* States, simply because they are not equal States.' Lorimer 1884, p. 260. From this viewpoint Lorimer derives his infamous tripartite ranking of international society, of (i) civilized, European states which merit full recognition; (ii) barbaric communities that at most warrant a partial recognition of their sovereign status as well as the partial application of international legal rules (this included inter alia Turkey, Japan, and China); and (iii) savage nations, which were not recognized as sovereign entities and as such outside the legal framework in terms of sovereignty and rights/duties.

[65] Conditions of Admission of a State to Membership in the United Nations, Advisory Opinion, ICJ Reports 1948, p. 57.

is a rogue state which possesses weapons of mass destruction?). The invariable quality of sovereign equality of the member states is also expressed in the 1970 Declaration on Principles of International Law.[66] Together with the outlawing of the use of force against the territorial integrity of any state, this translates in another fundamental norm within the UN framework, the principle of nonintervention (Article 2(7) UN Charter).

While the prominence and sacrosanctity of these principles of sovereignty, equality and non-intervention can be understood in light of the (qualified) right to self-determination, how to govern the international society remains a challenging, contested, and evolving issue. In particular since the end of the Cold War, the liberal pluralist premises of the UN framework have been challenged by competing norms in the international order. While most discussions highlight the emergence of cosmopolitan values in this regard, and the shifting balance between human rights and state sovereignty, there is also another more 'conservative' trend, emphasizing more communitarian values as basis for the New World Order. Toward the end of the twentieth century, a new generation of liberal internationalism increasingly emphasized that law, peace, and freedom within international society cannot be established only on the basis of rules of nonintervention and sovereign autonomy combined with the liberal principle of *laissez-faire*. Not all members prove to be reliable fellow-states and good citizens of the international society facilitating the peaceful living-apart-together of sovereign states.[67] Ironically then the alleged victory of liberalism and the emerging New World Order also set the course for a potential shift toward a less inclusionary society, in which equality is not so much a matter of principle, but conditional upon appropriate sovereign behavior.

Particularly relevant for the current discussion is a shift that can be identified within a contemporary liberal internationalism (version 3.0),[68] pertaining to a qualification of membership rules of international society. To put it differently, in this particular vision of international society, which Simpson has characterized as liberal antipluralism,[69] sovereign equality becomes the ground for making distinctions between states on the basis of their performance as members of that society.[70] The Wilsonian progressive vision of international society as a universal, natural, and cooperative coexistence of equal members operating on the basis of

[66] 'All States enjoy sovereign equality. They have equal rights and duties and are equal members of the international community, notwithstanding differences of an economic, social, political or other nature... States are juridically equal ... Each state enjoys the rights inherent in full sovereignty.' Declaration on Principle of International Law Concerning Friendly Relations and Cooperation among States in Accordance with the Charter of the United Nations, GA Resolution 2625 (XXV), October 24, 1970.

[67] For an analysis of states as citizens, see Kustermans 2011b.

[68] Terminology adopted from Ikenberry 2009. Liberal internationalism 2.0 is the version operational during the Cold War and not relevant to the argument pursued here.

[69] Simpson 2004, Chap. 10.

[70] Aalberts and Werner 2008; Aalberts 2012.

self-restraint and reciprocity is replaced by an understanding of a liberal order that needs to be 'built'. Hence liberal internationalism 3.0 assumes that in order to be proper members of the society, states need to be disciplined to exercise their sovereignty rights and freedom in a responsible way. This results in a particular blend of law, peace, and freedom combined with inequality and the use of force to safeguard the liberal order, or 'forging a world of liberty under international law': '[l]iberty requires order, and order, at some level, must be able to harness force'.[71] This reasoning in turn leads to a distinction between good sovereigns, who adhere to the rules of the international society they together constitute, versus bad states, who need to be disciplined to become proper citizens and thus to restore the normal international *order*.[72]

Since the end of the Cold War this discussion mainly revolves around two different types of 'bad' states: failed states on the one hand, and rogue regimes on the other, with the one lacking the ability, and the other lacking the will to play the sovereignty game properly. Whereas the former category facilitated the (commonly accepted) legal justification of the intervention in Afghanistan as a matter of US self-defence,[73] the category of the rogue state played an important and more controversial role in the justification for the Iraq war. As such it also formed the background of the second strand of justification by the Dutch government in its political support for the invasion. Although predating the post 9/11 war on terror, this discourse reached a notorious apogee with George W. Bush's identification of the 'Axis of Evil' as the preamble to the invasion in Iraq.[74] While the Dutch government distanced itself from this pejorative labelling,[75] it does connect to the more general identification of irresponsible regimes, which oppose the international pursuit of a just world order 'freer from the threat of terror, stronger in the pursuit of justice and more secure in the quest for peace'.[76] This sets the rogue states, 'those that not only do not have a part in the international system, but whose very being involves being outside of it and throwing, literally, hand grenades

[71] As formulated by the Princeton Project on U.S. National Security in the 21st Century by The Woodrow Wilson School of Public and International Affairs, Princeton University. Ikenberry and Slaughter 2006, p. 20.

[72] Werner 2004; Kustermans 2011b.

[73] Aalberts and Werner 2008.

[74] In terms of frequency of use, the label rogue states actually belongs to Clinton (who used it to push the ratification of the Chemical Weapons Convention treaty by the US senate) more than to George W. Bush. See Hoyt 2000; O'Reilly 2007.

[75] See Letter of the MoFA (then Minister van Aartsen), 19 March 2002, *Kamerstukken II,* 27925/52. See also Verslag van een Algemeen Overleg d.d. 7 Februari 2002, *Kamerstukken II,* 21501/02; *Handelingen II,* 2001/2002, Aanhangsel nr. 868.

[76] These terms were used by George Bush senior to introduce the notion of the New World Order in his address to the Congress on September 11, 1990. Address Before a Joint Session of the Congress on the Persian Gulf Crisis and the Federal Budget Deficit, available at http://en.wikisource.org/w/index.php?title=Toward_a_New_World_Order).

inside in order to destroy',[77] apart from the decent members of international society, who adhere to and protect its shared norms and values on the basis of their common interest in peace and justice.[78]

The popularity of the rogue statehood terminology originates with the US Ministry of Defence, which focuses on the real threat to (inter)national security of the potential possession of weapons of mass destruction by such regimes, who have a history and reputation of aggressive behavior and/or (financial) support to terrorist organizations.[79] The term soon was adopted in the broader political discourse, which also entailed a broadening of its meaning to combine (i) material security threats with a reference to (ii) illiberal regimes who enslave their citizens and who in particular (iii) refuse to meet their international obligations, reject international law, and break their promises.[80] In the discourse these elements are often lumped together, leading to indiscriminatory use of recalcitrant, outlaw, or illiberal statehood.[81] Yet, two alternative versions of liberal antipluralism can be distinguished: a more substantive one, focusing on democratic governance as the basis for international order, peace, and security; and a more moderate version that focuses on procedural justice and the criminalization of persistent violators of international law.[82] Both versions of anti-pluralism imply a distinction between good citizens of the international society and its outcasts, and call for qualifying the norm of equality on the basis of sovereign performance, as well as legitimizing more far reaching (forceful) interventions to forge the rule of law and restore the normalcy of the international legal order.[83] Key in this line of argumentation is that rogue regimes owe the forfeiting of their sovereignty rights to their own recalcitrant behavior—operating at the fringes of international society as alleged

---

[77] Madeleine Albright, 'Remarks at University of South Carolina', 19 February 1998, available at http://secretary.state.gov/www/statements/1998/980219c.html.

[78] Rawls uses the term 'decent states' to identify (internally) illiberal states, who nevertheless respect the operational rules of the sovereignty game (such as diplomatic norms and *pacta sunt servanda)* in their external relations with fellow-states, thus respecting the procedural justice of the international legal order. In his scheme Iraq would qualify as an outlaw state, being both illiberal domestically and aggressive on the international plane. Rawls 1999.

[79] Klare 1995; O'Reilly 2007; Kustermans 2011a.

[80] *Cf.* O'Reilly 2007, pp. 307–308.

[81] Simpson 2004, p. 281. The post 9/11 securitization discourse also often includes failed states within the same category as rogue regimes, while they allegedly are each other's negatives in terms of effective sovereignty, as the former UK Foreign Secretary, Jack Straw, proclaims: '[f]rom one perspective, totalitarian regimes and failed or failing states are opposite ends of the spectrum. But [in the doctrine of the international community] there are similarities: one is unable to avoid subverting international law; the other is only too willing to flout it. Jack Straw, 'Principles of a Modern Global Community', 10 April 2002, quoted by Aalberts and Werner 2008, p. 143.

[82] Simpson 2004, pp. 279–282.

[83] Within academic discourse this debate is propagated by inter alia Rawls 1999; Slaughter 1995; Téson 1992; Walzer 1977. For a discussion of their different versions of liberal antipluralism see e.g. Simpson 2004; Janse 2006.

criminal states, they outlaw themselves: '[t]he breaches of international law committed by these states contribute to outlaw status and this outlaw status determines the legality of measures taken against these states (combined with a concomitant loss of immunities)'.[84] The age of weapons of mass destruction adds an urgent call and imminent threat to this discussion, in particular since the 9/11 attacks. Indeed, in this context President George W. Bush developed his notorious doctrine which combined both versions of liberal antipluralism and consisted of four components: unilateralism; attacking countries that harbor terrorists; pre-emptive (read preventive) strikes; and democratic regime change.[85] In effect, it entails the criminalization of countries that belong to the 'axis of evil'.

This discussion on the criminalization of states is not just a form of hegemonic foreign policy or academic philosophizing, but has entered both international legal discourse and international practice. In this context Simpson discusses the International Law Commission's work on State Responsibility, and its attempts to define and incorporate the idea of state crime in the 1996 Draft Articles.[86] Whereas the 2001 Articles on State Responsibility have deleted the category of crime, it does invoke state responsibility in case of 'gross and systematic failure' of peremptory norms of international law obligations (article 40 Articles on State Responsibility).[87] While refraining from developing a full scale criminal regime, the 2001 Articles do identify 'special consequences' for such violations other than ordinary breaches of international law. Moreover, the Articles allow states not directly affected (i.e., non-injured states) to invoke the responsibility of a state who is in serious breach of its international obligations (Article 48(1)b Articles on State Responsibility) and to 'take lawful measures ... to ensure cessation of the breach'

---

[84] Simpson 2004, p. 340; Saunders 2006. See also point 6 of the commentary of the International Law Commission to the now superseded Article 52 of the 1996 Draft Articles on State Responsibility, available at www.lcil.cam.ac.uk/Media/ILCSR/rft/Sr52.rtf.

[85] US National Security Strategy 2002, published 20 September 2002, available at http://georgewbush-whitehouse.archives.gov/nsc/nss/2002/index.html. See also Davids Committee 2010, p. 155. For a controversial legal justification of the Iraq war on the basis of anticipatory self-defense see Yoo 2003.

[86] 1996 Draft Articles on State Responsibility (provisionally adopted by the Commission on the first reading), available at www.lcil.cam.ac.uk/projects/state_responsibility_document_collection.php. In the displaced Article 19(2) it defined crime as a bread of an international obligation 'so essential for the protection of fundamental interests of the international community that its breach is recognized as a crime'. Draft Article 52 read that the commission of such a crime would deprive the outlaw state of some aspects of its sovereign equality—although the ILC explicitly excluded forfeiting the right to territorial integrity, by forbidding the use of force as a way to restore normalcy.

[87] ILC Articles on Responsibility of States for Internationally Wrongful Acts (2001). The category of peremptory norms (*ius cogens*) is itself underdetermined within international law. Described as 'a norm accepted and recognized by the international community of States as a whole as a norm from which no derogation is permitted' in the 1969 Vienna Convention on the Law of Treaties (Article 53), so far an exclusive list of *ius cogens* is lacking. Usually the prohibition on use of force, genocide, and slavery are mentioned as examples.

(Article 54 Articles on State Responsibility).[88] In terms of international practices of criminalization via stigmatization, repression, sanctioning, and surveillance, Simpson identifies three 'great international law projects of criminalisation'.[89] All cases concern criminalization after aggressive wars: Versailles, Nuremberg, and the sanctions imposed on Iraq under UNSC 687 after its invasion in Kuwait. The Iraqi case not only includes the economic sanctions regime, but also far-reaching measures of policing and surveillance which stood at odds with the principle of territorial integrity. In the latter case the Security Council hence has operated beyond its mandate as an institution of constraint, and more as an institution of criminal repression, adopting quasi-judicial practices and assigning fault and responsibility. Overall it can be concluded that while the idea of state crime remains controversial and the category of the outlaw or rogue state has no legal significance to date,[90] as a discourse it proliferates in policy, academic, and legal circles alike. This forms the background of the second justification strand by the Dutch government.

6.3.2 Legitimacy Through Synergy

While refraining from explicit pejorative labeling and stigmatization, the Dutch government did characterize the Iraqi regime according to the aforementioned rogue characteristics, by repeatedly describing it as an aggressive and brutal dictatorship, which not only possesses weapons of mass destruction, but also had proved to use them against both its neighbors and its citizens, causing over a million deaths.[91] As formulated by the then MoFA, van Aartsen, in his response to the identification of the 'Axis of Evil' by George W. Bush in the 2002 State of the Union: '[h]is vocabulary was probably not ours but we can support the vision that these words represent'.[92] However, time and again the government took explicit distance from 'regime change' as a goal of any international action because it does not fall under the authority of the Security Council, and hence could not be legitimized by any resolution whatsoever. It could only be a (positive) unintended consequence of potential military action.[93] Instead, the Dutch government took a 'moderate antipluralist' stance by pinpointing the third characteristic of rogue

---

88 The right for countermeasures by both the injured State and States not directly injured is carefully demarcated and for instance does not suspend the prohibition on the use of force (Articles 50–52). See also Crawford 1999, Crawford et al. 2000.

89 Simpson 2004, pp. 291–293.

90 Arend 2002.

91 Letter of the MoFA, 25 September 2002, *Kamerstukken II,* 28618/5, *Handelingen II,* 30 January 2003, 38/2821–2849, *Handelingen II,* 12 February 2003 (43/2992–3038), *Handelingen II,* 18 March 2003, 50/3275–3327.

92 See Letter of the MoFA, 19 March 2002, *Kamerstukken II,* 27925/52.

93 *Handelingen II,* 25 September 2002, 5/284–307. See also Letter of the MoFA, 4 September 2002, *Kamerstukken II,* 23432/56.

statehood, i.e., the refusal to play the sovereignty game according to the rules of the international society, in its justification for the invasion in Iraq.[94] Thus, it highlighted Iraq's pattern of non-compliance over more than a decade, although the number of violated resolutions varies in the different accounts.[95] This persistent non- (or at least very late and minimal) compliance with the series of binding resolutions issued by the Security Council since the beginning of the 1990s proved that Saddam Hussein did not take the international community, and the Security Council in particular, seriously, and rendered him an unreliable partner, as the MoFA concluded in his letter on the eve of the invasion. He also called the Parliament's attention to the fact that '[t]he judgement of the way in which Iraq meets its obligation to disarm should take into consideration that we are dealing with a regime which has managed to shirk Security Council resolutions. Saddam Hussein is a recidivist whose behaviour has been totally consistent over the course of years. It is clear that, without serious military pressure, resolutions of the Security Council do not impress him at all.'[96]

Together, this raised an 'incredibly difficult dilemma' and 'highly moral-ethical question' for both the Dutch government and the international community at large, as the MoFA formulated in his deliberations to the Parliament, namely how to handle 'this type of states': '[w]hat do you do as a world community with dictators who posses weapons of mass destruction and who ultimately do not listen to that world community?'.[97] It is this combined characteristic of cruelty, aggression, and violation which led the international community to the adoption of UN Resolution 1441.[98] Acknowledging the importance of the UN track, the Dutch government emphasized that the Resolution puts the fate of Iraq in Saddam Hussein's own hands: not only does he get a 'final opportunity', but the burden of proof (regarding the disarmament) is also his call.[99] Emphasizing the paramount importance of procedural justice that too was interpreted as being on Saddam's table—it is he who has to abide by the international rules and fulfill his international obligations in the first place: '[t]he Dutch government stands behind the United Nations' track. Resolution 1441 must be taken seriously. Saddam Hussein must at last adhere to the will of the

[94] Neither did the government play the humanitarian card. When the humanitarian issue was discussed it was in terms of the possible consequences of an invasion, rather than as a justification or rationale for the intervention itself. See, for instance, Letter of the MoFA, 10 February 2003, *Kamerstukken II,* 23432/76.

[95] *Cf. Handelingen II,* 5 September 2002, 95/5648–5671; Verslag van Algemeen Overleg d.d. 19 November 2002, *Kamerstukken II,* 23432/66; *Handelingen II*, 30 January 2003, 38/2821–2849; *Handelingen II*, 12 February 2003, 43/2992–3038; *Handelingen II*, 19 February 2003, 46/3085–3120; *Handelingen II*, 18 March 2003, 50/3275–3327.

[96] Letter of the MoFA, 18 March 2003, *Kamerstukken II,* 23432/94.

[97] *Handelingen II*, 30 January 2003, 38/2821–2849, p. 2837; *Handelingen II*, 12 February 2003, 43/2992–3038, pp. 3013, 3027.

[98] *Handelingen II*, 30 January 2003, 38/2821–2849, p. 2833.

[99] This was explicated by MoFA de Hoop Scheffer through the metaphor that the weapon inspectors should not need to use a torch light looking inside bunkers and shelves; Saddam should turn on the light. Handelingen II, 12 February 2003, 43/2992–3038.

international community'.[100] In this context, Prime Minister (PM) Balkenende also objected to the general framing of the debate:

> [i]nternational public opinion is currently often focused on the question: war or peace? I have said that this really should not be fore grounded in first instance, because the main issue is the question whether Iraq can be impelled to comply at last with what Resolution 1441 demands Iraq to do. This is what the international community has to deal with.[101]

In other words, the use of force paradigm (i.e., its prohibition safe the exceptional cases of self-defense or Security Council authorization) is the wrong framework to deal with this issue. It focuses on the possible consequences as opposed to the cause of the problem; rather than a question of war or peace the main issue is whether international obligations were met. Moreover, the main focus should not be on the international community's compliance with international law in reaction to Iraq's non-compliance, but on Iraq's persistent violation of international obligations as the instigator of the whole situation. By framing it as a matter of war or peace the discussion basically addressed the wrong subjects of procedural justice: it is not the international community who is violating its own norms, but Iraq who refuses to respect the operational rules of the international society. Hence, it is the difference between Iraq's compliance and non-compliance which determines the difference between peace and war, not the procedures followed by the international community: '[t]his is why I have also said in the company of Kofi Annan that the discussion is now often focused on the [wrong] question: war or no war? It should rather be: Iraq has to comply with… If that condition is fulfilled, the other discussion is off the table'.[102] Once it became clear that Saddam Hussein was not fully complying with the terms of Resolution 1441, PM Balkenende declared that its continued failure to live up to these international obligations meant that Iraq had kindled the possibility of 'serious consequences' against itself—he was not a victim but its instigator.[103] In other words, Iraq had outlawed itself, forfeiting its rights as a sovereign member of the international society, and military action became unavoidable now that Saddam Hussein failed to cooperate.

---

[100] PM Balkenende, *Handelingen II*, 12 February 2003, 43/2992–3038, p. 3027.

[101] PM Balkenende, *Handelingen II*, 19 February 2003, 46/3085–3120, p. 3102. In yet another instance, the PM linked this to the other characteristics of the Iraqi rogue regime: '[m]y objection to the discussion is often that it is war or peace. The quintessence, however, is the disarmament of an aggressor who possesses weapons of mass destruction and in any case does not answer the questions that the international community poses. We are dealing with a regime that is responsible for hundred thousands deaths. That is the reality too and that is what we are discussing.' *Handelingen II*, 18 March 2003, 50/3275–3327, p. 3326.

[102] PM Balkenende, *Handelingen II*, 19 February 2003 46/3085–3120, p. 3119. PM Balkenende: '[i]t is a brutal regime. If Iraq fulfils its obligations [under Resolution 1441 and its predecessors] there will not be any military action. This is in fact the signal.' *Handelingen II*, 19 February 2003, 46/3085–3120, p. 3103.

[103] PM Balkenende, *Handelingen II*, 18 March 2003, 50/3275–3327, p. 3275. See also the statements of US Secretary of State Powell before the Security Council, referred to by the MoFA de Hoop Scheffer in his letter of 10 February 2003, *Kamerstukken II*, 23432/76.

Moreover, taking military action became unavoidable for the international community too, because not only Saddam Hussein but also the Security Council has to take its own resolutions seriously. Procedural justice of the UN track in this perspective hence means that Resolution 1441 had to be executed to its ultimate consequences by both Saddam Hussein *and* the international community alike. As reiterated by PM Balkenende: 'I have explained the importance of the UN track and of a credible compliance with the resolutions by Iraq. Until now, these have not been taken seriously at all. No military action is needed if Iraq is fulfilling its obligations.'[104] In the original text, the PM used the impersonal Dutch pronoun '*men*' ('people') in the second sentence as the subject who was not taking the resolutions seriously.[105] Whereas this most probably referred to the Iraqi government, in a broader context it could also refer to the Security Council itself, which was not taking its own resolutions serious enough in this view. This view was put in so many words in a letter by the MoFA de Hoop Scheffer on the eve of the military intervention, in which the government summarized the position it adopted since the beginning of the whole debate, emphasizing inter alia that acting against the possession of weapons of mass destruction is primarily a responsibility of the UN collectively, in casu the Security Council; that the Security Council had obligated Iraq to disarm itself already in 1991 and had issued numerous resolutions since to compel Iraq to comply with its international obligations; and that 'the Security Council itself is now also held to take its own resolutions seriously, in particular the unanimously accepted Resolution 1441'.[106] Its failure to do so formed the basis of a third strand of justification, as will be discussed in the next section.

The characterization of the Iraqi regime and the emphasis on its persistent non-compliance with the numerous resolutions of the Security Council can be classified as justification by synergy. It combines arguments based on the Charter framework—notably the binding character of Security Council resolutions—with extra-Charter values. The Davids Committee also mentions this second argument on the basis of the (further) material breach by Iraq of its obligations to disarm and fully cooperate with the inspectors. In a short discussion it confirms that this material breach had indeed been established by the Security Council from Resolution 707 (15 August 1991) onwards up until Resolution 1441. However, the Committee continues, pursuant to the Vienna Convention on the Law of Treaties only contracting parties have the right to take countermeasures in case of non-compliance. In this case it was the Security Council that could do so, and there was no legal ground for unilateral enforcement. Moreover, on the basis of Article 25 and Chapter VII of the UN Charter, the Security Council has exclusive discretion to determine whether Iraq's conduct qualified as 'further material breach' under Resolution 1441.[107]

---

104 *Handelingen II*, 19 February 2003, 46/3085–3120, p. 3104.

105 'Ik heb gezegd wat het belang is van het spoor van de Verenigde Naties en van een geloofwaardige naleving van de resoluties door Iraq. Men heeft daar tot nu toe steeds een loopje mee genomen.' *Handelingen II*, 19 February 2003, 46/3085–3120, p. 3104.

106 Letter of the MoFA, 18 March 2003, Kamerstukken II, 23432/94.

107 Article 60, Vienna Treaty on the Law of Treaties 1969; Davids Committee 2010, pp. 272–273.

Hence this argument did not provide sufficient legal ground to justify the support of the invasion. However, as aforementioned, this line of argumentation pursued by the Dutch government was not a legal one *pur sang*. It hooks up to the discussion on rogue states and their position within the international community, whose rules they disrespect. The issue of state roguery, and Iraq's qualification as such, is only mentioned in the margins of the Davids Report and instantly dismissed as expressions of sentiment.[108] I would argue, however, that rather than an emotional charge, the frequent references to Iraq as a rogue state by the Dutch government should be understood against the backdrop of a normative discourse on the New World Order in the twenty-first century that calls for a qualification of the principle of sovereignty, making it conditional upon appropriate sovereign conduct. While a widespread discourse in diplomatic, legal, and academic circles, so far this is not embedded in the UN framework. This second line of argumentation put forward by the Dutch government hence can be identified as an example of justification by synergy. As such it relied on extra-Charter values and linked Iraq's persistent non-compliance with the corpus of Security Council resolutions to the normative discourse on the criminalization of states. In this context the Dutch government identified one of the moral-ethical dilemmas that face the international community in the twenty-first century: how to deal with (rogue) regimes, which not only possess weapons of mass destruction and thus threaten international peace and security, but also persistently ignore and disrespect their international obligations, and as such pose a threat to the authority of the Security Council and the international legal order at large? Moreover, in light of the Security Council's exclusive authority to determine the further material breach and define its consequences, the Dutch government developed a third line of argumentation, by emphasizing the Council's failure to live up to its responsibilities to uphold the international legal order.

6.4 Claiming Legitimacy (2): The Dutch Vision on International Community

6.4.1 Politics, Credibility, and Responsibility of the Security Council

Within the international society as defined by the UN framework, the Security Council is the highest authority of the international community, and the only actor authorized to deal with the enforcement of international peace and security.[109]

---

108 Davids Committee 2010, p. 116.

109 In this context 'international society' is the normative and institutional context or forum within which states operate (see also the definition *supra*, note 63); 'international community' refers to the (collective) agency.

This was also emphasized time and again by the Dutch government in its deliberations with the parliament, singling the Security Council out as the appropriate body to deal with the issue of Iraq's disarmament. As discussed above, in basically all its correspondence and communication the importance of the UN track, with the legal procedure of Security Council authorization under Chapter VII, was highlighted. However, apart from identifying the corpus theory as being within the legal confines of the Chapter VII procedure, from the very beginning the MoFA also considered another characteristic of the Council, namely that it is permeated with political considerations.[110] Far from a court of independent judges, it is at the bottom-line a political body, 'doing politics and making political choices'.[111] In other words, the legally correct procedures (of obtaining a Security Council authorization for forceful interventions under Article 39 and 42 UN Charter) sometimes are blocked by politics within the authority itself. This issue of the politics of the Security Council was also put forward in the discussion on the interpretation of Resolution 1441, and in particular the usage and meaning of 'serious consequences' in the resolution text. That formulation was ultimately a political compromise in order to avoid a French veto of the resolution, as was discussed above. And when it became clear that there would be no agreement on the second resolution, PM Balkenende addressed the politics of the Security Council again: '[o]ne has to keep an eye on the position of different states in the Security Council and on the way in which power politics works. Ultimately the question has to be answered: did Saddam meet his international obligations, and if not, does it have serious consequences?'[112]

There were two elements to the argument. One is that Saddam Hussein should not benefit from the inability of the Security Council to come to a decision, and continue to get away with his persistent breach of international obligations. With an indirect reference to the criminalization discourse, the government maintained that 'the incapacity of the Security Council cannot result in the impunity of Saddam Hussein'.[113] This would not only make him the 'laughing outsider',[114] but it also 'gives a wrong message to other countries that would like to undermine the international legal order'—thus linking the Iraqi case to the general problem of state roguery within contemporary international society.[115] Ultimately, the threat

[110] Letter of the MoFA, 25 September 2002, *Kamerstukken II*, 28618/5; *Handelingen II*, 5 September 2002, 95/5648–5671; *Handelingen II*, 25 September 2002, 5/284–307.

[111] *Handelingen II*, 30 January 2003, 38/2821–2849, p. 2835; Verslag van Algemeen Overleg d.d. 18 December 2002, *Kamerstukken II*, 23432/74. This argument is mentioned by the Davids Committee as part of an advice of the deputy Director General Political Affairs to the MoFA, but is not further analyzed as part of the justification for the political support for the war. Davids Committee 2010, p. 247.

[112] *Handelingen II*, 18 March 2003, 50/3275–3327, p. 3302.

[113] *Handelingen II*, 18 March 2003, 50/3275–3327, p. 3308 (emphasis added). See also Letter of the MoFA, 18 March 2003, *Kamerstukken II*, 23432/94.

[114] *Handelingen II*, 18 March 2003, 50/3275–3327, pp. 3275, 3276, 3299 and 3306.

[115] Letter of the MoFA, 18 March 2003, *Kamerstukken II*, 23432/94.

of Iraq was not only to international peace and security, but also to the international legal order and credibility of the Security Council in the face of such states that do not behave as good citizens of the international society.[116] Moreover, the Council's credibility had already suffered a significant blow after more than a decade of inaction for lack of political bone in the face of non-compliance of Iraq to its resolutions.[117] This history of inaction also related to the second element of the argument, namely the duty of the Security Council to take its own resolutions seriously and push them to their ultimate consequences. As the primary authority to take further decisions following the conditions formulated in Resolution 1441, the Security Council not only enjoys this privilege but should also take its responsibilities on the basis of the 'serious consequences'. Just as Saddam Hussein should take Resolution 1441 seriously, so should the Security Council, as the MoFA again emphasized on the eve of the invasion.[118]

Stating its disappointment in the failure of the Security Council to live up to its responsibility and come to a new collective declaration, this translated into a charge on the Council for making Hussein's malbehavior possible in the first place through the inability to come to a consensus, as was suggested by PM Balkenende.[119] Whereas the PM in this context referred to Saddam's conduct of the past few months in particular,[120] this allegation by extension held for his persistent non-compliance with and disrespect for the international community during the whole decade. This was put in so many words by MoFA de Hoop Scheffer later on in the debate: '[i]f the regime of Mr. Saddam Hussein would have been tackled root and branch 13 years ago, we would not be having this discussion'.[121] Moreover, this responsibility of the Security Council also reaches beyond this particular case to warranting the future of multilateral cooperation at large.[122] In this context the government had previously referred to Secretary General Kofi Annan's and President Bush's statements at the 57th plenary session of the General Assembly (12 September 2002).[123] Both had called upon the Security Council to live up to its responsibilities in case Iraq's defiance of mandatory resolutions would continue. This was reiterated at the Security Council meeting of

---

[116] Verslag van Algemeen Overleg d.d. 3 December 2002, *Kamerstukken II,* 23432/68; *Handelingen II*, 18 March 2003, 50/3275–3327.

[117] Verslag van Algemeen Overleg d.d. 19 November 2002, *Kamerstukken II,* 23432/66; *Handelingen II*, 19 February 2003, 46/3085–3120.

[118] Verslag van Algemeen Overleg d.d. 3 December 2002, *Kamerstukken II,* 23432/68; Letter of the MoFA, 18 February 2003, *Kamerstukken II,* 23432/85; *Handelingen II*, 19 February 2003, 46/3085–3120; Letter of the MoFA, 18 March 2003, *Kamerstukken* II, 23432/94.

[119] *Handelingen II*, 18 March 2003, 50/3275–3327, pp. 3275, 3275, 3299, 3300, 3306 and 3308.

[120] *Handelingen II*, 18 March 2003, 50/3275–3327, p. 3300.

[121] *Handelingen II*, 18 March 2003, 50/3275–3327, p. 3311.

[122] Letter of the MoFA, 18 February 2003, *Kamerstukken II,* 23432/85.

[123] Letter of the MoFA, 30 September 2002, *Kamerstukken II,* 23432/61, appendix; Letter of the MoFA, 18 March 2003, *Kamerstukken II,* 23432/94, appendix; Meeting records GA 57th plenary session, A/57/PV.2, available at www.un.org/ga/57/pv.html.

8 November 2002, at which Resolution 1441 was adopted.[124] Kofi Annan in this context linked Security Council's authority directly to its political will to act. Emphasizing the importance of multilateralism and rule of law, he also identified the maintenance of international order to be not only in every state's interest, but also everyone's responsibility. Bush identified the conduct of the Iraqi regime as a test for the international community, and the UN in particular—whether the Security Council would face its responsibility or be irrelevant: '[w]e will work with the Security Council for the necessary resolutions. But the purposes of the United States should not be doubted. The Security Council resolutions will be enforced, and the just demands of peace and security will be met, or action will be unavoidable, and a regime that has lost its legitimacy will also lose its power'.[125] As Berman notes, 'regime' in the latter sentence could refer to both the Iraqi government and the Security Council in the face of its failure to 'serve the purposes of its founding'. In this context the US president not only predicted that the UN would share an untimely grave with its predecessor, but indirectly even threatened to secure its imminent demise.[126]

Even before it was clear that it would be impossible to reach consensus on the second resolution, the Dutch government anticipated the situation by stating that the international community (at large) could not remain a bystander with its hand (legally) tied by lack of a new resolution by its supreme authority.[127] This argument was followed up after the draft second resolution was indeed withdrawn by the United States on the eve of the invasion, as a third justificatory argument to support the war in Iraq. It can be identified as a bid for legitimacy through defying the Security Council.

6.4.2 Legitimacy Through Defiance

Paradoxically, it is precisely the acknowledgment of the Security Council as the right authority to decide upon the Iraq issue that included the seeds for seeking legitimacy through defying the very Council. There were two elements to this justification—first, as identified above, having the formal authority means also having the obligation to execute that authority according to the demands of

[124] Meeting records S/PV4644, 8 November 2002; Verslag van Algemeen Overleg d.d. 3 December 2002, *Kamerstukken II,* 23432/68.

[125] Meeting Records GA 57th SESSION A/57/PV.2, 12 September 2002, p. 9. See also Davids Committee 2010, p. 239. At the Security Council meeting of the adoption of Resolution 1441, Kofi Annan adopted similar phrasing by identifying a time of trial for both Iraq, the United Nations and the international community. Meeting Records, SC session 4644, S/PV4644, 8 November 2002, p. 2.

[126] Meeting Records GA 57th SESSION A/57/PV.2, 12 September 2002, p. 8; Berman 2005, p. 110.

[127] Verslag van een Algemeen Overleg d.d. 1 October 2002, *Kamerstukken II*, 23432/61.

international peace and security. This implication was emphasized by PM Balkenende in his statement that

> [t]he primary responsibility for the further decision-making lies with the Security Council … The Security Council has already tried for twelve years to force Iraq to answer [the questions of the weapon inspectors]. This raises the stakes of the credibility of the Security Council, as Kofi Annan also indicated [in his statement before the European Council on 17 February 2003]: [i]f Iraq is not complying, the Security Council will have to take a difficult decision. In that case there is only one option: the Council has to take its responsibility, no matter how painful it is.[128]

Hence, the Security Council is not only the principal authority but also bears the primary responsibility.[129] Secondly, the identification of the primary responsibility also implies, according to the Dutch government, that in second instance (i.e., when the Council fails to live up to it) this responsibility—and hence the authority to take action—can move elsewhere.[130] In other words, rather than violating the procedural norms of the international society, the United States and United Kingdom were taking up the gauntlet dropped by the Security Council by bringing the 'serious consequences' of Resolution 1441 to bear. They were willing to take their responsibility as members of the international community, where the member states of the Security Council failed to do so.[131] In his letter of 18 March 2003, the MoFA even pushed this further by claiming that, as all Security Council member states bear responsibility for the lack of consensus about the second resolution, they also all share in the responsibility for the unilateral action.[132]

Asserting that the politics in the Security Council could not and should not mean that the international community cannot take action, and letting Saddam get away with his continuous material breach of international obligations by escaping the 'serious consequences'; and that all other diplomatic measures and peaceful remedies, including Resolution 1441, had been exhausted, the Dutch government maintained that it had to consider its own role and responsibility, as a good member of the international community so to speak: '[t]he question that The Netherlands has to answer again [as in 1998] is, simply, not whether military

---

[128] *Handelingen II*, 19 February 2003, 46/3085–3120, p. 3101—note that the PM was not taking the distinction between 'consider' and 'decide' into consideration here.

[129] This is indeed how the functions and power of the Council are formulated in the UN Charter. Article 24(1) UN Charter reads: '[i]n order to ensure prompt and effective action by the United Nations, its Members confer on the Security Council primary responsibility for the maintenance of international peace and security, and agree that in carrying out its duties under this responsibility the Security Council acts on their behalf.'

[130] This conclusion was not drawn by Kofi Annan, who rather explicitly stated as late as 10 March 2003 at a press conference in The Hague that '[i]f the US and others were to go outside the Council and take military action it would not be in conformity with the Charter.' Available at www.un.org/apps/sg/offthecuff.asp?nid=394. See also Davids Committee 2010, p. 248.

[131] *Handelingen II*, 18 March 2003, 50/3275–3327, p. 3307.

[132] Letter of the MoFA, 18 March 2003, *Kamerstukken II,* 23432/94.

intervention is allowed, but if it is required'.[133] Like the US and the UK, the Dutch government maintained that the international community could not remain idle and had to defy the UN Security Council for the sake of international peace and security. In the face of the inaction of the Security Council, enforcement became a responsibility of all individual members of the international community:

> [a]t a certain moment [the UN track of resolutions and new deadlines] is finished. That is the reality. When [the Gordian] knot has to be cut because clarity is required, then you have to ask yourself what you do with the "serious consequences". That is not simplicity, but the consequence of the discussion and decision-making and of the question whether the UN takes itself seriously. A United Nations that has been busy for twelve years to make Saddam move and that is dealing with 1441 for months now without any concrete results, is loosing its credibility. That is the major issue. At a certain point you have to say: and this is it.[134]

This understanding of shifting responsibilities also transpires clearly from PM Balkenende's statement to the Davids Committee: '[w]hen it comes to enforcement of 1441, we stepped up to our responsibilities'.[135] While thus politically supporting the US/UK initiative, the Dutch line of argumentation differed in at least two accounts from the US standpoint. While Bush was issuing threats to the survival of the UN itself, juxtaposing the demands of international order to the niceties of international law, the Dutch government postulated the need to use force in order to *save* the international legal order: '[l]aw once in a while needs force to be law(ful)' ... [A]t the bottom line, [it is] about securing the international legal order'.[136] Moreover, contrary to the Bush doctrine as a typical illustration of a neoconservative mix of offensive Realpolitik combined with a democratic peace logic, the Dutch government was arguing for the survival of the international (legal) order rather than its own self-preservation and national interest narrowly defined. As such, its position was more akin to Blair's doctrine of the international community (DIC).[137] Launched at the end of the 1990s, the DIC propagated a 'Third Way' in international politics—combining the strengthening of international rules and norms via an ethical foreign policy, with the explicit option that it sometimes requires the use of force to uphold them—multilaterally when possible, unilaterally if need be. Parallel to the discourse on state roguery and equally linked to the notion of the New World Order, the DIC was based on a conception of good international citizenship—this not only means that all members should abide by the rules, but also maintains that being a member of the international society at

---

[133] Verslag van een Algemeen Overleg d.d. 1 October 2002, *Kamerstukken II*, 23432/61; Letter of the MoFA, 18 March 2003, *Kamerstukken II*, 23432/94; *Handelingen II*, 19 February 2003, 46/3085–3120; *Handelingen II*, 18 March 2003, 50/3275–3327.

[134] *Handelingen II*, 18 March 2003, 50/3275–3327, p. 3303.

[135] Mail regarding telephone call between Bush and MP Balkenende, 28 February 2003, quoted in Davids Committee 2010, p. 101.

[136] Verslag van Algemeen Overleg d.d. 3 December 2002, *Kamerstukken II*, 23432/68.

[137] Wheeler and Dunne 1998.

once entails moral responsibilities to promote international order and justice against deviant states.

In light of these substantial different visions on the international order and how its particular vision informs the justifications put forward by the Dutch government, it is a shame that this British perspective, or Blair's doctrine as the DIC is popularly referred to, is not more explicitly distinguished from the Bush doctrine in the Davids Report. The Committee mainly focuses on the Atlantic reflex, and only mentions in passing that, given their shared stronger preferences for a multilateral track, the Dutch government's position was closer to Blair than to Bush.[138] It should be clear that given its status as a policy guideline, the DIC does not have any impact on the legality question of the invasion which the Davids Committee was assigned to answer. However, engaging with these discourses would have enabled the Committee to explore the nexus between legality and legitimacy which shapes any justification of international action, and which is informed by different conceptions of international society and how to safeguard the international legal order. Moreover, it enables a move beyond the law versus politics debate as it is traditionally casted in terms of interests (Logic of Consequences) versus norms (Logic of Appropriateness).[139]

The dichotomy between politics/interests versus law/norms most explicitly comes to the fore in the notorious dissenting opinion of committee member van Walsum. While he endorses the conclusion of the Davids Committee that the *corpus theory* fails as solid legal ground for the support of the Iraq war, in his personal note van Walsum nevertheless refrains from concluding that hence the Dutch government was wrong in its political support for the invasion. In a remarkable mix of normative and empirical reasoning, he claims that

> a responsible government should allow itself to be led not only by the rules of international law but also by the demands of international politics. If the two considerations conflict, the government is faced with a dilemma but no government will accept that its vital political objectives should defer to international law under all circumstances.[140]

In other words, reviving the classical distinction between Realism and Idealism, van Walsum defines a responsible government as one that prioritizes its national interests, and violates international law if (inter)national politics requires it to do so. Hence, politics/interests ultimately trump law/values, and so it should be. This argument was never put on the table by the Dutch government, to the surprise of the Davids Committee. In his discussion of the Davids Report, Nollkaemper notes that this is not so surprising given the overall Dutch (and European) tradition to speak the language of law rather than hard politics. Nevertheless, he suggests that van Walsum's mitigating opinion might indeed be closer to the reality of Dutch

---

[138] Davids Committee 2010, p. 211.

[139] March and Olsen 1998. They use these terms to distinguish between policy-making on the basis of rational cost-benefit analysis and material interests and policy-making that incorporates shared values, norms, and ideas as an incentive.

[140] Davids Committee 2010, p. 270; translation in NILR 2010, p. 133 (emphasis added).

decision-making with regard to the Iraq invasion than the Committee concludes.[141] In this regard the Committee concludes that the question of legality was 'subsidiary' in the policy principles laid down by the MoFA in August 2002.[142] Moreover, it identifies Atlantic solidarity and policy continuity as the leading motives. However, the Committee found no evidence of commercial interests as a strategic incentive to express political support for the invasion.[143] What the real drivers for the Dutch support were is beyond the scope of this article. However, in light of the current analysis of its justifying arguments, it is less surprising that the Dutch government did not call upon its vital political objectives. Drawing on a particular discourse on the international order in the twenty-first century, the Dutch government postulated a different reading of what responsible government in the international society entails. At least in its justification for the support of the Iraq invasion it wore a different cloak of responsible statehood, which was not informed by Realist premises on state survival but by what it means to be a good citizen in the international society. And this not only made Iraq an outcast which had to be acted against, but also called upon the other members of the society to take their responsibility in safeguarding law, peace, and freedom in the contemporary international order—multilateral if possible, but unilateral if necessary.[144]

Although it was never casted in those terms by the Dutch government, what seems to transpire from the interaction of the corpus theory with the alternative strands of legitimacy is not so much the traditional divide between hard or soft politics, but a tension within a Logic of Appropriateness, namely between *lex lata* and *lex feranda.* At face value this resembles the justification scheme of the intervention in Kosovo, and its famous formula that the unilateral intervention had been 'illegal but legitimate'. However, throughout the run-up to the Iraq war, i.e., from August 2002 to March 2003, the Dutch government stuck to the legally untenable corpus theory to support its claim that unilateral enforcement in the case of Iraq would indeed be in accordance with international law.[145] This was not only untenable as the Security Council had clearly not approved it with the seal of legality; but it also resulted in an inconsistent body of arguments put forward by

---

[141] Nollkaemper 2010, pp. 149–150.

[142] Davids Committee 2010, conclusion no. 8.

[143] Davids Committee 2010, conclusions nos. 14 and 15.

[144] At the same time, it did not go so far as to provide military support; yet as this analysis has shown the unilateral enforcement by the US and the UK (as great powers with great responsibilities) was justified in these terms.

[145] Also after the publication of the Davids Report it did not explicitly take distance from it. At least two other distinctions with the Kosovo war are of relevance. First, the Kosovo intervention was casted in terms of cosmopolitan ethics against the background of the developing international practice of humanitarian intervention, whereas in the Iraqi case the Dutch government rather pinpointed more conservative communitarian values as the basis of the international society of sovereign states. Moreover, the US government was not successful in its attempt to regularize the defiance rhetoric *ex post facto* by putting a Security Council imprimatur on the Iraq occupation and transforming it into a Chapter VII operation as happened in the Kosovo case. Berman 2005, p. 116.

the Dutch government. On the one hand, the government argued that the invasion was legal because the Security Council had already authorized the use of force in the 1990s; on the other hand it also claimed that the Charter framework had to be defied because the Council failed to live up to its responsibility to authorize force (again). While in the Kosovo case the questions of legality and legitimacy were kept strictly separate, in the Iraq case the Dutch government combined them in an incompatible mix and as such undermined its own case for justification.[146]

6.5 Epilogue

'The UN Charter is not an instruction manual that gives ready-made advice on how the Security Council and the member states should act in any given situation', the Davids Committee concluded in its analysis of the legal justification of the Dutch support for the Iraq war. 'Instead, the Charter forms the normative framework within which these actors should operate and legal developments and state practice can be manifested in reaction to strongly felt new convictions and vital national and international interests.'[147] This article has analyzed how such convictions or visions on international society, including the common interest to forge and uphold the international legal order interacted with the legal framework of the UN Charter in the Dutch justification for its political support of the Iraq invasion. To be sure, this does not alter the conclusion that the invasion of Iraq (and hence the political support by The Netherlands) was illegal on the basis of positive international law, and this article underwrites the solid and faithful work of the Davids Committee.[148] However, the current analysis does lay bare that the answer to the legality question is not predetermined by positive international law per se but is part of a process of deliberation in which it also interacts with different strands of justification, which together are the stakes for seeking international legitimacy for political decision making.

Recognizing that law as a scheme of legal argumentation always requires interpretation, this article has presented an alternative perspective on the debate regarding the justification for the Iraq war by deconstructing the different lines of argumentation put forward by the Davids Committee and Dutch government. The fact that law is always an interpretive enterprise, however, does not mean that any argument is as good as any other, or that legal argumentation can be reduced to

---

[146] This is not to say that it would have been more successful had it invoked the argument of 'illegal legal reform'. See Buchanan 2003. It should only be noted that whereas it claimed consistency over time both in its standpoint toward the 2003 invasion, as in its overall Iraq since the 1990s. See Davids Committee 2010, conclusion 14. The Dutch position was not consistent by and of itself.

[147] Davids Committee 2010, p. 268; translation in NILR 2010, p. 132.

[148] It should be noted that the Committee itself never uses the word 'illegal' but only refers to the 'lack of a mandate'. For a critique, see Nollkaemper 2010.

'opinions' as PM Balkenende in a rather unfortunate and highly criticized first reaction to the report stated.[149] Just because different lines of legal argumentation are possible, it does not mean that they all carry the same weight and law is whatever anyone wants it to be. Such a view turns international law into a caricature, and neglects that as a scheme of interpretation it is one that serves and addresses a particular audience. Above all, it is a regime to regulate international intercourse, and hence the 'international community' ultimately is its judge. In this context the debate in the UN can be seen as the expression of a hegemon's unsuccessful attempt to interpret pre-existing rules in a new manner and legitimize unilateral intervention against corrupting elements within the international society.[150]

Some have portrayed the political support for the unlawful intervention in Iraq as a shame on the Dutch identity as the prosecutor of international rule of law, with its government seating in the legal capital of the world. However, as Mertens and van Dinther also explain, what might be at stake is less a conflict between hard politics and soft law, but a tension between positive international law and the promotion of the international legal order.[151] The latter is a constitutional duty for the Dutch government, but as also argued by Mertens and van Dinther, this duty to promote the international order in fact could entail both *lex lata* and *lex feranda,* and is aimed to encompass the main policies of the time.[152] This is precisely what the current analysis of the Dutch justification with regard to the Iraq war has exposed. Together with the discussion of liberal internationalism 3.0 and the normative discourse on the status of rogue states in the New World Order, this provides a more in-depth understanding of the argumentation of the Dutch government to politically support the Iraq war. While the conclusion of the Davids report regarding the illegality of the invasion was confirmed, this analysis has argued that it is too simplistic to conclude that because the war was illegal it automatically follows that the Dutch government was trumping law with politics, ignoring international norms for the sake of national interest narrowly defined.[153] Rather, this article has revealed how the different positions are based on different conceptions of the international society and how to forge the international rule of law in the twenty-first century. These conceptions in turn translate in contrasting approaches to sovereignty, responsibility, international society, and the nature and operation of the international legal order. Overall this translation results in a more nuanced understanding of the Dutch position based on a particular vision on how the international legal order is best safeguarded in an international reality in which law and politics are not neatly isolated domains but inherently interwoven.

---

[149] Video of the press conference by PM Balkenende on 12 January 2002 is available at http://nos.nl/video/128696-reactie-balkenende-op-rapportdavids.html.

[150] Press-Barnathan 2004, p. 206.

[151] Mertens and van Dinther 2012.

[152] Article 90 of the Dutch constitution. Mertens and van Dinther 2012. See also Besselink 2003.

[153] To be sure, this is not what the Davids Committee explicitly does in its report, but it does refer to the traditional zero-sum conception of law and politics within both International Relations and International Law.

References

Aalberts TE (2012) Constructing sovereignty between politics and law. Routledge, London

Aalberts TE, Werner WG (2008) Sovereignty beyond borders: sovereignty, self-defense and the disciplining of states. In: Adler-Nissen R, Gammeltoft-Hansen T (eds) Sovereignty games. Instrumentalising state sovereignty in Europe and beyond. Palgrave, Houndmills, pp 129–150

Anghie A (2005) Imperialism, sovereignty and the making of international law. Cambridge University Press, Cambridge

Arend AC (2002) International law and rogue states: the failure of the Charter framework. N Engl Law Rev 36:735–753

Berman N (2005) Legitimacy through defiance: from Goa to Iraq. Wis Int Law J 23:93–125

Besselink LFM (2003) The constitutional duty to promote the development of the international legal order: the significance and meaning of article 90 of The Netherlands constitution. Neth Yearb Int Law 34:118–135

Buchanan A (2003) Reforming the international law of humanitarian intervention. In: Holzgrefe JL, Keohane RO (eds) Humanitarian intervention: ethical, legal and political dilemmas. Cambridge University Press, Cambridge, pp 130–174

Bull H (1995) [1977] The anarchical society. A study of order in world politics, 2nd edn. MacMillan, London

Crawford J (1999) Revising the draft articles on state responsibility. Eur J Int Law 10:435–460

Crawford J, Bodeau P, Peel J (2000) The ILC's draft articles on state responsibility: toward completion of a second reading. Am J Int Law 94:660–674

Davids Committee (2010) Rapport Commissie van onderzoek besluitvorming Irak. Boom, Amsterdam

Gong GW (1984) The standard of 'civilization' in international society. Clarendon Press, Oxford

Hoyt P (2000) ''Rogue states'' and international relations theory. J Confl Stud 20:68–79

Ikenberry GJ (2009) Liberal internationalism 3.0: America and the dilemmas of liberal world order. Perspect Politics 7:71–87

Ikenberry GJ, Slaughter A-M (2006) Forging a world of liberty under law. U.S. national security in the 21st century (Final report of the Princeton project on national security). The Woodrow Wilson School of Public and International Affairs, Princeton University

Janse R (2006) The legitimacy of humanitarian interventions. Leiden J Int Law 19:669–692

Klare MT (1995) Rogue states and nuclear outlaws: America's search for a new foreign policy. Hill and Wang, New York

Koskenniemi M (2006) [1989] From apology to utopia. The structure of international legal argument. Cambridge University Press, Cambridge

Koskenniemi M (2007) The fate of public international law: between technique and politics. Mod Law Rev 70:1–30

Kustermans J (2011a) The category rogue. Paper presented at the 6th ECPR General conference, Reykjavik, 24–27th Aug 2011

Kustermans J (2011b) The state as citizen: state personhood and ideology. J Int Relat Dev 14:1–27

Lorimer J (1884) The institutes of the Law of Nations. A treatise of the jural relations of separate political communities. Volume II. Blackwood, Edinburgh

March JG, Olsen JP (1998) The institutional dynamics of international political orders. Int Organ 52:943–969

Manusama KM (2012) Between a rock and a hard place: providing legal advice on military action against Iraq. Neth Yearb Int Law 42:95–121

Mertens T, van Dinther J (2012) Whose international order? Which law? Neth Yearb Int Law 42:123–138

NILR (2010) Report of the Dutch committee of inquiry on the war in Iraq—Chapter 8: the basis in international law for the military intervention in Iraq. Neth Int Law Rev 57:81–137

Nollkaemper A (2010) Na de Commissie Davids: Nederland, Irak en het volkenrecht. Nederlands Juristenblad 3:144–150

O'Reilly KP (2007) Perceiving rogue states: the use of the "rogue atate" concept by US foreign policy elites. Foreign Policy Anal 3:295–315

Press-Barnathan G (2004) The war against Iraq and international order: from Bull to Bush. Int Stud Rev 6:195–212

Ralph J (2011) After Chilcot: the 'doctrine of international community' and the UK decision to invade Iraq. Br J Politics Int Relat 13:304–325

Rawls J (1999) The law of peoples. Harvard University Press, Cambridge

Saunders EN (2006) Setting boundaries: can international society exclude "rogue states"? Int Stud Rev 13:23–53

Simpson GJ (2004) Great powers and outlaw states. Unequal sovereigns in the international legal order. Cambridge University Press, Cambridge

Slaughter A-M (1995) International law in a world of liberal states. Eur J Int Law 6:503–538

Stahn C (2007) Responsibility to protect: political rhetoric or emerging legal norm? Am J Int Law 101:99–120

Téson FR (1992) The Kantian theory of international law. Columbia Law Rev 92:53–102

Walzer M (1977) Just and unjust wars: a moral argument with historical illustrations. Basic Books, New York

Werner WG (2004) From justus hostis to rogue state. The concept of the enemy in international legal thinking. Int J Semiot Law 17:155–168

Wheeler NJ, Dunne T (1998) Good international citizenship: a third way for British foreign policy. Int Aff 74:847–870

Yoo J (2003) International law and the war in Iraq. Am J Int Law 97:563–576

Chapter 7
'Public' International Law? Democracy and Discourses of Legal Reality

Philip Liste

Abstract When democracies wage war, they 'know' that they have the law on their side. The same holds true when they condemn war. But what if democracies take divergent legal positions to one and the same war? Relying on governmental and public 'Iraq' discourses in the United States and Germany, this article argues that governments can no longer define the law in isolation from their societal environments. The critical relation of 'politics,' 'law,' and 'democracy' is increasingly established not only in the political centers of states but also in the periphery: in the public discourse. This discursive process of international law becoming 'public' cannot be ignored. However, the patterns of meaning of international law vary remarkably. While there is public politics of international law in democracies, a per se 'democratic' politics of international law is hardly recognizable.

Keywords Discourse · Politics of international law · Germany · United States of America · Democracy · Civil society

Contents

P. Liste (✉)
Faculty of Economics and Social Sciences, University of Hamburg,
Hamburg, Germany
e-mail: philip.liste@wiso.uni-hamburg.de

I. F. Dekker and E. Hey (eds.), *Netherlands Yearbook of International Law 2011*,
Netherlands Yearbook of International Law 42, DOI: 10.1007/978-90-6704-849-1_7,

7.1 Introduction

Discourses of international law are no longer limited to the professional community that has been called the 'invisible college of international lawyers'.[1] The conditions of possibility of forming legal arguments are rendered by a diversity of actors referring to 'the law,' including those in the legal peripheries like public intellectuals,[2] commentators in daily newspaper,[3] or protesters like the mothers of the disappeared at the Plaza de Mayo in Buenos Aires.[4] The discourse surrounding the 2003 Iraq war was just another manifestation of this widening of legal discourses. This paper argues that these phenomena have repercussions for the formulation of the states' *politics of international law*. In principle, state actors can no longer escape from their societal environments, even more so when these environments are structured along democratic imaginaries or expectations.

In this regard, international law is facing the emergence of new 'politico-legal spaces' of discourse. While used as a surface of criticism in diverse arenas, including the public spheres, public international law obtains an increasingly *public* character; public international law becomes 'public' international law. The aim of this paper is to describe the 'legal' practice within these newly emerging spaces and to ask for the political repercussions of corresponding civic articulations of international law. Yet, civil society must not be misunderstood as 'good' corrective to 'bad' state politics and, thus, cannot be preassumed as being per se well minded towards international law. To the contrary, attempts to subordinate international law to the rationalities of *Realpolitik* can, in principle, also find support in civil society. Societal contexts are constructed *more or less* 'convenient' for international law-related argumentation. I argue that the sensibility of discourses to the language of international law has to do with the way particular 'elements of discourse' are interrelated.[5] 'Law' means different things in different spaces. Its meaning cannot be taken for granted and cannot be understood without taking into account how it is usually related to other *elements* like 'politics' or 'democracy'. The *common sense* of international law is not created in a void.

---

[1] Schachter 1977.

[2] Jürgen Habermas and his intervention in the debate on humanitarian intervention during the Kosovo crisis in 1999 might be a good example, see Habermas 1999.

[3] Critical: Friel and Falk 2004.

[4] Fischer-Lescano 2005.

[5] Laclau and Mouffe 2001.

It springs from a social process. As a discursive *element*, 'international law' receives its meaning from a societal practice of *inter-relation*—with remarkable consequences for the argumentative possibilities of relying on it. Coming from this discourse-oriented perspective the paper asks: How is the *meaning* of international law constructed in diverse discourses? How are governmental scripts of politics formulated against the backdrop of the societal *common sense* of international law? In addition, a focus will be on the 'democratic quality' of societal international law talk by asking whether there is one imaginary of international law which can be understood as being essentially 'democratic.'

In order to find some answers to those questions, the paper compares the societal dimension of politics of international law in the US and Germany. The focus of the observation is on the discourses on the Iraq war from summer 2002 until spring 2003, the time of the beginning of the military intervention.[6]

7.2 Discourse and the Common Sense of International Law

In his early writings as a young legal scholar, Hans Morgenthau rejected the possibility of isolating international law from its sociological environment by stating that '[l]es notions de politique et de juridique ne forment nullement un couple antithétique.'[7] Any analysis of international law would have to take into account the whole spectrum of political action. A critical part of international law-related political action would emanate from the obvious necessity to take part in a certain language game of diplomacy and he called this type of action 'Völkerrechtspolitik,' the politics of international law.[8] In this paper, I follow Morgenthau insofar as he takes the nexus of politics and law as 'the' starting point. Arguing somehow with Morgenthau against Morgenthau; however, I will not try to discover the 'real' interrelationship between international law and politics, but to describe how the nexus of the two elements is socially constructed within discourses.

The concept of politics of international law that now has been taken up by diverse scholars[9] can be understood in a twofold sense. First, it refers to state practice that relates to the political formation of international law (negotiation of treaties, articulations of legal opinions, etc.). Basically, state practice can either perpetuate established international legal norms (including their established interpretation) or promote the emergence, implementation, and interpretation of new legal norms.

---

[6] For a more detailed, book-length analysis, see Liste 2012.

[7] Morgenthau 1933, p. 26.

[8] Morgenthau 1929, p. 170.

[9] Fischer-Lescano and Liste 2005; Koskenniemi 1990; Reus-Smit 2004.

Second, the notion of politics of international law might be reopened for considering an extended understanding of 'international' legal discourse including global realms of the public. In world society, state politics of international law are not without constraints. Governmental scripts of foreign policy are semantically embedded in societal environments, even when referring to categories of international law. In diplomatic circles, international legal scripts cannot easily be articulated this way today and that way tomorrow. In quite a similar way, arguments building upon international law will hardly be recognized as relevant in a public sphere where international law is permanently determined as being an irrelevant category, meaningless to the 'realities' of power politics—and this might even be so when articulated by members of the government. In turn, a governmental policy of breaking international legal obligations will hardly be recognized as appropriate course of action where international law is commonly understood as cornerstone to a nation–state identity or normative foundation of world politics. Thus, referring to international law, ascribing meaning to it, relating it to other elements (like 'politics' or 'democracy'), and determining its status is itself a 'political' practice, a *discursive politics of international law*.

This differentiation between state and non-state or governmental and civic forms of international law-related talk has some practical implications. The first dimension of politics of international law is characterized by attempts to modify particular international legal norms. As a minimum condition, this modification of international law, of course, necessitates on the side of individual actors an expertise in 'good' legal argumentation.[10] The second dimension of politics of international law does not operate as legal discourse in the strict sense of the term. What is at stake here is not a formation of particular international legal norms and thus a modification of international law, but rather the social status of international law as such. While the first dimension focuses on the meaning of particular norms within the webs of legal text (juridical practice in the narrow sense), the second dimension is less technical. Its focus is on the role of international law in 'the social', the *common sense of international law*.[11]

The spheres where this commonsensical state of international law is reproduced are diverse and divergent. As mentioned above, the meaning of discursive elements like 'international law' or 'democracy' cannot be taken for granted; meaning is the result of a social process. It is generated in and in between discourses as the articulations of government officials and the discourse of the mass media do not proceed in a self-contained manner but relate to each other on a daily basis. In the following section, the analysis of this textuality will begin with a focus on the positions taken by the US and German Governments, the

---

[10] Koskenniemi 2006; Ress 2002.

[11] Following Antonio Gramsci, common sense is 'the conception of the world which is uncritically absorbed by the various social and cultural environments in which the moral individuality of the average man is developed.' See Gramsci 1971, p. 419.

governmental discourses. Section 7.4 will then focus on the governments' *societal environments* by relying on media discourses.

7.3 Governmental Politics of International Law

A vast body of literature has interpreted the Iraq moment as severe crisis of international law increasingly under normative pressure of US hegemonic power.[12] In part, and in the US in particular, this diagnosis has also been undergirded in a normative sense.[13] In turn, international law was referred to in the global public realm to a remarkable and perhaps unprecedented extent.[14] The public legal discourses in the environments of the political centers, however, cannot be evaluated without a critical appraisal of governmental discourses of justification. This section focuses on the law-related narratives of the US and German Governments reproduced while the Iraq crises grew more and more acute.

7.3.1 Politico-Legal Practice in the US

With respect to the Iraq war, US politics of international law have been relatively straight forward. Deviating from common wisdom, however, preventive self-defense (or preemption) has not been the core of argumentation. Instead, the US Government focused on the *enforcement* of international law. With respect to its official legal position on the military intervention in Iraq, the Bush Administration has not entered a terrain of 'no law.' Even the so-called Bush Doctrine—i.e. the 'pre-emptive strikes policy' articulated in September 2002—was, in part, articulated as a legal concept.[15] Additionally, the doctrine was not pushed all the way through the process. In a letter addressing the President of the UNSC, the administration stated to enforce several resolutions of the UNSC adopted since 1990. In particular, the legal argument comprises a 'very creative' combination of resolutions 678 (1990), 687 (1991), and 1441 (2002);[16] i.e. these resolutions taken together provide the legal basis for the war.

Against the established narrative background, the status of international law follows only from its effect. Enforcement is constructed as cornerstone in any engagement with international law. Its necessity is not addressed as emanating

[12] Habermas 2004. For a useful discussion of the notion of 'hegemony' in international law (from a Gramscian or 'neo-Gramscian' perspective), see Buckel and Fischer-Lescano 2009.

[13] Glennon 2003; Goldsmith and Posner 2005.

[14] Brunnée and Toope 2010; Koskenniemi 2004.

[15] White House, National Security Strategy of the United States, September 2002, p. 15.

[16] For the whole argument, see Taft and Buchwald 2003. For criticism, see Bothe 2003.

from the law itself but from the national interest. As regards the situation in Iraq, attempts to solve the issue on the level of the UN are evaluated in the negative. Against the backdrop of a 'war on terror', continuation of this UN approach is taken as being no longer acceptable. The status of the UN and international law in general is determined within this politico-legal narrative. In this regard, the UN is facing a challenge and can only endure as a meaningful institution when succeeding in effective enforcement.[17] By the same token, the US ranges as a warrantor of international law enforcement and thus of international law as such. The relevance of the UN is, in turn, limited to a very specific scenario in which the US is legitimized to operate as warrantor and thus as hegemon. Where there is no consent to the US performing this function, the international legal process tends to lose value.

Even the putative change of strategy during February 2003 (abandoning the plan to legitimize military action via a 'second resolution' in the UNSC) did not consist in any semantic shift.[18] The governmental discourse was marked by a temporal narrative that constructed a military intervention as a mere consequence of the historical path since 1990, by a certain law and power nexus coupling the status of international law with its effective enforcement, and a blurring of boundaries between the two concepts of international law enforcement on the one hand and (preventive) self-defense on the other.[19]

7.3.2 Politico-Legal Practice in Germany

As Minister of State Bury put it in May 2003, 'the Federal Government does not comment on jurisprudential debates.'[20] This refusal, however, might be interpreted as a meaningful position in itself. Time and again, the Schröder Administration had emphasized the paramount importance of a continuation of the diplomatic process at the level of the UN. The practice of silence, however, is but a manifestation of German ambivalence. In particular, two figures of discursive signification do characterize the German governmental discourse: first, the continuation of the international legal process and, second, the perpetuation of international law as a *monument.*

The goal of a continuation builds on a particular narrative of the conflict between Iraq and the international community of states. But different from the

---

[17] President Bush, Speech at the UN General Assembly, 12 September 2002, UN-Document A/57/PV.2.

[18] President Bush, Remarks at Swearing-In Ceremony for William Donaldson as the New Chairman of the Securities and Exchange Commission, White House, 18 February 2003.

[19] Secretary Rumsfeld, Beyond Nation Building, 11th Annual Salute to Freedom, Intrepid Sea-Air-Space Museum, New York City, 14 February 2003.

[20] Minister of State Bury, Bundestag, 16 May 2003, BT-Drucksache 15/988, p. 2 (translation by the author).

US American narrative of ongoing failure, the international management of the Iraq crisis is represented as being a difficult and complex process with some light at the end of the tunnel. Following this line of argumentation, the containment of Iraq had worked; a new level of threat could not be identified.[21] Against the background of this narrative, the abort of the international process made no sense. The military use of force was localized beyond the scope of sense making practice.

Furthermore, the debate about the German position to the Iraq war was marked by issues of German–US relations. In the course of events, the traditionally established narrative coupling the promotion of international law with the partnership with the US turned out to be difficult to uphold.[22] In this vein, the difficulty of bringing the two concepts together did challenge the identity of a major aspect of German foreign politics. Facing this identity being at risk, members of the Schröder Administration did not stop articulating the reconcilability of the two narratives[23] and, in so doing, trying to countervail the tendency of an increasing difference between 'International Legalism' and 'Americanism.'

7.4 The Struggle for International Law in the Social

Relating to the Iraq crisis, the public discourses in both the US and Germany were deeply concerned with international law and show a similar trend with international law-related contributions to newspapers increasing during the period under analysis.[24] While this civic reliance on the 'international law of world society' is acknowledged in the literature as unexpected support for international law,[25] types of signification can be expected to operate differently in different sites. Civil society might also lay the discursive ground for the (governmental) negation of international law.

The discourse analysis this paper relies on focuses on Editorials and Op-Eds that referred to international law and were published between August 2002 and March 2003 in four daily newspapers, the US American *New York Times* and *Washington Post* and the German *Frankfurter Allgemeine Zeitung* and *Süddeutsche Zeitung*.

---

[21] Interview with Bundesaußenminister Fischer, 'Ich sehe keine Verbindung zwischen Irak und Al-Qaida,' *Süddeutsche Zeitung*, 7 August 2002, p. 9.

[22] For the concept of chain of equivalence: Laclau and Mouffe 2001, p. 131.

[23] Interview with Bundesaußenminister Fischer, 'Was nun?' ZDF (German TV channel), 26 February 2003.

[24] Liste 2012.

[25] Brunnée and Toope 2010; Habermas 2004; Koskenniemi 2004.

7.4.1 USA

Before the military attack on Iraq was launched in March 2003, the public discourse of US foreign politics was still affected by a presence of a terrorist threat in general and the terrorist attacks of September 11, 2001, in particular. Nevertheless, and operating in parallel to the governmental discourse, the analyzed contributions establish a narrative of continuity that couples the historical situation of the present (including the 9/11 moment) to that of the 1990s. It is only this narrative context, in which it does make sense to use military force as an attempt to bring an end to a history of failure. Furthermore, international law is relied upon on a regular basis as yardstick for action of other states and individuals. In turn, the same cannot be said when it comes to the evaluation of US foreign policy. Rather, open-mindedness towards international law is under attack, e.g., when those applying the law are addressed as only passing 'resolution after resolution [...] and then repaired to the lounge for drinks'[26] or the UN is represented as 'toothless debating society' and 'duty-free store on the East River'.[27] But even those contributions that are more sympathetic to international law and the UN offer a relatively clear policy rationale when arguing on the feasibility of *legal* strategies for the US under the *given* situation. Thus, the common sense of international law tends to be instrumentalist. There might, indeed be occasions when reliance on international law is prudent and those where it is not. In this vein, international law receives a meaning as a potentially adequate tool but not as an end in itself.[28] In a *Washington Post* Op-Ed from September 2002, Robert Kagan, in a similar way characterized US American sensibilities on multilateralism arguing that:

> [f]or most Americans, getting a few important allies on board is multilateralism. [...] To most American multilateralists the U.N. Security Council is not the final authority. It is a blue-ribbon commission. If it makes the right recommendations, it strengthens your case. If not, you can always ignore it.[29]

In sum, the rather instrumentalist approach towards international law established in the governmental discourse appears to be tight-fitting within its societal environment. The interrelation of law and politics is marked by an obvious hierarchy. The two elements are differentiated as modes of action whereas the mode of international law and the UN is characterized as a losing game. In turn, an effective, resolved and prudent politics is taken as the opposite and thus adequate course of action. As a matter of fact, this attitude towards international law becomes most obvious through positions supporting the policy of the Bush Administration:

---

26 Richard Cohen, 'Ready for War,' *Washington Post*, 10 October 2002, A33.

27 Richard Cohen, 'A Winning Hand for Powell', *Washington Post*, 6 February 2003, A37.

28 For a historical argument on how President Truman has prudently kept in mind both the US allies and questions of international legitimacy, see Thomas E. Mann, 'What Bush Can Learn from Truman,' *New York Times*, 6 October 2002, p. 13.

29 Robert Kagan, 'Multilateralism, American Style', *Washington Post*, 13 September 2002, A39.

> [c]ritics rarely grant the administration the credit it deserves for casting a spotlight on the deadly obsolescence and weakness of international bodies and global rules to deal with the modern threats of weapons of mass destruction and nihilistic terrorism. If the speeches and doctrinal statements about preemption and counterproliferation shake the United Nations and other bodies out of their state of inaction and bring a new international legal architecture into being, the rhetoric will have been worth it.[30]

Outright respect towards international law is an attitude that makes no sense against this discursive backdrop. What is needed is a wake-up call of politics pointing international law to the realities of the twenty-first century. International law and international organizations like the UN represent utopia, while the US administration is said to reflect reality and thus work against this utopian paralysis. Even more, it is power politics that could lead international law on the path to reality by backing it up with force. As Richard Cohen points out, 'if international law is to mean something, then the international community has to back it up. [...] For the sake of international law [...] war may be the only course.'[31] Through articulations like these, international law and the deployment of armed force are not constructed as oppositional. Rather, the meaning of international law emanates from its relation to power. The use of military force is represented as a means of safeguarding the relevance of international law and the UN. In this respect, international law receives its validity from politics marked by the readiness to use force—a clear-cut subordination of law to politics.

As regards international law and democracy, the corresponding interrelation between the two elements is constructed as difference, i.e. the two elements are represented as not always going together. By the same token, democracy is obviously privileged in the discourse so that it becomes a sense-making practice to reject international law on democratic grounds. This configuration becomes most obvious through normative considerations of political processes, particularly with regard to the Administration's decision-making practice on Iraq.

> The president has no power to pick and choose among the laws that bind him—unless Congress tells him otherwise. This is what makes the precise terms of any Congressional authorization for war against Iraq so important. According to judicial precedents, treaties like the United Nations Charter can be trumped only by subsequent legislation. The Charter would lose its status as governing domestic law if Congress explicitly authorizes the president to make war in violation of its terms.[32]

Although international law is in principle represented as binding law, this status depends on a domestic legislative act. Although, in other words, the President is described as being bound by international law, the implicated international legal obligation follows not from international law as such but could be overruled through the legislative branch. The domestic political process is not taken as subordinated to international obligations of the state. A similar configuration of

[30] Jim Hoagland, 'Foxed by Illusionist Partners', *Washington Post*, 22 December 2002, B07.

[31] Richard Cohen, 'Ready for War', *Washington Post*, 10 October 2002, A33.

[32] Bruce Ackerman, 'The Legality of Using Force,' *New York Times*, 21 September 2002, p. 15.

democracy and 'the international' appears in the course of more foundational considerations and becomes very clear in a juxtaposition of the US sensibilities to that of 'the Europeans'. Francis Fukuyama in an Op-Ed from September 2002 engages with the relation of the nation-state and the international community including international institutions and the corresponding sources of legitimacy. As he puts it:

> [b]ut the European idea that legitimacy is handed downward from a disembodied international community rather than handed upward from existing democratic institutions reflecting the public will on a nation–state level invites abuse on the part of elites, who are then free to interpret the will of the international community to suit their own preferences.[33]

Obviously, there are doubts concerning the legitimacy of international law emanating from the fact that it, at least in part, comes into being without an institutional reflection of the public will—with no democratic process—and is interpreted by foreign elites not accountable to the democratic public. The international community is given no agency under this narrative; it is rather addressed as a nebulous idea open to diverse variants of hypocrisy and not matching the liberal democratic imaginary. The imperatives of international law might be incompatible to the rationales of democracy—democracy, in turn, is represented as a good reason not to obey international law.

7.4.2 Germany

While in Germany a debate on a proactive German military engagement in Iraq was not under way, the discourse had its particular points of reference. In particular, the primary question was not whether or not to intervene in Iraq, but rather concerned the relation to the US, i.e. whether or not to support the major ally. In this regard, the 'Iraq' is often represented in the discourse as not being the core problematique. Instead of signifying the Iraqi regime as a serious threat, 'Iraq' operates as signifier for a transatlantic conflict concerning world order. What was seen to be at stake was the future orientation of Germany and Europe towards the US and the world.[34]

As a consequence, the *fixity* of the discourse is rather weak, i.e. there seems to be no discursive hegemony, no structural subordination of one concept to the other. Articulations of German 'Americanism' are paralleled by those of 'openness towards international law'. While there is consensus in the analyzed media that the identity of German foreign politics is clearly marked by both concepts, it remains far from clear what to do in a situation when the two contradict each other. In this context, the issue is commonly addressed as puzzling for any formulation of a

---

[33] Francis Fukuyama, 'U.S. vs. Them', *Washington Post*, 11 September 2002, A17.

[34] Nikolas Busse, 'Wer in der Welt bestimmt', *Frankfurter Allgemeine Zeitung*, 11 March 2003, p. 1.

'German' foreign policy. What is important, there is no dominant mode of coping with the challenge; the puzzle is solved differently by different discursive contributions. In the discourse the signifier 'Germany' is *overdetermined*,[35] i.e. there are divergent determinations of the identity of German foreign politics floating freely in the discourse. The *fixity* of an established identity suffers from the ongoing presence of this variety of significations.

This state of discursive ambivalence also affects the signification of 'international law'. In particular, there are two types of signification to be mentioned. First, international law is represented as a monument; though a now internationally contested monument. Nevertheless, and in part as remedy to this state of contestation, this monumental character is perpetuated, e.g., by an ongoing notice of its paramount importance in world order. The putative crisis of international law is addressed through *counterfacticity*, a type of emphasizing the relevance of law even against the factual presence of power. Despite its contested nature under the socio-political situation, this type of articulation clings to international law.[36] This, however, is paralleled by articulations that point to the facts of power and, in so doing, signify international law as being too idealistic. The mentioned *counterfacticity* is facing a normative representation of the facts. Breaches of the law are implicitly justified by pointing to *Realpolitik* and thus the 'reality' of international law.[37] A clear discursive hegemony of either of the two positions is not recognizable.

The two mentioned types of signification do already point to the diversity in the construction of an interrelation of law and politics. On the one hand, law is signified as part of a canon of liberal values and thus receives a status as being able to constitute politics. On the other hand, it is obvious how particularly the more conservative contributions to the discourse do make a difference between *political* and *legal* perspectives and, in the course of their argumentation, privilege the former as the more prudent and realistic course of action.[38] Here, the foundations of international law are basically seen in power politics.

Both, conservatives and more liberal commentators, however, were critical of how the Schröder Administration referred to international law and the international legal process. For example, Günther Nonnenmacher writing for the *Frankfurter Allgemeine Zeitung* and Heribert Prantl writing for the *Süddeutsche Zeitung* both take the German Basic Law as the vantage point of their argumentation to problematize the governmental politics of international law—but differ in their results. Politics undermines the law in secret and in conflict with its ideal foundation, is the answer provided by Prantl;[39] international legal obligations are not

---

[35] For the discourse theoretic concept of over-determination, see Laclau and Mouffe 2001.

[36] Stefan Ulrich, 'Im Club der Unbeugsamen', *Süddeutsche Zeitung*, 17 March 2003, p. 4.

[37] Berthold Kohler, 'Mit Amerika', *Frankfurter Allgemeine Zeitung*, 25 March 2003, p. 1.

[38] Berthold Kohler, 'Noch ein Grund', *Frankfurter Allgemeine Zeitung*, 21 March 2003, p. 1.

[39] Heribert Prantl, 'Recht bleibt Recht, aber nur solange es passt', *Süddeutsche Zeitung*, 22 March 2003, p. 4.

sufficiently determined, state actors must recognize the given scope of interpretation and take the corresponding political opportunity, is that provided by Nonnenmacher.[40]

International law and democracy are coupled in the discourse in two ways. First, the conflict between Western states and Iraq is represented as conflict between democracy and non-democracy while it is the former regime type that, in principle, is characterized as promoter of an international legal process.[41] Similarly, the international (legal) process is taken as a process that should operate in a 'democratic' way, which means that less powerful states should not be squeezed to follow the will of power.[42] Second, compliance with international law is represented as the usual case and thus the adequate course of formulating foreign policy in the democratic state.[43] In this respect, international law and democracy form a *chain of equivalence*, they are structurally addressed as inherently going together. As a matter of fact, foreign policies that act in breach of international legal obligations are differentiated from democracy or the realm of 'democratic' action. Thus, international law receives a status as a strong normative criterion of democratic will formation. In other words, acting in accordance with international law is an essential value of democratic state practice. Although there are certain deviations from this type of signification, it seems to be relatively fixed in the German discourse.

7.5 Conclusion

It does not come as surprise that German and US American discourses differ to a remarkable extent. It is commonplace that the US approaches to international law and the UN are instrumentalist and power oriented; by the same token, the promotion of international law is said to be part and parcel of the identity of German foreign politics. Indeed, international law is usually framed as tool of prudent US foreign politics that can be applied for the benefit of the national interest and that even should be applied wherever possible. By contrast, over a wide spectrum of discursive contributions in Germany international law ranges as value in itself so that it receives a status as a normative measurement of an adequate foreign policy. In this regard, the discourse analyses do verify common wisdom.

In turn, and on the basis of a more detailed assessment, the US discourse cannot be characterized as ignorant towards international law; there is consideration of

---

40 Günther Nonnenmacher, 'Rechtszweifel', *Frankfurter Allgemeine Zeitung*, March 22, 2003, p. 1.

41 Nikolas Busse, 'Wer in der Welt bestimmt', *Frankfurter Allgemeine Zeitung*, 11 March 2003, p. 1.

42 Stefan Ulrich, 'Mut zum Nein', *Süddeutsche Zeitung*, 26 February 2002, p. 4.

43 Patrick Bahners, 'Willensfrage', *Frankfurter Allgemeine Zeitung*, 14 February 2003, p. 31.

international law also as a normative frame of political and military action. Although in the US harsh rejections of 'legal' criticism often prevailed on the part of the governmental discourse,[44] the media commentary on the course of the Administration indeed implied that international law is to be taken seriously—even when, in the end, it is assumed that legal assessment would have to be fair to the 'real' political circumstances. In Germany, the often assumed subordination of foreign politics to the regime of international law, although dominating the political debate, is repeatedly qualified, particularly in conservative contributions to the discourse.

Most importantly, in both countries the approaches to international law were interrelated to the democratic identity of foreign politics. Hence, both the US 'rejection' as well as the German 'embracement' of international law flow from a 'democratic politics of international law.' As a result, any linear notion of a causal relationship between the democratic regime type and the attitude towards international law must be rejected. 'Fidelity' to international law[45] can follow from the 'democratic' discourse as can deep skepticism. However, the result of a discourse analysis like this could be taken as a vantage point for developing a typology, whereas the two cases under analysis, Germany and the US, should not be misunderstood as approximations to two opposing ideal types. While there is a hegemony of a certain signification of international law in the US, a comparable state of hegemony cannot be observed by analyzing the German discourse. With respect to key concepts of the debate, there is a semantic intersection, including the hegemonic positions in the US on the one hand and a remarkable amount of the more conservative contributions to the German discourse on the other.

Additionally, the picture of the 'democratic quality' of the politics of international law looks somehow different if the normative criterion of *societal embeddedness* is taken into account. The ways the governmental types of signification are embedded within the public discourses differ to a remarkable extent. While the positions taken by the US Administration can be smoothly localized in the semantic hegemonies of society, the discursive determinations of the German Administration, first, operated in a field of lacking determinacy and, second, even tend to 're-couple' those elements usually divided within the media discourse (particularly the political orientation to the US as partner and the normative orientation to international law). While the US Administration's articulations can be localized within the societal field of discursive hegemony, the discursive practices of the German Administration could be understood as attempts to 'hegemonize' the discourse by rationalizing their decision to prioritize international law through reliance on the people (or an assumed *volonté générale*). While this, of course, can be understood as the duty of an elected government, it can still be argued that from

---

[44] E.g. Secretary Rumsfeld replying during an interview that 'any country has the right to do anything, so I don't know what the meaning of your question is', Secretary Rumsfeld, Interview with LBC TV and *Al Hayat* Newspaper, 4 December 2002.

[45] For the concept of fidelity, see Brunnée and Toope 2010.

a democratic point of view German foreign policy has not been as inevitable as has often been proclaimed. Taken this different structure of two 'national' discourses, 'the Germans', as democrats, might have been good international lawyers, but 'the Americans', as international lawyers, might have been the better democrats.[46]

References

Bothe M (2003) Der Irakkrieg und das völkerrechtliche gewaltverbot. Archiv des Völkerrechts 41:255–271

Brunnée J, Toope S (2010) Legitimacy and legality in international law. Cambridge University Press, Cambridge

Buckel S, Fischer-Lescano A (2009) Gramsci reconsidered: hegemony in global law. Leiden J Int L 22:437–454

Fischer-Lescano A (2005) Globalverfassung: die geltungsbegründung der menschenrechte. Velbrück, Weilerswist

Fischer-Lescano A, Liste P (2005) Völkerrechtspolitik: zu trennung und verknüpfung von politik und recht der weltgesellschaft. Zeitschrift für Internationale Beziehungen 12:209–249

Friel H, Falk R (2004) Record of the paper: how the New York Times misreports US foreign policy. Verso, London

Glennon M (2003) Why the Security Council failed. Foreign Affairs 82:16–35

Goldsmith J, Posner E (2005) The limits of international law. Oxford University Press, Oxford

Gramsci A (1971) Selections from the prison notebooks of Antonio Gramsci. International Publishers, New York

Habermas J (1999) Bestialität und humanität. Ein krieg an der grenze zwischen recht und moral. Die Zeit, 29 April 1999. http://www.zeit.de/1999/18/199918.krieg_.xml. Accessed 10 Aug 2011

Habermas J (2004) Hat die konstitutionalisierung des völkerrechts noch eine chance? In: Habermas J (ed) Der gespaltene esten. Kleine politische schriften X, Suhrkamp, Frankfurt am Main, pp 113–193

Koskenniemi M (1990) The politics of international law. Eur J Int L 1:4–32

Koskenniemi M (2004) What should international lawyers learn from Karl Marx? Leiden J Int L 17:229–246

Koskenniemi M (2006) From apology to utopia: the structure of international legal argument (reissue with new epilogue). Cambridge University Press, Cambridge

Laclau E, Mouffe C (2001) Hegemony and socialist strategy: towards a radical democratic politics. Verso, London

Liste P (2012) Völkerrecht-sprechen: zur konstruktion demokratischer völkerrechtspolitik am beispiel der Vereinigten Staaten von Amerika und der Bundesrepublik Deutschland. Nomos, Baden-Baden

Morgenthau H (1929) Stresemann als schöpfer der deutschen völkerrechtspolitik. Die Justiz: Monatsschrift für Erneuerung des Deutschen Rechtswesens 5:169–176

Morgenthau H (1933) La notion du 'politique' et la théorie des différends internationaux. Libraire du Recueil Sirey, Paris

Ress G (2002) Interpretation. In: Simma B (ed) The charter of the United Nations: a commentary. Oxford University Press, Oxford, pp 13–32

[46] I owe this formulation to Lothar Brock.

Reus-Smit C (2004) The politics of international law. In: Reus-Smit C (ed) The politics of international law. Cambridge University Press, Cambridge, pp 14–44
Schachter O (1977) The invisible college of international lawyers. Northwest Univ Law Rev 72:217–226
Taft W, Buchwald T (2003) Preemption, Iraq, and international law. Am J Int L 97:557–563

Chapter 8
Does Might Still Make Right? International Relations Theory and the Use of International Law Regarding the 2003 Iraq War

Bertjan Verbeek

Abstract Theories of International Relations take various positions regarding the role of international law in international politics. This article identifies four different perspectives on that role by making two distinctions: first, between approaches that assume that states act on the basis of a cost-benefit analysis and approaches that assume that states act upon shared ideas; second, between theories that assume that sovereign states are the only relevant players in international politics and theories that allow for the possibility that domestic and transnational players may affect international politics as well. Subsequently, the article investigates the choices made by France, Italy, the Netherlands, the United Kingdom and the United States prior to the 2003 war against Iraq. The four perspectives on the role of international law provide different interpretations of the weight these states attached to international law when considering the use of violence against Iraq.

Keywords International relations theory · Iraq war · Rationalism · (Social) constructivism · Globalization · Non-state actors

Contents

B. Verbeek (✉)
Institute for Management Research, Radboud University Nijmegen,
Nijmegen, The Netherlands
e-mail: b.verbeek@fm.ru.nl
URL: www.ru.nl/fm/verbeek

B. Verbeek
Crismart, Swedish National Defence College, Stockholm, Sweden

I. F. Dekker and E. Hey (eds.), *Netherlands Yearbook of International Law 2011*,
Netherlands Yearbook of International Law 42, DOI: 10.1007/978-90-6704-849-1_8,

8.1 Introduction

This contribution presents an overview of the debate among scholars of International Relations (IR) regarding the question to what extent the major members of the international political system, sovereign states, take international law into account when they decide to make use of violent means. In particular, it seeks to examine how this debate helps account for the choices several states made during the chain of events leading up to the 2003 war against Iraq. The major claim of the article is that, although states can still choose to ignore the requirements of international law, they do so at increasing political costs, both domestically and internationally. Furthermore, it is important to take into account that states differ in the ways they seek to build power in the international system: by consequence, international law may play a different role to different states in that process of power accumulation. The questions raised in this article reflect a growing interest in bridging the gap between the disciplines of international law and IR.[1]

8.2 International Relations Theory and the Importance of International Law

Since the end of the twentieth century two major debates have characterized IR theory. One has been held between so-called rationalist and (social) constructivist scholars.[2] It focuses on the explanatory mechanism behind the behaviour of the

[1] See, in particular, Byers 2000; Collins and White 2011; Evangelista 2008; Goldstein et al. 2000; and Lake 2010.

[2] Various other approaches characterize IR theory, such as Critical Theory, Post-Modernism, Neo-Marxism, Neo-Gramscian, the English School, and Post-Structuralism. For an over view, see Dunne et al. 2007; the major debate nowadays is between rationalists and (social) constructivist, although some prefer a juxtaposition of rationalists and so-called reflectivists, who fundamentally differ on epistemology, allowing constructivists to be closer to either, while adopting a social rather than a material ontology (Christiansen et al. 1999).

major actors in world politics and on the ways to study them. The second debate relates to the precise role played by sovereign states. It centres around the notion that sovereign states are of decreasing relevance when accounting for global events. In particular, it is argued that globalisation has increased the weight of so-called non-state actors.[3] Both debates offer different perspectives on the question whether states take into account international law.

8.2.1 Rationalism Versus (Social) Constructivism

The starting point of nearly all scholars of IR is that the international political system is characterised by anarchy. Anarchy refers to the absence of an institution that possesses the legitimate monopoly on violence in international society and that could enforce rules and agreements.[4] However, from that common point of departure perspectives widely diverge. In particular, scholars differ on the nature of this anarchical system and its inhabitants. By consequence, they disagree about the effects anarchy has on the behaviour of the members of the international political system. These different perspectives entail diverging assessments of the role international law plays in international relations.

Rationalist scholars of IR assume that members of the international political system try to advance their self-interest and do so by calculating narrowly which policy option best serves that interest. The major rationalist currents are neorealism and neoliberalism.[5] Neorealists argue that only states can survive under the conditions of anarchy.[6] Because anarchy is, what they call, a 'self-help system' in which—deep down—no one can be trusted in the absence of an enforcement mechanism, states seek survival and thus must be constantly on their guard. The best guarantee for survival is to acquire power. However, because all states can be expected to seek power, states must be prepared for the eventuality of war. This basic condition of insecurity precludes states from engaging in long-term cooperation. Neorealists contend that these conditions of anarchy need not necessarily lead to violent conflict as long as states conduct a policy of maintaining, or restoring, the balance of power. Proper balancing will deter states from actually employing violent means. However, balancing implies that only short-term cooperation will be possible because the constantly shifting distribution of power forces states to changing alliances.

---

[3] Cf. Reinalda 2011.

[4] Exceptions to this point of departure are those scholars who argue that the nature of the international political system itself is the product of, and depends on, the underlying structure of global economic relations. They include (neo-)Marxists and some Critical Theorists. Cf. Dunne et al. 2007.

[5] A third, much smaller, brand of rationalists can be found among those scholars who explain a state's behavior in the international political system by the objective of a state's leadership to preserve their domestic power situation. This will be discussed in Sect. 8.2.2.

[6] The major proponents of neorealism are Waltz 1979; Walt 1985; Mearsheimer 2001.

This perspective leads neorealists to have a pessimistic, or at best an instrumental, view on international law.[7] Some neorealists reason that international law is the product of the distribution of power within the international political system. They would say that international law, and, subsequently, intergovernmental organizations, serve the interests of the most powerful states. To them, the UN system largely reflects the power relations between the victors of the Second World War. Similarly, the current pressure of states like Brazil, Russia, India, China, and, to a lesser extent, Germany and Japan, to alter some of the elements of the UN system, reflects the changing distribution of power in the world. Moreover, these scholars would argue that states will tend to ignore international law if it runs against their vital interests. The United States chose to go to war against Iraq in 2003 despite the absence of a Security Council resolution explicitly authorising the use of force. Other neorealists would take a less radical view and claim that states will observe some rules of international law because they facilitate the vital game of the balance of power. They point to the rules of international diplomacy which underpin the system of sovereign states. Diplomacy is essential to detecting the vital interests of other players in the system and to careful manoeuvring in the balance of power game. If states break these basic rules, they run into serious trouble: witness Iran's international isolation after it permitted students to storm the American embassy in Tehran and to hold hostage more than 60 American diplomats in 1979–1980; or Syria's predicament when its government turned a blind eye on the storming of several embassies in November 2011.

A second major strand of rationalist scholars can be found in neoliberalism (or neoliberal institutionalism).[8] Neoliberals accept the premise of anarchy but disagree with the neorealists' pessimistic view on cooperation. They argue that international institutions will allow states to move beyond the fear of constant conflict. Neoliberals reach this conclusion because they assume that states will seek material gain in order to generate welfare rather than power. International institutions allow states to meet other states on a regular basis, to discover their intentions, and, most importantly, to build up trust among states by monitoring the observance of agreements. Although violent conflict may still occur from time to time, their recurrent engagement in international institutions will teach states that long-term cooperation may be beneficial. By consequence, they eventually will be prepared to forego short-term gains from defection because they value the long-term benefits of cooperation through international institutions: regularly cheating on agreements makes a state an unreliable partner in the future, which will deter other states from future cooperation. In order to support their claims, neoliberals will point to the prolific rise of the number of intergovernmental organisations and international treatises dealing with pressing transborder issues and their relative success in establishing inter-state cooperation.[9]

---

7 This position is eloquently presented in Mearsheimer 1994/1995.

8 The major proponents of neoliberalism include: Keohane 1984; Axelrod and Keohane 1985.

9 See, e.g., Murphy 1994.

Not surprisingly, neoliberals take a more optimistic view on the role of international law. To them, international law is essential to establishing a framework which facilitates the long-term cooperation of states through international institutions. Moreover, whereas neorealists would never expect states to observe international law if it runs against their interests, neoliberals would expect states to comply, because states value the longer term benefits of cooperation. It is important to realise that for neoliberals states need not 'accept intrinsically' international law; rather, like the neorealists, they claim that states make a cost-benefit analysis of obeying international agreements. States may accept short-term losses, but only because they value the benefits of long-term cooperation over the loss of reputation as a reliable partner when they refuse to comply in the short run. Ultimately, this is explained by the neoliberal assumption of states seeking welfare rather than survival.

Social constructivists differ from rationalists in a radical way.[10] Rationalists basically accept anarchy as a given outside condition, which offers constraints and opportunities to states: it is like the ocean in which they have to swim. For constructivists, by contrast, the very condition of anarchy is partly product of what states (and other players) do: states 'construct' anarchy because they develop a common understanding of, or shared meaning regarding, the situation in which they operate. Subsequently, they act on the basis of that common understanding. For them, 'anarchy', in the famous words of Alexander Wendt, 'is what states make of it'.[11] The absence of a central authority in the international system may be an objective condition, but it only has effect through the shared meaning attached to that condition by the majority of the members of that system. That means that under certain conditions anarchy may resemble the pessimistic situation as depicted by the neorealists. However, for a constructivist the weight attached to the balance of power and to international diplomacy would resemble the dominant common understanding of states of how to deal with the situation. Similarly, the value neoliberals attach to international institutions becomes rooted in shared values. For a constructivist, it would thus be possible that states (and other players) develop a common global culture in which the use of force and cost-benefit calculations give way to norms and rules which states value in their own right, or, in constructivist terms, which states have fully internalised. Social constructivists thus incorporate change into their concept of IR, whereas rationalists tend to focus on a relatively frozen objective condition of anarchy. Constructivist thinking thus in principle would allow for a future transformation into a situation of world government. At the same time, the constructivist perspective does not exclude a reversal into a Hobbesian state of nature. Such changes depend on the extent to which states are interdependent, perceive to share a common fate, and are prepared to show self-restraint in their behaviour.[12]

---

[10] The major proponents of social constructivism are Onuf 1989; Wendt 1999; and Zehfuss 2002.

[11] Wendt 1992, p. 391.

[12] Wendt 1999, pp. 343–366.

Constructivism adopts an open attitude towards the role of international law in international relations. This approach clearly allows for the possibility that states formulate norms and rules because they intrinsically value them and will be prepared to sacrifice their individual interest in order to respect and strengthen them. At the same time constructivism recognises that interests and power matter. Indeed, respecting international law may prove an important source of soft power for states, which will enable them to enhance their reputation and pursue their interests in a relatively inexpensive way. Although all states attempt to acquire soft power, it may prove an important tool particularly for small states, which, per definition, possess relatively few hard power resources.[13] The emphasis on respect for international norms and the promotion of The Hague as the capital of international law not only testifies to the intrinsic value the Netherlands attaches to these positions, but also provide reputational strength that can be used to build coalitions in various diplomatic settings. Constructivists would also emphasise that the process, which produces common understandings among states, may not be uniform and that various meanings compete for acceptance. International law will thus always be subject to battles of meanings and interpretation. For a constructivist, framing the agenda of such discussions and building coalitions among like-minded players would be the main subject of investigation.

8.2.2 The Role of Sovereign States

So far, the discussion mainly focused on sovereign states, their attitude towards the condition of anarchy, and its consequence for the role of international law. The second debate, however, raises questions regarding the utility of this focus on sovereign states. Of course, international law has traditionally been built by sovereign states, or by organisations which are intergovernmental in character. It seems only logical to identify the state with an individual, or, in IR jargon, to conceive of the state as a unitary actor. At the same time, scholars of IR have since long pointed out that the behaviour of states is partly determined by players within the state as well as by transnational players.[14]

The sub-discipline of Foreign Policy Analysis emphasises that the relationships between politicians, civil servants, interest groups, and the wider public affect the foreign policy choices of states. Again, here we find scholars who take a rationalist approach and those who adopt a constructivist view.[15] Rationalists would focus on leaders who want to maintain their power position. In democracies this might

---

[13] On soft power, see Nye 2004.

[14] For domestic actors, see Allison 1971; Snyder et al. 1962; for transnationalism, see Keohane and Nye 1971.

[15] For a rationalist account, see Bueno de Mesquita and Lalman 1992. For a constructivist approach, see Weldes 1999.

entail pleasing the electorate in order to win elections. In more autocratic regimes it might involve buying off powerful players, such as the army, or the bureaucracy. Rationalists would assume that political parties, interest groups and bureaucratic organisations seek to advance their own interests. Foreign policy may thus reflect a compromise to keep domestic players happy rather than a clear response to an international situation. Constructivists would maintain that domestic actors may be driven by shared understandings of desirable state of affairs, such as respect for specific international norms and rules, or that different understandings compete for dominance.

Scholars of Foreign Policy Analysis would investigate the role of international law by investigating how actors employ international law in their efforts to affect a state's foreign policy. Rationalists would focus on the instrumental use of international law by domestic players: these actors are expected to tailor their arguments in order to strengthen their power position in the policy-making process leading to a foreign policy decision. At the same time these actors will make use of the 'self-binding' character of adopting a certain international legal position: once a certain perspective is shared it becomes possible for interest groups and the media to track the government's performance and to 'shame them' in case their policies deviate from the chosen international legal path. The power game thus continues after the foreign policy choice. Constructivists put forward that at least some domestic players may be intrinsically motivated by considerations of international law. Depending on their position in the policy-making process they may thus affect critically a state's foreign policy position. Such players are usually expected to be found among interest groups, such as Amnesty International, or among certain branches of the bureaucracy, in particular the legal branches of the Ministry of Foreign Affairs and the Office of the Prime Minister. Although all states contain significant domestic actors, democracies are expected to be particularly 'vulnerable' to the impact of such actors on foreign policy because of their system of accountability through elections.

IR scholars who pay attention to transnational actors claim that non-state actors operating across national borders have become salient players in world politics, particularly since their numbers have increased dramatically after the end of the Cold War and with the advent of globalisation. Such non-state actors include transnational corporations such as Toyota, Google, and Gazprom, but also international non-governmental organisations (NGOs), such as Oxfam and Greenpeace. Increasingly, the international bureaucracies of intergovernmental organisations have managed to obtain a degree of policy autonomy *vis-à-vis* their sovereign member states and thus count as a different kind of transnational non-state actor.[16] Such transnational non-state actors are considered to have become significant players in world politics. States cannot easily ignore their preferences in order to pursue their interests. This runs against neorealist and neoliberal notions of IR, which assume that sovereign states are the only relevant players.

[16] See Reinalda and Verbeek 1998.

Rationalist accounts of transnational actors focus on the material sources of influence that such players may possess in their relationship to states: transnational business has the power to affect production and consumption and is decreasingly bound by geographical limitations; international NGOs are able to mobilise domestic (and international) public opinion and thus are able to put pressure on the positions of states; international bureaucracies often possess crucial technical information that states need in order to formulate their policy positions. Constructivist research into transnational actors highlights the capacity of such players to build coalitions of like-minded organisations in various member states and their potential capacity to persuade states to adopt specific positions at international conferences. International bureaucracies are capable of 'empowering' such non-state actors by allowing them to be official participants at international conferences and thus to affect the dominant policy frame. Constructivists emphasise that many such non-state actors are intrinsically motivated by international norms and rules.

Transnational actors thus do affect the specific role that international law plays in international relations: they may affect international conferences of sovereign states directly, because they have been given access to the formal deliberations. They may do so indirectly by forging coalitions with like-minded players within the states, thus pushing them to observe international law through the domestic system of democratic accountability. Obviously, the weight of these channels of influence has been significantly enhanced by the spread of global media and social networks which make state representatives immediately aware of changes in the mood of international and domestic public opinion.

The above discussion is summarised in Table 8.1, representing the two debates and their implications for the role of international law in international relations.

8.3 States, International Law and the 2003 Iraq War

From the perspective of the IR discipline the most interesting issue regarding the Iraq war is why similar states made different choices regarding the significance of Security Council Resolution 1441, adopted on 8 November 2002. With some taking the position that Resolution 1441 provided a sufficient legal basis for the use of violence against Iraq and others arguing that a new resolution explicitly condoning the use of violence was required. Western states felt threatened in a similar way by the events of 9/11 and, in the first instance, shared serious fears that countries like Iraq would ally with terrorist groups and pose a threat to them, if not now, then in the near future. Indeed, the invocation of Article 5 of the NATO Treaty on 13 September 2001 testifies to the common fate experienced by Western countries.[17]

[17] See, http://www.nato.int/docu/update/2001/1001/e1002a.htm; cf. the testimony of senior NATO official Edgar Buckley, available at http://www.nato.int/docu/review/2006/issue2/english/art2.html, accessed on 19 October 2011.

Table 8.1 Two debates on international relations and international law

		Debate 1: Fundamental approach to international relations	
		Rationalism	**Social Constructivism**
Debate 2: main players in the international political system	Sovereign states	International law is the product of the distribution of power between states and reflects the interests of the major states States make instrumental use of international law Effects of precedence are possible	International law is the product of a common understanding by states regarding proper international norms and rules States compliance is possible under conditions of interdependence; perception of common fate; and self-restraint
	Sovereign states plus domestic and transnational players	Domestic and transnational players use international law to advance their own interests by pressurising states State behaviour is the outcome of a struggle between all players	Domestic and transnational players, as well as states may be motivated by common understandings regarding proper international norms and rules State behaviour is framed by the dominant shared perspective on the proper role of international law

This section examines five countries which made different choices nonetheless: the United Kingdom and the Unites States decided to wage war without a new Security Council resolution. The Netherlands and Italy decided to offer political support, but refrained from participating in the *Coalition of the Willing*. France rejected the position of the United States outright and remained outside the conflict. By examining these different choices, we will draw some conclusions from the different positions in the IR debate on international law presented above.

8.3.1 United States

The United States consistently argued that a second Security Council resolution was unnecessary in order to use violence against Iraq. First, let us assume a statist perspective. On face value, a rationalist approach to this attitude seems to offer an easy explanation: the United States, as the only remaining super power after the end of the Cold War, has little to fear from disregarding international regulations. Given its vital interests in the region, be that the prevention of terrorist groups from gaining access to weapons of mass destructions in Iraq, or control over natural resources, the United States is expected to protect these interests, if need be with violent means. Interestingly, however, this seemingly neorealist position was not shared by America's leading realist scholars (apart from Henry Kissinger): in a paid advertisement in the New York Times on 26 September 2002 they argued that war against Iraq was not in the national interest of the United States, because Iraq did not pose a threat to the United States and because there was no proof of cooperation between Al Qaeda and Iraq.[18]

Also from a neoliberal point of view the American position seems puzzling: going ahead without a second Security Council resolution entailed the risk of alienating many friendly states and splitting the NATO alliance, thus making it more difficult to mobilise future support for America's foreign policy in international institutions. In this respect, going at great lengths to argue that SC Resolution 1441 provided sufficient legal basis in order to limit future diplomatic damage implies that even super powers cannot simply brush aside legal arguments, but have to cast their policies in careful legal terms in order to contain future risks.

A constructivist argument might be based on the work of Alexander Wendt. Wendt argues that the objective condition of anarchy cannot be self-explanatory. We still need to know how states view each other bilaterally (what is their collective identity), as well as which view of anarchy is dominant in the entire system. States give meaning to the condition of anarchy in three different ways. First, they may share the notion of anarchy as a state of nature, as depicted by Thomas Hobbes in his *Leviathan*. In such a culture of anarchy states consider each

18 'War with Iraq is Not in America's National Interest', *New York Times* 2002. For Kissinger's position, see Kissinger 2002.

other enemies that have to be defeated at all costs. Second, when states consider each other as rivals, Wendt speaks of a Lockean culture: states have developed a system of communication and contracting, which allows them to pursue their individual goals. In this shared notion of anarchy states may still resort to force, but only as the last resort. The third culture of anarchy is labelled Kantian because in this culture states see each others as friends, meaning that they will not make use of force to settle their disputes.[19]

Applied to Iraq, it could be maintained that the United States and Iraq held a Hobbesian collective identity defining each other as enemies rather than rivals in the international political system. To the United States, at least, Iraq was not an honest member of the Lockean culture in which states, although rivalling each other, respect the norms and rules of international diplomacy. Evidence of this relationship is America's labelling of Iraq as part of the 'Axis of Evil' in January 2002. From this perspective, a second SC resolution would seem unnecessary because the United States perceives Iraq not to play the game according to the established rules.

When other actors than sovereign states are taken into account, the American legal position seems to reflect the policy vision of a group of American policy-makers, often labelled 'neoconservatives', who in 2001 happened to hold key positions in the Administration of President George W. Bush (2001–2009). These neoconservatives, amongst whom Richard Cheney, Richard Perle, Donald Rumsfeld, and Paul Wolfowitz, had maintained since the end of the Cold War that the United States should use its military superiority to serve America's long-term interests. Regime change in Iraq was seen as serving that objective. The group saw international law and its institutions as instrumental to America's needs and as something to ignore if so needed. It found powerful allies in the American Congress which is very wary of any suggestion that American sovereignty is delegated, or, worse, lost to international institutions, such as the United Nations. From a constructivist point of view, this neoconservative understanding of US objectives had to compete with a set of players who saw the United States as part of international society and who considered respect for international law at a minimum essential for achieving long-term goals. The major proponents of this line of reasoning could be found within the State Department. Rationalists would point out that the 2000 Presidential elections elevated many neoconservatives to important foreign policy positions. The attacks of 9/11 created the window of opportunity to link regime change in Iraq to the War on Terror. The neoconservatives hurried to put regime change in Iraq on the agenda, if needed by military means. Their opponents at the State Department, initially with support from British Prime Minister Tony Blair, hindered the neoconservative strategy by making the United States initially take the UN route.[20] Yet, by the Fall of 2002 the major representative of the legal route within President Bush's inner circle, Secretary of

19 Wendt 1999.

20 Mazarr 2007, p. 8.

State Colin Powell, had accepted essential elements of the neoconservatives' outlook.[21]

The different lenses thus offer different perspectives on the role of international law in United States' foreign policy towards Iraq in 2002–2003. If foreign policy is seen as the product of the struggle of domestic groups competing for the dominant definition of the national interest, it is clear that international law mattered to the United States, as long as the 'State Department faction' had access to the President's inner circle. After Powell gave up resistance the neoconservatives' perspective of tailoring international law to one's needs gained the upper hand. From a statist perspective the neoconservatives' perspective is reinforced if—via constructivist logic—Iraq is defined as a state that does not play by the rules of international diplomacy. The neoliberal view that respect for international law is to be preferred in order not to alienate one's allies does not offer a sufficient explanation: it helps account for supporting SC Resolution 1441, but not for the refusal to compromise on a second resolution. At the same time, however, it is clear that even a super power goes to great lengths in arguing that its behaviour is in compliance with international law.

8.3.2 United Kingdom

The United Kingdom officially decided to support United States policies towards Iraq. It deemed a second Security Council resolution desirable, but not indispensable. The British government deployed the largest number of troops second to the United States (some 47,000) and was heavily involved in military planning throughout 2002. The British case poses some interesting puzzles. At the beginning of 2003, 60% of British public opinion wanted explicit UN authorisation of the use of force. Meanwhile, in Parliament Prime Minister Tony Blair was facing mounting opposition from Members of Parliament of his Labour Party. Interestingly, in February 2003, when the adoption of a second SC resolution seemed less and less likely, President Bush offered Blair the possibility to withdraw from the alliance.[22] The United Kingdom thus could have chosen a different path: it might have given into public opinion or to parliamentary opposition at little international cost.

However, Prime Minister Tony Blair chose not to withdraw from the alliance. In his assessment the United Kingdom could only exert influence on the United States' course if it joined the coalition. This attitude was founded on a common British understanding of Great Britain's place in world politics: too weak to be an individual player, too weary of a truly independent European foreign policy and

---

[21] For a reconstruction of the policy process within the United States, see Mazarr 2007; Badie 2010. The neoconservatives' instrumental view of international law regarding the use of torture and the role of the American Supreme Court are described in Cole 2008.

[22] Davidson 2011, p. 134.

therefore influential only as America's junior partner with a substantive military contribution. This rationalist calculation of state interest underlies British foreign policy in 2002 and 2003. Yet, within those parameters the United Kingdom pushed the United States towards walking the proper path of international law and the United Nations throughout 2002. In his talks with President Bush and Vice-President Richard Cheney on 7 September 2002, Prime Minister Blair persuaded his counterparts that the UN road would be politically expedient, at least.[23] This path, however, halted at SC Resolution 1441. Blair accepted SC Resolution 1441 as a proper legal basis. He refused to let the United Nations Monitoring, Verification and Inspection Commission (UNMOVIC) conclude its work in Iraq (as proposed by France), partly for military reasons: postponing the war risked having to fight under unfavourable summer conditions in Iraq.[24]

Blair's official support for international law created a difficult situation for him at home, when doubts arose whether Iraq indeed possessed weapons of mass destructions and when legal scholars started arguing that SC Resolution 1441 was insufficient to justify a war against Iraq and that a second SC resolution authorising the use of force was required. Because of the support of the Conservative Party, Blair never had to fear defeat in the House of Commons. Yet, he faced opposition among his own parliamentary backbenchers, including Speaker of the House and Former Foreign Secretary Robin Cook.[25] These opponents had a powerful ally in Blair's Cabinet, Minister for International Development Clare Short.[26] Blair had to use all his talents of persuasion to prevent short from resigning and to keep the number of backbench opponents to a minimum. A sizeable number of Labour MP's voting against their own Prime Minister would severely damage Blair's domestic reputation and efficacy as a leader. The testimony of Attorney General Lord Goldsmith that SC Resolution 1441 provided a sound legal basis, proved essential to success.[27] Eventually, on 18 March 2003 the House of Commons accepted the choice for war. Blair met with a substantial opposition from his backbenchers, but not as many as whispered in the weeks before, thus limiting the immediate damage to his domestic political standing, but sowing the seeds for unrest in the years to come.

The UK's attitude towards international law in the Iraq case cannot be readily attributed to one IR approach or another: the parameters seem set by a neorealist calculation of how Great Britain can exercise power in the international system, leading to an early choice to join the United States. Yet, by emphasising the path of international law to its American ally the UK seems to fit the neoliberal approach. At the same time, this very policy choice creates enormous domestic

---

[23] Woodward 2004, pp. 177–179.

[24] Davidson 2011, p. 145. Cf. Danner 2006.

[25] Backbenchers are MP's of the governing party who do not occupy a formal position in the government. Usually, these governing positions number around 60–80 MP's.

[26] Cook 2003; Short 2004.

[27] Stothard 2004, pp. 54–55.

difficulties for the Blair government, requiring it to couch its legal argument in such a way as to prevent too much internal dissension. Overall, democratic middle power states like Great Britain typically face these conflicts between *Innenpolitik* and *Aussenpolitik*, more so than small or super powers. They want to play a significant international role, but are to an important extent dependent on domestic support. In the British political system, this implies that international law will be part of the domestic political battle between the Cabinet and its Parliamentary supporters.

A constructivist approach would point to the phenomenon of the so-called special relationship between Great Britain and the United States. American and British policymakers like to portray the cooperative nature of the relations of their two countries as a particular, durable friendship, based on a shared history, language and values.[28] This common identity has resulted in more intensive forms of cooperation than between most allies, even those within NATO. This is particularly the case in defence and intelligence. Diplomatically, this has resulted in special American attention to its British friends, for instance, in regular summits between American Presidents and British Prime Ministers. However, as in private life among friends, shared values and language do not imply perfect shared understandings. The British idea of the special relationship does not always correspond with the American perspective. The British often compared themselves to the ancient Greeks tutoring and advising the Romans. This sometimes caused them to neglect the American perspective in favour of the British.[29] Regarding the war against Iraq, the special relationship helps to explain Blair's easy access to President Bush as well as Blair's optimism in 'steering' the Americans. Similarly, it partially accounts for Blair's decision to stick with the Americans, also when the international legal route was closed and the neoconservatives' perspective gained the upper hand.

In sum, the constructivist perspective of the special relationship is important in understanding the influence Britain could have on the United States. Blair's advocacy for international law, however, is not the product of international law being a cornerstone of the value system shared by Americans and British. Rather, it stems from his political dependence on a sizeable majority among his Labour parliamentarians, many of whom demanded an international legal approach. This constellation initially helped bring about United States support for SC Resolution 1441. However, once the United States decided to go ahead without a second resolution Great Britain was entrapped in its special relationship with the United States. This predicament forced Blair to go to great lengths to persuade dissenters within his party that SC Resolution 1441 constituted a sufficient legal base for military intervention.

---

[28] Reynolds 1985–1986.

[29] See Verbeek 2003, esp. pp. 42–60.

8.3.3 Italy

In 2002–2003 Italy faced a dilemma between foreign and domestic priorities similar to Tony Blair's. Capitalising on his personal relationship with President George Bush, Italian Prime Minister Berlusconi had made it a priority to raise Italy's international status by siding with the United States. After 9/11 this had resulted in sending 3,000 Italian soldiers to Afghanistan as part of Operation Enduring Freedom. In the course of 2002, it seemed that becoming a preferred partner of the United States might entail following the Americans to Iraq. Eventually, the second Berlusconi-government (2001–2006) decided not to join the *Coalition of the Willing*, but rather to provide political support in March 2003. Less visibly, Italy allowed the United States to make use of its bases and ports, and agreed to send 1,000 additional troops to Afghanistan substituting American troops that were being redeployed to Iraq.[30] From a neorealist point of view, Italy's position can be explained by its attempt to stay close to the United States without alienating France and Germany, which also serves to explain Italy's position on the international legal issue. It sought to act as a bridge between the United States, France and Germany by insisting on Security Council authorisation. However, once the opposition of the latter two to the position hardened at the beginning of 2003, and a second Security Council resolution became increasingly unlikely, Italy remained within the borders of the legal path it had chosen by offering political, but not military support.[31] It becomes once again clear that international law reduces the number of options available to states once they have chosen a specific international legal path. A constructivist would readily acknowledge such a mechanism of rhetorical entrapment.

If we adopt a perspective that allows for many different players, the domestic constraints on Berlusconi's position become clear. In Italy a strong pacifist current, uniting (many) Christian-Democrats and (former) Communists, has been present since the end of the Second World War. In addition, in some domestic political quarters, such as among Berlusconi's ally the *Lega Nord*, hostility towards foreign entanglements and the United Nations, is growing.[32] This domestic opposition against the deployment of Italian troops in wars, supported by Roman Catholic church's condemnation of the pending war, was strengthened by Italy's international diplomacy promoting the United Nations and a second Security Council resolution. When a second resolution proved unlikely, however, it became much more difficult for the Berlusconi government to commit Italian troops. Indeed, this had to wait until April 2003 when Berlusconi promised Italian troops for the reconstruction of Iraq. In order not to arouse domestic opposition, however, this contribution had to be couched in terms of a peacekeeping operation. Clearly, then,

[30] Davidson 2009; Romano 2006.

[31] Nuti 2003.

[32] See Evangelista 2011; Andreatta 2001.

Italy walked a tight rope between international and domestic constraints. Its emphasis on international law limited its options abroad as well as at home.

8.3.4 France

From January 2003, on it slowly became clear that France would resist a new Security Council resolution that would authorise war. Foreign Minister Dominique De Villepin, in particular, engaged in an active lobby at the United Nations to prevent such a resolution.[33] At the beginning of March 2003, British Prime Minister Tony Blair attempted to bridge the gap by seeking a resolution that would give UNMOVIC some more time, but which would entail a clear and immediate military response in case Iraq did not initiate compliance within 7 days. The United States' military were opposed to such a formula because it risked having to fight during the Iraqi Summer heat. Before President Bush had decided, however, it had become clear that France would not support any resolution that might authorise the use of force. The prospect of a French veto in the Security Council deterred Great Britain and the United States from seeking further Security Council authorisation.[34] From a realist point of view, France's interest in reaffirming, or even reinforcing, its ties with the United States was not as important as it was for Great Britain, Italy or, as we shall see, the Netherlands. On the contrary, France's interests lie in North Africa and Russia (energy sources) and in promoting a European Union that acts independently from the United States. Moreover, France did not perceive Iraq as a threat to these interests.[35]

Traditionally, France often employs rhetoric that puts emphasis on international law and morality. In the case of Iraq, France's hammering on the legal and moral dimensions of the issue dovetailed with its long-term interests in world politics. It stayed close to Russia; within the European Union it operated with Germany as the leading opponents against the United States' policies; it exposed Great Britain as a country which takes its lead from the United States; and it helped countries such as Italy and the Netherlands to take a middle position of political instead of military support for the war against Iraq. Not surprisingly, therefore, France stated that only UN inspectors could determine whether Iraq was in breach of previous Security Council resolutions, and opposed policies that would lay such judgement in the hands of the Security Council.

The French case comes closest to the neorealist position that international law serves the interests of the state. In the case of France this is to be expected because it aspires to play a leading role in world politics. In the case of the Iraq war playing the legal card strengthened France's position *vis-à-vis* the United States and one of

[33] Davidson 2011, p. 147.

[34] Blair 2010, pp. 429–432.

[35] Davidson 2011, pp. 147–157.

France's major rivals for leadership: the United Kingdom. Domestic players were hardly relevant to French decision-making, which was dominated by President Jacques Chirac and Minister of Foreign Affairs Dominique de Villepin. A constructivist perspective does not add to understanding the role of international law in France's foreign policy. France considers itself a leading European nation in international affairs. It considers giving Europe an independent voice as its major mission. It will thus seek to counter any attempts at cultural or political hegemony, such as an American hegemony. Such a position, which aims at promoting French interests while covering them in European wrapping paper, entails a vision of the United Nations as a guardian against world hegemony. The Security Council, with France as a permanent member, serves as a shield against any hegemon. France's identity in international affairs thus reinforces the instrumental view of international law that the neorealist predicted.[36]

8.3.5 The Netherlands

On 18 March 2003 the Netherlands, like Italy, decides to give political rather than military support to the war against Iraq. Formally, this choice is explained by the lack of an overwhelming parliamentary majority and by the fact that the government had formally been a caretaker government since the parliamentary elections on 22 January 2003. At the same time, the Dutch Government offered Dutch troops for the reconstruction of Iraq after the war, preferably under UN authority. Considerations of international law played an important role during the decision-making process leading up to the decision of 18 March 2003. The perspective of Foreign Policy Analysis, with its focus on domestic players, seems best suited to tackle the complicated Dutch policy process.

First, the political context of the policy process in 2002–2003 mattered.[37] In the summer of 2002, after a turbulent campaign in which one party leader, Pim Fortuyn, was murdered, Prime Minister Jan Peter Balkenende led an unstable coalition cabinet consisting of Christian-democrats (CDA), economic liberals (VVD) and a new anti-political establishment party (LPF). The Prime Minister's preoccupation with domestic politics allowed Minister of Foreign Affairs Jaap de Hoop Scheffer to take the lead over Iraq. By October 2002 the LPF had left the coalition, turning the Cabinet into a caretaker government until May 2003 when Balkenende formed a new coalition with CDA, VVD and the left-liberal party D66. Between the elections of January 2003 and early March 2003 policy-making was constrained by the coalition talks between Christian-democrats and social-democrats (PvdA). The latter party had a strong international law abiding policy resisting any war without authorisation by a new Security Council resolution.

---

[36] de Villepin 1995.

[37] Cf. Rapport Commissie 2010, pp. 81–82.

Second, given the central role of the Minister of Foreign Affairs it is important to take into account the internal divisions within the Ministry of Foreign Affairs. Interestingly, the department's directorate responsible for legal advice (DJZ/IR) was present at a major policy meeting only once (at a so-called brainstorm session on 9 August 2002) and was never again close to decision-making until the final decision on 18 March. The brainstorm session was attended by de Hoop Scheffer, as well as representatives from the Ministry's major Directorates (Political Affairs [DGPZ], Africa and the Middle East [DAM], United Nations [DVF] and Legal Affairs [DJZ]). The meeting proved important to what eventually would become the dominant line of the Dutch Government: a new Security Council resolution was desirable but not indispensable. This view was not shared by DJZ/IR, but it became the dominant position of the Ministry and the Cabinet nonetheless, even before the adoption of Security Council Resolution 1441 on 8 November 2002. De Hoop Scheffer's subsequently limits the room of manoeuvre for the Dutch Cabinet: shortly after the brainstorm session he informs US Ambassador Sobel of the Dutch position regarding the use of violence; early September he accepts DGPZ's sharp formulation of a letter to the Dutch Lower House, which would reach Parliament before the Cabinet had time to discuss its contents.

Indeed, the full Cabinet would not discuss Iraq comprehensively until 15 November 2002.[38] At no instance until its final decision of 18 March 2003 would the Cabinet explicitly discuss the arguments in favour or against the dominant legal position, or discuss what exactly would entail a breach of SC Resolution 1441.[39] Indeed, the internal memo drafted by DJZ that discussed the legality of a war never reached the Cabinet. The memo argued that the legal argument in favour of war without explicit authorisation was extremely thin. The legal advisers also expected that the International Court of Justice was not likely to support the dominant perspective.[40] Interestingly, the Cabinet's letter of 18 March 2003 to the Dutch Parliament did not contain one justification of its decision in terms of international law.

Here, a Foreign Policy Analysis perspective helps explain the Dutch predicament. First, during the first months of 2003 the Cabinet's position was constrained by the coalition talks between Christian-democrats and social-democrats. Because the latter opposed war without a new resolution, the Cabinet ducked the legal issue as long as these coalition talks still seemed viable. Second, because of the Ministry of Foreign Affairs' early dominance of the policy process the official legal perspective, which framed the Cabinet's discussions, reflected the perspective of the dominant player within the Ministry, i.e., DGPZ, which dominated the flow of information within the Ministry. DGPZ's perspective was dominated by a strengthening of the international status of the Netherlands, which required a close

---

[38] Ibid., pp. 83–89 and 92.

[39] Ibid., pp. 255–258.

[40] In April 2003 DJZ would elaborate its position in a leaked paper; see, Memorandum Irak 2003.

relationship with the United States. The legal department DJZ, which held a very nuanced view on the role international law should play in the present case, had no access to these major players.[41]

The other perspectives seem to shed less light on the Dutch decision for political rather than military support. A neorealist would have expected the Netherlands to follow the United States more closely. This position had already become problematic in the 1980s and 1990s when the Netherlands opted to contribute to military missions in the Persian Gulf region through the Western European Union rather than as a formal ally of the United States. Although the neorealist position suggests that it would be difficult for the Netherlands to outrightly oppose the United States, it cannot account for the specific policy choices within the room of manoeuvre that the Netherlands still enjoys as a member of the Atlantic alliance. Constructivists would point to the self-image that the Netherlands projects abroad, as the country of international law. Even if this image affects the terms of the foreign policy debate in the Netherlands, it cannot fully explain its specific policy choice or its adherence to the claim that SC Resolution 1441 offered sufficient justification for the use of violence. Such an explanation requires the incorporation of the domestic struggle and the perspective on international law held by the dominant groups in that struggle.

8.4 Conclusions

The major conclusion of this contribution may be disappointing: there is no clear-cut answer to the question of how international law and international politics are related. The two major debates held in the IR discipline shed some light on the precise nature of the relationship. Depending on our assumptions regarding states' motives, we may formulate different predictions regarding the role international law may play in an anarchical world. Similarly, if we allow for the possibility that domestic players can be salient actors in addition to sovereign states, the attitude of states towards international law will depend on the relative openness of the state to pressures from such players. The choices a state makes will then be the product of the struggle between competing perspectives. This choice may be leaning either more towards respect for international law or towards the instrumental use of international law. Importantly, one should not assume that those 'allegedly cynical realists' and 'pro international law groups' are always pitted against each other: in the United States they were united in their opposition against the 2003 Iraq War. On the whole, however, it is important to pay attention to the possibility of rhetorical entrapment: once states decide to cast their policies in a certain international legal light, they can be expected to be monitored for consistency: not just by other sovereign states, but also by domestic players. From this follows, that we

[41] Rapport Commissie van Onderzoek Besluitvorming Irak 2010, pp. 243–251.

might expect democracies to be more sensitive to such 'naming and shaming': their systems of accountability may make politicians pay an electoral price for not living up to their own international legal claims.

The five case studies of the role of international law in decisions regarding the 2003 Iraq War allow for some interesting qualifications. First, in today's unipolar world even the world's most powerful state does not profess that might makes right. A neorealist perspective would suggest that, 'when the crunch comes', great powers will subject international law to their vital interest no matter what. Assuming that Iraq posed a threat to American vital interests (an assumption not shared by most neorealists), it remains puzzling why, for a long time, the United States pursued a second Security Council resolution. When that proved impossible, it went to great lengths to argue that SC Resolution 1441 provided sufficient legal basis. Of course, one may sweep it aside as simple instrumental use of international law. Neoliberals rightly point to the effect adherence to international law may have in building a broad, effective coalition. The very fact that the United States weakened its position by going against the wishes of various (potential) allies illustrates the constructivist argument that international law nowadays is an important source of soft power and that the United States resented the damage it suffered in terms of international standing. None of these perspectives then offer a complete account of the choices the United States made. They need to be supplemented with tools from Foreign Policy Analysis which point at the domestic struggle of competing groups with diverging views on the role international law should play.

Second, middle powers seem particularly troublesome: Italy and Great Britain had an interest in improving their status by bandwagoning with the leader; France had an interest in improving its status by balancing against the United States. In the latter case respect for international law served that purpose. In the British and Italian cases it required taking into account domestic constituents. In Great Britain Tony Blair's persuasive powers mobilised enough Labour MPs behind a narrow interpretation of international law. In Italy, the necessity to stay close to the United States, as well as France and Germany provided room to domestic actors requiring a second Security Council resolution and entailed that the Berlusconi government could only offer political support. Third, a state's position in an international legal debate is increasingly the product of a competition between international and domestic players. Some intrinsically value international law; others see it as a state instrument. Powerful coalitions may cause the state to take a specific view: the dominance of DGPZ within the Dutch Ministry of Foreign Affairs early in the policy-making process, supported by the Minister of Foreign Affairs and the relative absence of the Prime Minister in the early stages, set the stage for effective Dutch acceptance of SC Resolution 1441 as sufficient ground for the use of force. The coalition talks between Christian-democrats and social-democrats in early 2003 rendered a formal embracement of that position more difficult. In this sense domestic might did make right.

All in all, the perspectives presented in this contribution offer different accounts of when and why states attach importance to international law in international affairs. The war against Iraq in 2003 demonstrates that nowadays it has become increasingly difficult for states to ignore international law. For IR theory, this means that international law restricts the range of legitimate options available to states. At the same time, legal discourse gives ammunition to non-state actors in their attempts to affect the preferences and behaviour of states. The more open the political systems of these states, the more international legal concerns are likely to be part of policy considerations. In that sense, the growth of the number of democracies looks auspicious. At the same time, international law remains open to competing interpretations. The specific choices states make thus remain difficult to predict. Witness the Security Council resolution authorising a no-fly zone over Libya in 2011:[42] it was designed in such a way as to prevent a veto from China and Russia. Once adopted, however, the text allowed for different interpretations ranging from protecting civilians to promoting regime change, thus serving different interests. From an IR perspective, although international law may have become more salient to states' considerations, their actual policies will remain the product of political battle; a battle which is increasingly also conducted by non-state actors.

References

Allison G (1971) Essence of decision. Explaining the Cuban missile crisis, Little Brown, Boston

Andreatta F (2001) Italy as a crossroads. The foreign policy of a medium power at the end of bipolarity. Daedalus 130:45–65

Axelrod R, Keohane R (1985) Achieving cooperation under anarchy: strategies and institutions. World Politics 38:226–254

Badie D (2010) Groupthink, Iraq, and the war on terror: explaining US policy shift toward Iraq. Foreign Policy Anal 6:277–296

Blair T (2010) A journey. Arrow Books, London

Bueno de Mesquita B, Lalman D (1992) War and reason. Yale University Press, New Haven

Byers M (ed) (2000) The role of law in international politics. Oxford University Press, Oxford

Christiansen T, Jørgensen K, Wiener A (1999) The social construction of Europe. J Eur Public Policy 6:528–544

Cole D (2008) Justice at war. The men and ideas that shaped America's war on terror. New York Review Books, New York

Collins R, White N (eds) (2011) International organizations and the idea of autonomy. Institutional independence in the international legal order, Routledge

Cook R (2003) The point of departure. Diaries from the front bench. Simon and Schuster, London

Danner M (2006) The secret way to war. The Downing Street memo and the Iraq war's buried history. New York Review Books, New York

Davidson J (2009) Italy-US relations since the end of the cold war: prestige, peace, and the transatlantic balance. Bull Italian Politics 1:289–308

Davidson J (2011) America's allies and war. Kosovo, Afghanistan, and Iraq. Palgrave Macmillan, Houndmills

de Villepin X (1995) Quel ONU pour la France? In: Lewin A (ed) La France et l'ONU. Collection Panoramiques, Condé-sur-Noireau, pp 69–78

Dunne T, Kurki M, Smith S (eds) (2007) International relations theories. Discipline and diversity. Oxford University Press, Oxford

---

[42] SC Resolution 1973/2011.

Evangelista M (2008) Law, ethics, and the war on terror. Polity Press, Oxford
Evangelista M (2011) Atomic ambivalance. Italy's evolving attitude towards nuclear weapons. In: Giacomello G, Verbeek B (eds) Italy's foreign policy in the 21st century: the new assertiveness of an aspiring middle power. Lexington, Lanham, pp 103–124
Goldstein J, Kahler M, Keohane R, Slaughter A (eds) (2000) Legalization and world politics. Int Org 54:xi–xiii, 385–703
Keohane R (1984) After hegemony. Cooperation and discord in the world political economy. Princeton University Press, Princeton
Keohane R, Nye J (eds) (1971) Transnational relations and world politics. Harvard University Press, Cambridge
Kissinger H (2002) War on terror: Iraq is phase II. http://www.theage.com.au/articles/2002/09/05/1031115911092.html. 6 Sept 2002. Accessed 19 Oct 2011
Lake D (2010) Rightful rules: authority, order, and the foundations of global governance. Int Stud Quart 54:587–614
Mazarr M (2007) The Iraq war and agenda setting. Foreign Policy Anal 3:1–23
Mearsheimer J (1994/1995) The false promise of international institutions. Int Secur 19:5–49
Mearsheimer J (2001) The tragedy of great power politics. WW Norton, New York
Memorandum Irak—Rechtsbasis militair ingrijpen (2003) kenmerk DJZ/IR/2003/158, 29 Apr 2003
Murphy C (1994) International organization and industrial change: global governance since 1850. Polity Press and Oxford University Press, Oxford
New York Times (2002) War with Iraq is not in America's national interest. Paid advertisement, 26 Sept 2002. http://mearsheimer.uchicago.edu/pdfs/P0012.pdf. Accessed 5 Sept 2011
Nuti L (2003) The role of the US in Italy's foreign policy. Int Spectator 38:91–101
Nye J (2004) Soft power. The means to succeed in world politics. Public Affairs, New York
Onuf N (1989) World of our making. Rules and rule in social theory and international relations. University of South Carolina Press, Columbia
Rapport Commissie van Onderzoek Besluitvorming Irak (2010). Boom, Amsterdam
Reinalda B (ed) (2011) The Ashgate research companion to non-state actors. Ashgate, Aldershot
Reinalda B, Verbeek B (eds) (1998) Autonomous policymaking by international organizations. Routledge, London
Reynolds D (1985–1986) A 'special relationship'? America, Britain and the international order since the Second World War. Int Aff 62:1–20
Romano S (2006) Berlusconi's foreign policy: inverting traditional priorities. Int Spectator 42:101–107
Short C (2004) An honourable deception? New Labour, Iraq and the abuse of power. Simon and Schuster, London
Snyder R, Bruck H, Sapin B (1962) Foreign policy decision-making. The Free Press, New York
Stothard P (2004) Thirty days: an inside account of Tony Blair at war. Harper Collins, New York
Verbeek B (2003) Decisionmaking in Great Britain during the Suez crisis. Small groups and a persistent leader, Ashgate
Walt S (1985) Origins of alliances. Cornell University Press, Ithaca
Waltz K (1979) Theory of international politics. McGraw Hill, New York
Weldes J (1999) Constructing the national interest. The United States and the Cuban missile crisis. University of Minnesota Press, Minneapolis
Wendt A (1992) Anarchy is what states make of it: The social construction of power politics. Int Organ 46:391–425
Wendt A (1999) Social theory of international relations. Cambridge University Press, Cambridge
Woodward B (2004) Plan of attack. The definitive account of the decision to invade Iraq. Simon and Schuster, New York
Zehfuss M (2002) Constructivism in international relations: The politics of reality. Cambridge University Press, Cambridge

Chapter 9
Libya and Lessons from Iraq: International Law and the Use of Force by the United Kingdom

Nigel D. White

Abstract Those countries, including the United Kingdom, using force in Libya in 2011 have taken much greater care to ensure that their actions are underpinned by legality. This suggests a return to respect for the jus ad bellum, but as the operation against Libya unfolded it became clearer that some of the problems that undermined the legality and legitimacy of the invasion of Iraq 8 years earlier had not been avoided, which raises the question of how such operations can be kept within the strict bounds of the law.

Keywords Libya · Use of force · United Kingdom · Responsibility to protect · Security Council resolutions · War powers

Contents

This article is based on evidence given to the House of Commons Political and Constitutional Reform Committee, 31 March 2011. This article was completed towards the end of June 2011 while the Libyan revolution and operation was, contrary to initial expectations, still in progress.

N. D. White (✉)
Public International Law, University of Nottingham, Nottingham, UK
e-mail: nigel.white@nottingham.ac.uk

I. F. Dekker and E. Hey (eds.), *Netherlands Yearbook of International Law 2011*,
Netherlands Yearbook of International Law 42, DOI: 10.1007/978-90-6704-849-1_9,

9.1 Introduction

In mid-February 2011, within the wider context of unrest and revolution in North Africa and the Middle East, an uprising began against the regime of Colonel Muammar Gaddafi, ruler of Libya since 1969. The uprising gained momentum but was resisted by the regime and forces loyal to him, violence increased, leading to an internal armed conflict between rebels with their base in the eastern city of Benghazi, and Gaddafi forces from their stronghold in the western capital of Tripoli. The imbalance between the sides (particularly in heavy weaponry and attack aircraft), and the reported systematic attacks on unarmed civilians by government forces, led to debate in Western capitals about the imperative of protecting civilians, initially primarily by means of the imposition of a no-fly zone aimed at preventing Gaddafi's airforce from attacking civilians, but the hidden pretext was to stop his forces blocking a successful rebellion.

The main protagonists in favour of the use of military force against Libya, France and the UK, were mindful of the lessons from Iraq, both in terms of the legality of the 2003 invasion (when the main protagonists were the UK and the US) and its state-building consequences. This short article considers, from the British perspective, whether those lessons have resulted in a use of force in 2011 against Libya, the legality and legitimacy of which is a significant improvement on the use of force in 2003 against Iraq. While the evidence presented at the Iraq Inquiry being held in the UK strongly indicates that the use of force against Iraq was unlawful,[1] the UK has taken much greater care in 2011 to ensure that its actions against Libya are underpinned by legality. This suggests a return to respect for the *jus ad bellum* by the UK, but as the operation against Libya has unfolded it has become clear that some of the problems that undermined the legality and legitimacy of the invasion of Iraq have not been avoided, which raises the question of how such operations can be kept within the strict bounds of the law. Nevertheless, with politicians in the UK debating the use of force in the Spring of 2011, almost exactly 8 years after the invasion of Iraq, they are looking back to that

---

[1] UK Prime Minister Gordon Brown announced the establishment of the Iraq Inquiry in the House of Commons on 15 June 2009, its terms of reference being 'to consider the period from summer 2001, before military operations began in March 2003, and the UK's subsequent involvement in Iraq up to the end of July 2009. The Prime Minister told the House of Commons: 'the Iraq Inquiry will look at the run-up to the conflict, the conflict itself and the reconstruction. The objective is to learn the lessons from the events surrounding the conflict', available at http://iraqinquiry.org.uk/faq.aspx. See evidence given to the Inquiry by Sir Michael Wood, Foreign Office Legal Adviser in 2003, on 26 January 2010, available at http://www.iraqinquiry.org.uk/media/43614/100126am-wood.pdf; and by Elizabeth Wilmshurst, Deputy Legal Adviser at the FCO in 2003, available at http://www.iraqinquiry.org.uk/media/44211/20100126pm-wilmshurst-final.pdf. Both considered the use of force against Iraq in 2003 to be illegal as a matter of international law. For Lord Goldsmith's (the Attorney-General at the time) more equivocal evidence of 27 January 2010, available at http://www.iraqinquiry.org.uk/media/43803/100127-goldsmith.pdf.

controversial episode to learn crucial lessons, including lessons about the importance of international law.

9.2 UN Security Council Resolutions on Libya

Prior to the use of force by aircraft drawn from member states of the North Atlantic Treaty Organization (NATO), on 26 February 2011 the United Nations Security Council (UNSC) unanimously agreed to the imposition of an arms embargo against the whole of Libya and of targeted sanctions against Gaddafi and his supporters in the form of an assets freeze and travel ban.[2] That Resolution (1970) also referred the situation in Libya since 15 February 2011 to the Prosecutor of the International Criminal Court (ICC) after considering that the widespread and systematic attacks taking place in Libya may amount to crimes against humanity. Without any sense of irony the Resolution decided that the Libyan authorities shall cooperate fully with the ICC, while recognising that states not party to the Rome Statute on the ICC (including the USA, Russia and China from the five permanent members of the Security Council—P5) have no obligations under the Statute.

Considerations that a travel ban and a referral to the ICC may well have made Gaddafi more intransigent and trapped did not prevail, and with the Libyan authorities failing to adhere to the obligation to end the violence imposed by Resolution 1970, but also at a point when Gaddafi's forces were about to attempt the recapture of Benghazi from rebel forces, the UK, France, the US and Lebanon persuaded the UNSC to authorise military action in Resolution 1973 on the 17 March 2011.[3] This Resolution's provenance can be traced back to the Korean War in 1950 and Operation Desert Storm in 1991, when the UNSC authorised US-led Coalitions of the Willing to deal, by taking necessary measures (UN-speak for the use of military force), with breaches of international peace and security.[4] This form of authorisation has been recognised in UN practice and in most jurisprudence as a lawful delegation of power to member states to take military action under Chapter VII, Article 42 of the Charter, to deal with threats to or breaches of the peace as a recognised exception, along with the right of self-defence, to the ban on the threat or use of force in the UN Charter.[5]

In Resolution 1973, after repeating its statement in Resolution 1970 that the Libyan government had the responsibility to protect the population, the UNSC authorised member states to take all necessary measures, 'to protect civilians and civilian populated areas under threat of attack' in Libya, including Benghazi,

---

2 UNSC Res. 1970, 26 February 2011.

3 UNSC Res. 1973, 17 March 2011.

4 UNSC Res. 83, 28 June 1950; UNSC Res. 678, 29 November 1990.

5 Articles 2(4), 42 and 51 of the UN Charter. For discussion see White and Ulgen 1997, p. 378; Blokker 2000, p. 541.

'while excluding a foreign occupation force of any form on any part of Libyan territory'. As is common with such authorisations to use force under Chapter VII of the Charter, the obligation on member states to the UNSC was a reporting one, in this case to the United Nations Secretary-General (UNSG), of the measures taken pursuant to the resolution. Resolution 1973 also imposed a no-fly zone in Libyan airspace 'in order to help protect civilians', and authorised member states 'to take all necessary measures to enforce compliance' with the no-fly zone.

Resolution 1973 thus contained an enforceable no-fly zone, a measure that had been mooted since early in the crisis, but it also allowed NATO states to go further and take military action to protect civilians, leading to an on-going debate in the UK as to whether this could include, for example, the targeting of Gaddafi himself on the basis that he was the ultimate source of the problem for civilians.[6] When an armed conflict is occurring between states or within a state, as was the case in Libya where there was both an internal armed conflict between rebels and government forces and an international one between Libya and the 'Coalition' or 'Allies' acting under Resolution 1973, then soldiers and their commanders are legitimate targets under the laws of war,[7] and in this sense Colonel Gaddafi was a legitimate target, but the law of war was not the only legal regime applicable here. Indeed, it was arguably qualified by the UNSC resolution which authorised the prosecution of the war,[8] and which does not so readily bear such a wide interpretation. Indeed, at the UNSC meeting, at which Resolution 1973 was adopted,[9] there was controversy surrounding the common understanding of the Resolution suggesting that great caution should be exercised when subsequent attempts were made to place meanings on it that are difficult to reconcile with the text and background to the Resolution; bearing in mind that the paragraph in the Resolution that authorised the protection of civilians was seemingly added late to the text to enable NATO forces to stop what appeared to be an imminent and brutal attack by Gadaffi forces on Benghazi.

---

[6] At Prime Minister's Question Time on 23 March 2011, the leader of the opposition, Ed Miliband asked the Prime Minister to 'clarify the Government's position on the targeting of Colonel Gaddafi? It is important that we stick to the terms of the UN resolution as we seek to maintain the coalition we have built on that resolution'. In response David Cameron stated that 'all our targets must be selected to be absolutely in line with UN Security Council resolution 1973. That allows us to take "all necessary measures" to enforce a no-fly zone and to put it in place as safely as possible as well as to take action to protect civilian life. All targets should be in line with that but I do not propose to give a running commentary on targets or, frankly, to say anything beyond that', *Hansard,* HC, Vol. 525, Col. 943, 23 March 2011. NATO clearly targeted Colonel Gaddafi and senior members of his regime, *BBC News*, 20 June 2011, available at http://www.bbc.co.uk/news/world-africa-13846128.

[7] Dinstein 2004, pp. 88–94.

[8] On the overriding effects of Article 103 see Liivoja 2008, p. 583. This has been interpreted too broadly by UK Courts as overriding inconsistent human rights obligations in *R (Al Jedda)* v *Secretary of State of Defence* [2007] UKHL 58.

[9] UNSC 6498th mtg, 17 March 2011.

Thus even though there was a clear and current authorisation to use force against Libya in Resolution 1973, there were shades of the debate that occurred in 2003 in relation to Iraq concerning the interpretation of older resolutions going back to Resolution 678 of 1990.[10] Nevertheless, there is a vast difference between the argument made by the UK in relation to Iraq in 2003, namely that a 1990 authorisation to use force to implement Security Council resolutions in the context of removing Iraq from Kuwait was still a valid authority 13 years later for invading Iraq and removing Saddam Hussein as well as his Weapons of Mass Destruction (WMD);[11] and the interpretation of a Resolution adopted in March 2011 sanctioning necessary measures to protect civilians and enforce a no-fly zone, which was being implemented by states within a week of its adoption by the UNSC.

The legal basis for the Libyan action is exponentially so much stronger, but the Libyan operation has not eliminated some fundamental problems of the UN collective security 'system' so starkly revealed by the Iraq crisis of 2003. The system is rudimentary and depends upon political consensus between the P5 being present, which it was in March 2011, but not in March 2003; but that precious Resolution of 2011 (1973) was, at the time of writing, likely (though not definitely),[12] to be the only source of authority for the use of force against Libya and therefore was subject to greater and greater demands placed upon it, potentially stretching the Resolution beyond its meaning and contrary to the collective understanding of that resolution. The problem is that the veto-dominated negotiating system is too unwieldy to allow nimble executive responses to constantly changing security situations. This means that decisions on implementation of Resolution 1973 take place at the regional level in NATO, or between France and the UK, or indeed within the political systems of each and every state contributing to the air cam-

---

[10] White 2004, p. 645.

[11] See the Attorney General's advice given to the House of Commons immediately prior to the invasion on 17 March 2003, which was to the effect that the authority to use force against Iraq given in SC Resolution 678 (1990) was revived by a material breach by Iraq of Resolution 1441 (2002) and earlier disarmament resolutions; see *Hansard*, HC, Vol. 401, Col. 760 (18 March 2003) when Prime Minister Tony Blair relied on this argument in proposing a substantive vote. The Attorney General's full advice was not released until 28 April 2005, in which, in contrast, he concluded that 'if the matter ever came before a court', that court 'may well' conclude that Resolution 1441 did require a 'further Council decision in order to revive the authorization' in Resolution 687, *The Guardian*, 28 April 2005, available at http://www.guardian.co.uk/politics/2005/apr/28/election2005.uk.

[12] See discussion about the EU possibly seeking UNSC authority for a humanitarian aid military mission—EUFOR Libya—at the beginning of April, *The Guardian Weekly*, 2 April 2011, p. 5.

paign over Libya.[13] While this is to be expected, the absence of any control at the UN level is at the same time both alarming and unsurprising.[14]

During the UNSC meeting on 17 March at which Resolution 1973 was adopted,[15] the unanimity behind Resolution 1970 was broken, but not to the extent of disabling the adoption of Resolution 1973, by 10 votes to 0 with 5 abstentions (Brazil, China, Germany, India, Russia). Those abstaining were not only the usual advocates of nonintervention (China and Russia) but equally important states, each with a strong case for permanent membership themselves. The change within the UNSC from the situation in Kosovo in 1999 where the UNSC could not agree on military action to protect the Kosovars,[16] to Libya in 2011 is marginal, but sufficient to give the initial action a sound legal basis. That marginal push may have been helped by the emergence in the early twenty-first century of the idea that there is a responsibility to protect (R2P) on the part of the international community, when a state has failed to protect its population from crimes against humanity or other similar egregious acts.[17] The UN World Summit Outcome Document of 2005 placed this responsibility squarely on the UNSC if a state had failed to protect its population.[18] Both UNSC Resolution 1970 and 1973 on Libya stated in the preamble that the Libyan authorities bore responsibility to protect the population of Libya, which could be seen as a reference to R2P, though tellingly neither Resolution went on to state that since the Libyan government had failed to protect

---

[13] In a letter to national newspapers in France, the UK and US, President Obama, Prime Minister Cameron and President Sarkozy made it clear that 'our duty and our mandate under UN Security Council Resolution 1973 is to protect civilians, and we are doing that. It is not to remove Gaddafi by force. But it is impossible to imagine a future for Libya with Gaddafi in power. The International Criminal Court is rightly investigating the crimes committed against civilians and the grievous violations of international law. It is unthinkable that someone who has tried to massacre his own people can play a part in their future government. The brave citizens of those towns that have held out against forces that have been mercilessly targeting them would face a fearful vengeance if the world accepted such an arrangement. It would be an unconscionable betrayal'. *BBC News*, 15 April 2011, available at http://www.bbc.co.uk/news/world-africa-13090646.

[14] Towards the end of June 2011 there had been 8 further formal meetings of the UNSC on Libya since the adoption of UNSC Resolution 1973 on 17 March. These consisted of briefings by the UNSG, the representative of the UNSG, the Chairman of the Committee established by UNSC Resolution 1970, the prosecutor of the ICC, by UN officials on humanitarian aid and post-conflict rebuilding, and by the AU. See UNSC 6505th mtg, 24 March 2011; 6507th mtg, 28 March 2011; 6509th mtg, 4th April 2011; 6527th mtg, 3 May 2011; 6528th mtg, 4 May 2011; 6530th mtg, 9 May 2011; 6541st mtg, 31 May 2011; UNSC 6555th mtg, 15 June 2011.

[15] UNSC 6498th mtg, 17 March 2011.

[16] See UNSC Res. 1199, 23 September 1998; UNSC Res. 1203, 24 October 1998. Neither resolution expressly authorised 'necessary measures' to protect the people of Kosovo.

[17] See International Commission on Intervention and State Sovereignty, *The Responsibility To Protect* (International Development Research Centre, Ottawa, 2001); Report of the High Level Panel on 'Threats, Challenges and Change' (UN, 2004), recommendation 55; Report of the UNSG, 'In Larger Freedom: Towards Security, Development and Freedom for All' (UN, 2005), para 135.

[18] UNGA Res. 60/1, 24 October 2005, para 139.

its population, the UNSC had a responsibility to do so. Instead, the UNSC makes it clear in Resolution 1970 that its responsibility is for the maintenance of international peace and security, its traditional concern, making no reference to any other form of responsibility it might have. Thus while there is no doubt that the Libyan crisis will be lauded as a precedent for R2P, the Resolutions themselves do not bear such an interpretation.

It is informative to look at the reasons given by those abstaining on Resolution 1973. Germany expressed concern about being drawn into a protracted conflict and about the intervention causing more harm than it might prevent. India could not vote for the Resolution because of lack of clear information on the ground, and lack of clarity about the enforcement measures to be taken under Resolution 1973. Brazil's concern was that the resolution went beyond a no-fly zone, which was the measure being discussed up until that point, and was also concerned that the measures taken to protect civilians would cause more harm than good to those very people. Russia criticised the way in which the draft resolution 'morphed' before the eyes of Council members by going beyond a no-fly zone, and criticised the drafters for not answering questions about rules of engagement and limits on the use of force. China was generally against use of force in international relations, but because of regional support from the Arab League for a limited form of intervention as well as the special circumstances of Libya, had decided not to vote against. Thus there were clear warnings to NATO states to be careful about the nature and extent of their military operations. Just as the US and the UK should have heeded the concerns of many members of the Security Council when Resolution 1441 was adopted in November 2002 in the build-up towards military action by those states against Iraq, to the effect that the Resolution did not provide for the use of force,[19] so NATO states in the bombing campaign over Libya should have heeded the concerns of the members of the authorising body as to the extent of the use of force.

Having said that Resolution 1973 did allow for greater use of force than was anticipated in the build-up to its adoption. From the initial debates about an enforced no-fly zone, the end result was an authorisation to undertake a much greater use of force—necessary measures (mainly in the form of bombing) to protect civilians, necessitated by the imminent attack on Benghazi, thereby bringing it much closer to the military action over Kosovo in 1999 though that had not been authorised by the UNSC.[20] UNSC Resolution 1973 was rushed through even more quickly than is the norm, and promised much debate about its interpretation and meaning. The use of force by NATO planes towards the end of March and beginning of April seemed to be increasingly directed at supporting the rebels and in several respects went beyond the protection of civilians as mandated in Resolution 1973, by for example targeting battle tanks, though the argument was that these were being used to attack civilians and not simply in the fight

---

[19] UNSC 4644th mtg, 8 November 2002.

[20] *Supra,* note 16.

against the rebels.[21] What started out in appearance at least, though not so evident in political rhetoric or in the UNSC Resolutions themselves, as an application of the emerging 'responsibility to protect' doctrine,[22] seemed by mid-June to be heading towards another instance of regime change as in Iraq in 2003, with all the problems that entailed.

9.3 The UK and Libya

Early debates within the UK Parliament reflected this potential change in interpretation of Resolution 1973. Parliamentary debates on decisions to deploy troops to conflict zones have been shown by this writer elsewhere to provide a strong indication of the attitude towards international law within the political establishment in the UK.[23] This is not so much a search for *opinio juris* in a classical sense, but an examination of a particular state's understandings of, and in broad terms respect for, international law. Given the UK's leading role in many of the recent uses of force, including Iraq in 2003 and Libya in 2011, that understanding and respect becomes all the more important. This section will consider the debates on Libya within Parliament in March–June 2011 to discern what lessons had been learned from the invasion of Iraq in 2003.

On 28 February 2011, the Prime Minister, David Cameron, informed the House of Commons as to how the UK would implement Resolution 1970, but also mentioned that the government was planning for different scenarios including a no-fly zone.[24] On Friday 18 March following the adoption of Resolution 1973, the Prime Minister informed the House about the implementation of that Resolution, and spoke about the urgency of the situation and the imminent attack on Benghazi where Gaddafi had threatened to show no mercy.[25] At this stage the Prime Minister was clear that Resolution 1973 had limits; to protect civilian and civilian populated areas and did not permit an occupation force in any form.[26] He repeated this when asked, with Iraq in mind, about the problem of how UNSC Resolutions had been misinterpreted in the past.[27]

---

[21] In a TV interview the Prime Minister stated that the terms of UNSC Resolution 1973 made it difficult for NATO forces though they would stick to the terms of the Resolution, but this would allow them 'to actually take out Gaddafi's tanks and artillery and command and control that are unleashing this hell on people in Misrata in Brega, and other towns up and down the Libyan coast', *BBC News*, 17 April 2011, available at http://www.bbc.co.uk/news/uk-politics-13107834.

[22] On the responsibility to protect doctrine see Focarelli 2008, p. 191.

[23] White 2009, 2010, p. 814.

[24] *Hansard,* HC, Vol. 524, Cols. 23–26, 28 February 2011.

[25] *Hansard,* HC, Vol. 525, Col. 611, 18 March 2011.

[26] Ibid., Col. 612.

[27] Ibid., Col. 628 (Mark Tami MP).

Furthermore, the Prime Minister informed the House that the Cabinet had been given clear legal advice from the Attorney General, which he summarised for the House in terms that Resolution 1973, as a Chapter VII resolution clearly authorising necessary measures to protect civilians and enforce a no-fly zone, was a legally recognised basis on which to deploy and use force.[28] However, that legal advice did not appear to address the subsequent interpretation of Resolution 1973 and did not go to issues such as when force could be used to protect civilians; whether the arms embargo imposed in UNSC Resolution 1970 could be breached in favour of the rebels; and the issue of legitimate targets. Resolution 1973 stated that force could be used 'to protect civilians and civilian populated areas under threat of attack', which suggested that the standard was somewhat wider than self-defence of third parties, which usually requires an imminent attack,[29] but not as wide as simply destroying any military target on the basis that it might be the source of a future attack against civilians. David Cameron was asked by one MP whether the phrase in UNSC Resolution 1973, where necessary measures to protect civilians were authorised 'notwithstanding paragraph 9 of resolution 1970', which had imposed the arms embargo against the whole of Libya, would permit the arming of the rebels.[30] The Prime Minister thought that the arms embargo was still in place for the whole of Libya and not just against the government.[31]

One lesson from Iraq that does not seem to have been accepted in the Libyan crisis by the British government was the need for full advice on the international legal basis of the operation being made available to the House of Commons and not just to the Cabinet, before any debate leading to a vote in Parliament, in order to enable MPs to make an informed decision. Arguably such legal advice should draw upon wider expertise to ensure that it is balanced and represents an accurate view of international law to avoid the problems of Iraq, where there emerged several versions of the Attorney General's advice.[32] It is anticipated that the Iraq inquiry will show that most international lawyers in the UK agreed that the military action in Iraq in 2003 was unlawful,[33] yet the advice given to Parliament immediately before the invasion was that it had a clear legal basis.[34] In contrast to Iraq, there was a clear Chapter VII resolution, Resolution 1973, authorising the use of force in the case of Libya. Though a summary of the Attorney General's legal advice on the current action in Libya was released the process still seems the same as in Iraq in 2003. Though the legal basis was clear—a Chapter VII resolution

---

[28] Ibid., Col. 613 (David Cameron MP). Legal advice, 21 March 2011, available at http://www.politics.co.uk/features/foreign-policy/legal-advice-on-libya-mission-in-full-$21387896.htm.

[29] Fletcher and Ohlin 2008, pp. 63–72.

[30] *Hansard* HC, Vol. 525, Col. 627, 18 March 2011 (William Cash MP).

[31] Ibid. (David Cameron MP).

[32] *Supra*, note 11.

[33] See the Iraq Inquiry's invitation to international lawyers to make submissions on the legal basis of the 2003 military action against Iraq, 24 June 2011, available at http://www.iraqinquiry.org.uk/background/100602-submissions-from-international-lawyers.aspx.

[34] *Supra*, note 11.

authorising necessary measures to protect civilians and to enforce the no-fly zone—the legal advice did not anticipate the many problematic issues of interpretation and application that remain and were clearly foreseeable at the time of the Resolution's adoption. Unfortunately, the Attorney General's legal advice did not appear to be the full legal advice necessary for Parliament to make informed decisions.

During the initial Parliamentary debate David Cameron stated that the government 'will table a substantive motion for debate next week, but I am sure that the House will accept that the situation requires us to move forward on the basis of the Security Council Resolution immediately'.[35] Unlike in the case of Iraq where the slow build-up to conflict allowed for a substantive vote in the House of Commons in favour of the military action before the invasion commenced,[36] there was no vote before the RAF used force in Libya, although the leader of the opposition, Ed Miliband, did offer his party's support.[37]

The UK's deployment of force to Libya has reignited the debate sparked by the invasion of Iraq in 2003, about whether there needs to be a formalised convention (a 'war powers' resolution) or even an Act of Parliament enshrining Parliament's right to have a say in the deployment of troops, which still remains a prerogative power of the executive in the UK.[38] Even if this happens the content of any normative framework purporting to govern such decisions will contain exceptions for necessity, for example where the use of force is unavoidable ('leaving no choice of means or no moment for deliberation'),[39] either in self-defence or in cases of humanitarian necessity.

The prospect of enshrining the constitutional process of troop deployment in an Act of Parliament raises the prospect of judicial review of decisions to go to war,

---

35 *Hansard,* HC, Vol. 525, Col. 613, 18 March 2011.

36 *Hansard,* HC, Vol. 401, Cols 906–911, 18 March 2003.

37 *Hansard,* HC, Vol. 525, Col. 615, 18 March 2011.

38 Graham Allen MP raised the issue on the 21 March in a substantive debate 2 days after force had been used by the UK by stating that this 'House is not taking any decisions: the Government have already taken a decision and have graciously allowed us a debate today. Does he agree that if we are to ensure that we stay properly informed, which the Prime Minister and Leader of the Opposition have both talked about, we need to resolve the question of the House's rights in respect of when this country goes to war? As we are the elected Chamber there ought to be something in our Standing Orders or in the Cabinet manual or some other place that gives the Chamber the right to be consulted before or after an action takes place.' David Winnick MP stated 'I wish we could have had this debate before military action had been taken. I referred to that on a point of order and do not want to dwell on it because time is very short, but we must establish that, when military action is going to be taken, the House of Commons should debate the issue first. There is no doubt what the result of any vote tonight will be, and there would have been no difference if one had taken place on Saturday, but it would have been better if the House had so decided'. Foreign Secretary William Hague responded that 'We will ... enshrine in law for the future the necessity of consulting Parliament on military action,' *Hansard,* HC, Vol. 525, Cols. 739, 752, 799, 21 March 2011.

39 Following the criteria in the Caroline incident of 1837. See 29 *British and Foreign State Papers* 1137–11378; 30 *British and State Papers* 195–196.

which may help ensure that Parliament scrutinises the legality of any decision very carefully and is prepared not to vote for any proposed deployment or use of force that has no grounding in international law. But to do this Parliament must be given full legal advice, otherwise it is being asked to vote for a decision without being given the necessary information. However, the prospect, even if a distant one, of the Courts becoming involved in issues of troop deployment will probably deter MPs from voting for such a piece of legislation, therefore making a non-statutory war powers resolution the more realistic option. This would still instil a necessary democratic balance to conflict decision-making, but also would enable MPs to consider the legality as well as the wider objectives of the proposed war. They might, if given clear and full legal opinion, decide to vote against a war if the legality is doubtful; though they might disregard those legal doubts if it was felt that a use of force may not be clearly lawful but was nevertheless legitimate,[40] and they could do so without fear of being subject to judicial review. But again to be able to make this informed choice MPs must have full access to clear and comprehensive legal advice. By these means international law should become an important determining factor in political decisions to go to war or otherwise to use force, which is surely a positive, indeed unarguable, development. As yet, a war powers resolution remains unadopted.[41]

In contrast to debates during the build-up towards NATO's previous humanitarian-inspired bombing campaign in 1999 over Kosovo, when the UNSC was blocked by China and Russia, the Prime Minister saw the abstention of China and Russia on Resolution 1973 as a positive step forward for international law, stating that this would not have occurred in the past;[42] thereby suggesting the possible dawn of a new era of humanitarian intervention under UN authority. This issue was taken further when there was a full debate in the House on a substantive motion on Monday 21 March, 2 days after the RAF had become involved in the military action over Libya. The substantive motion debated and voted upon welcomed UNSC Resolution 1973, indicated that there was humanitarian necessity, regional support and a clear legal basis for action, and therefore supported the government in taking necessary measures to protect civilians and enforce the no-fly zone.[43] When asked why not intervene in other countries as well where on-going repression of discontent was brutal (Yemen was the example given),[44]

---

[40] This was essentially the view of the House of Commons Foreign Affairs Committee in its review of the Kosovo operation in 1999. See *Hansard*, HC, Foreign Affairs Committee, Fourth Report 1999–2000, HC 28-I, 7 June 2000, para124–44.

[41] In its report on the subject the Political and Constitutional Reform Committee of the House of Commons recommended that 'the Government should as a first step bring forward a draft detailed parliamentary resolution, for consultation with us among others, and for debate and decision by the end of 2011', Political and Constitutional Reform Committee, Eighth Report, 'Parliament's Role in Conflict Decisions', 17 May 2011.

[42] *Hansard*, HC, Vol. 525, Col. 627, 18 March 2011.

[43] *Hansard*, HC, Vol. 525, Col. 700, 21 March 2011 (David Cameron MP).

[44] Ibid., Col. 708, 21 March 2011 (Andrew George MP).

the Prime Minister replied that 'because we cannot do the right thing everywhere does not mean we should not do it when we have clear permission for and a national interest in doing so.'[45] He finished by saying that 'this is not going into a country and knocking over its Government, and then owning and being responsible for everything that happens subsequently. This is about protecting people and giving the Libyan people a chance to reshape their country.' He made it clear that UNSC Resolution 1973 'explicitly does not provide legal authority for action to bring about Gaddafi's removal from power by military means.'[46]

In order to emphasise the limited nature of the intervention and the desire to keep within the bounds of the law Foreign Secretary William Hague stated at the outset of the air campaign on 21 March 2011 that:

> [w]e are clear that we are engaged in this action to protect the civilian population and we were clear, as last week went on, that we had to act with all possible speed. That is why we moved heaven and earth, diplomatically, to pass the UN resolution on Thursday night. Yes, we took a risk in doing that because nine positive votes are required in the Security Council and there can be no vetoes. To have been defeated on that resolution would have made it hard to take any subsequent action, but any later would have been too late. Once the resolution was passed, we had to move with all possible speed. As the House knows, the Cabinet met on Friday morning to consider the UN resolution at length, with the legal advice of the Attorney-General in front of us for all members to read, and the Prime Minister came to the House at the earliest possible moment to state our intention. Some hon. Members have asked whether the House should have sat on Saturday to consider the motion; of course, in future instances, that can be considered, but they should be clear that to effect the situation, we had to give the orders for military action on Saturday afternoon. Other hon. Members have asked that there be no mission creep. I am happy to assure them that if the Government ever fundamentally change the nature of the mission that we have described to the House, we will return to the House for a further debate to consult it again.[47]

The motion was adopted by 557 votes to 13.

The matter returned to Parliament on a number of occasions in the period under review (until the end of June 2011), but no further votes were taken despite significant changes of events on the ground and an increasing range of targets being hit by NATO forces, including Colonel Gaddafi's compound. In these debates the government was very forceful in its statements that the military action was being taken to fulfil the purposes of UNSC Resolution 1973 in order to stop an 'Arab Srebrenica' in Benghazi,[48] and then the protection of civilians which remained the aim of the operation though the government left no doubt that the future of Libya was without Gaddafi.[49] The concerns of some Members of Parliament that the government was deliberately going beyond the terms of the Resolution and that such mission creep should lead to the government seeking

---

45 Ibid., (David Cameron MP).

46 Ibid., Col. 710–713.

47 Ibid., Col. 799 (William Hague MP).

48 *Hansard*, HC, Vol. 526, Col. 920, 5 April 2011 (Andrew Mitchell MP).

49 Ibid., Col. 966.

fresh Parliamentary endorsement did not prevail in the period under review. When the Foreign Secretary was reminded of the Prime Minister's statement to the House of Commons of 21 March 2011 that UNSC Resolution 1973 did not allow for the removal of Gaddafi by military means,[50] William Hague stated that the 'military mission remains defined by the UN Security Council resolution, and there has been no change in the Government's approach to that.' He also made it clear that another UNSC Resolution was unlikely as was the need for a further vote in the House of Commons,[51] thus removing the need for proper accountability for British military actions at both international and national levels. Given that the military action in Libya derives its constitutionality as well as its legitimacy from the UNSC at the international level, and the House of Commons at national level, such responses,[52] though entirely predictable, suggest less progress has been made since the Iraq crisis of 2003 than was commonly perceived at the time UNSC Resolution 1973 was adopted.

9.4 Conclusion: Lessons Learned or Lessons Ignored?

What such debates in the House of Commons on Libya showed was a government intent on not making the same mistakes as the previous government did in relation to Iraq in 2003, by securing UN authority for the use of force and by limiting the use of force to that necessary for the protection of civilians, thereby bringing itself at least initially fully within the *jus ad bellum* as well as the wider political consensus of there being a responsibility to protect when genocide or crimes against humanity are being committed. The swiftness of the diplomacy to secure an authorising resolution from the UNSC, and support from the House of Commons, was driven by humanitarian necessity—to have waited any longer would have led to the destruction of Benghazi and the potential deaths of thousands of civilians.

However, as with the more traditional doctrines of humanitarian intervention, this 'responsibility' did not stretch to other countries in the Middle East where violent repression was prevalent. It may be that the determination in Resolution 1970 that there was evidence of crimes against humanity being committed in Libya distinguishes that country from other Arab countries, though there was no attempt to determine whether such crimes had been committed elsewhere in North Africa and the Middle East during the so-called 'Arab Spring' of 2011. Selectivity is still the order of the day in the UN collective security system, but at least there

---

[50] *Hansard*, HC Vol. 527, Col. 37, 26 April 2011 (Douglas Alexander MP).

[51] *Hansard*, HC Vol. 527, Cols. 40, 47, 50, 26 April 2011.

[52] Repeated by government ministers. See *Hansard*, HC Vol. 528, Cols. 3–4, 16 May 2011 (Liam Fox MP); *Hansard*, HC Vol. 528, Cols. 779–784, 24 May 2011 (Nick Harvey MP); *Hansard*, HC Vol. 529, Col. 628, 14 June 2011 (William Hague MP).

was much greater effort to keep the military action within the parameters of international law. At the time of writing (towards the end of June 2011), the problem was that the longer the civil war in Libya continued, and the more NATO wanted to end it, the more problematic the military action became in reconciling it with the terms of Resolution 1973. The British government could bring the issue back to Parliament if it wished domestic approval to change its military strategy and tactics to include for instance ground troops (though by the end of June it had not done so at least by any formal vote), and further it could seek agreement with its allies and in NATO, but unless another UNSC resolution was sought and secured,[53] that military action would not then be authorised by the very body under which the UK and NATO were purporting to act—the UNSC.

The further in time the military action against Libya stretched away from UNSC Resolution 1973 adopted on 17 March 2011, the further it seemed to depart from the level of force authorised by that Resolution. Resolution 1973 was intended to authorise military action to prevent imminent attacks on Benghazi and other centres of civilian population such as Misrata. Instead of making it clear to Colonel Gaddafi and his forces, by statements and by action, that attacks or threats of attacks on civilian targets would not be tolerated, NATO, led by France and the UK, increasingly engaged government forces in a coordinated effort with rebel forces to defeat government forces and dislodge Gaddafi from power. The response to the crisis moved from an immediate and necessary protection of civilians towards regime change, illustrating that the UN collective security system does not appear to be capable of governing or regulating the use of force, even force which was initially taken under its authority, so that attaining a legally grounded UN collective security system increasingly seems as far away in 2011 as it did in 2003.

References

Blokker N (2000) Is authorization authorized? Powers and practice of the United Nations Security Council to authorize the use of force by coalitions of the able and willing. Eur J Int Law 11:541–568

Dinstein Y (2004) The conduct of hostilities under the Law of International Armed Conflict. Cambridge University Press, Cambridge

Fletcher G, Ohlin JD (2008) Defending humanity: when force is justified and why. Oxford University Press, Oxford

Focarelli C (2008) The responsibility to protect doctrine and humanitarian intervention: too many ambiguities for a working doctrine. J Confl Secur Law 13:191–213

Liivoja R (2008) The scope of the supremacy clause of the United Nation Charter. Int Comp Law Q 57:583–612

[53] 'Libya Conflict: France Eyes another UN Resolution', *BBC News*, 15 April 2011, available at http://www.bbc.co.uk/news/world-africa-13096829.

White ND (2004) The will and authority of the Security Council after Iraq. Leiden J Int Law 17:645–672

White ND (2009) Democracy goes to war: British military deployments under international law. Oxford University Press, Oxford

White ND (2010) International law, the United Kingdom and decisions to deploy troops overseas. Int Comp Law Q 59:814–823

White ND, Ulgen O (1997) The Security Council and the decentralized military option: constitutionality and function. Neth Int Law Rev 44:378–413

Table of Cases*

* The Table of Cases was compiled by Ms C. C. Diepeveen, Middelburg, The Netherlands. cdiep@zeelandnet.nl

I. F. Dekker and E. Hey (eds.), *Netherlands Yearbook of International Law 2011*, Netherlands Yearbook of International Law 42, DOI: 10.1007/978-90-6704-849-1,

Index*

A

* The Index was compiled by Ms C. C. Diepeveen, Middelburg, The Netherlands. cdiep@zeelandnet.nl

I. F. Dekker and E. Hey (eds.), *Netherlands Yearbook of International Law 2011*, Netherlands Yearbook of International Law 42, DOI: 10.1007/978-90-6704-849-1,

MIX
Papier aus verantwortungsvollen Quellen
Paper from responsible sources
FSC® C105338

If you have any concerns about our products,
you can contact us on
ProductSafety@springernature.com

In case Publisher is established outside the EU,
the EU authorized representative is:
Springer Nature Customer Service Center GmbH
Europaplatz 3, 69115 Heidelberg, Germany

Printed by Libri Plureos GmbH
in Hamburg, Germany